T^{HE} J_{AZZ} L_{IFE}

I

THE JAZZ LIFE

by
NAT HENTOFF

With a new Introduction by the Author

A DA CAPO PAPERBACK

Library of Congress Cataloging in Publication Data

Hentoff, Nat.
  The jazz life.

  (A Da Capo paperback)
  Reprint of the 1961 ed. published by Dial Press,
New York.
  1. Jazz music. I. Title.
[ML3561.J3H45 1978]   785.4'2'0973   78-9129
ISBN 0-306-80088-8

ISBN: 0-306-80088-8

First Paperback Edition 1978

This Da Capo Press paperback edition of *The Jazz Life* is an unabridged republica-
tion of the first edition published in New York in 1961 and in London in 1962.
It includes a new introduction written by the author for Da Capo's 1975 cloth
edition, and is reprinted by arrangement with the author.

Published by Da Capo Press, Inc.
A Subsidiary of Plenum Publishing Corporation
227 West 17th Street, New York, New York 10011

Introduction to
the 1975 edition

Introduction

In 1961, when this book was first published, that surgingly ecumenical force known as "rock" had not yet entirely established its hegemony over popular music. It soon did, however, and one result was a bleak decade for jazz.

Until the ascent of rock, there had been, among each new generation of the citizenry, a nucleus of the young that eschewed whatever trend in popular music was in favor among the majority of their peers and instead gravitated toward jazz. In addition to the manifest pleasure they obtained from the music, there was another dividend in being a jazz acolyte. It was something like belonging to a secret society. An elite secret society, because jazz aficionados, by and large, have always considered themselves as having vastly superior taste to those legions of their contemporaries who are uninitiated in the cabala of jazz and such of its avatars as Duke Ellington, Lester Young, Thelonious Monk, and Miles Davis.

It was this nucleus of new true jazz believers which kept replenishing the audience for jazz. During the 1960's, however, many of those young listeners—who might in earlier decades, have certified their hipness by joining the auditors and spectators of the jazz life—were lost instead to rock. Because rock was so multifarious (with some jazz and blues among its ingredients), and particularly because rock was being created *by* the young, (in contrast to previous popular music which had been crafted by adults working in Tin Pan Alley and the Hollywood studios), it was no longer square for a reasonably sophisticated young listener to dig the music that nearly everyone else in his generation was also grooving too.

Besides, there was a place for elitists in rock too—from those who divined mind-changing portents in the lyrics of Bob Dylan to others who became experts in the lore, sociological and otherwise, of the ancient (1950's) history of rhythm and blues and rock and roll.

A hardy few of the listeners coming up in the 1960's opted for jazz, but an index of how relatively few they were is the sharp decline in jazz record albums released during that decade in comparison to the outpouring of recorded jazz during the 1950's when jazz had shown some signs of reaching more of a mass popular audience (through Dave Brubeck, Shelley Manne, etc.) than ever before in its history.

In any case, there was a decided recession in the jazz life until the early 1970's. But by 1974, a regeneration of jazz appeared to be underway. First of all, a new fusion, "jazz rock"—as practiced by Chick Corea, Weather Report, Herbie Hancock, John McLaughlin's Mahavishnu Orchestra, Donald Byrd's Blackbyrds and Larry Coryell's The Eleventh House—was attracting large audiences. But there was also a markedly renewed interest in vintage jazz.

For instance, Teddy Wilson, the perennially precise swing-era pianist, declared his conviction, in the spring of 1974, that "The climate is changing. During the past couple of years, I've been getting requests for autographs as if I was back thirty-five years ago with Benny Goodman. And not only from people of my generation. College and high school students, and even some elementary school kids, have been coming up after a concert."

Teddy Wilson's son, Ted Wilson, a jazz drummer and an assistant professor of music at Kingsborough Community Kings College in New York, has also testified to the rejuvenation of interest in jazz in the 1970's. In one of his courses, he draws parallels between classical and jazz forms. "And what's especially interesting," Ted Wilson observes, "is the students' reactions when we begin to really explore jazz. When I play them recordings by King Joe Oliver with Louis Armstrong, the Benny Goodman quartet, and Duke, everybody flips out. In one of my classes, I had 42 students, and when we started to go into jazz, there were over a hundred people jammed into that room a few days later. It's all brand new to them. They haven't heard it on the radio, but once they're exposed to classic jazz, they begin to connect with it."

The senior Wilson's analysis is that the comeback, so to speak, of jazz among the young is an indication that many of them are growing out of rock. "What we play," Teddy Wilson agrees with his son, "is absolutely new to so many listeners whose tastes have been formed by the Beatles and groups like that since the early 1960's. Those of us who play jazz got hardly any air play during those years, so it's as if they have just discovered us. Furthermore, I do believe that any youngster who is genuinely interested in music eventually has to leave much of rock behind. I don't want to sound immodest, but what musicians like myself play is like Ph.D. music compared to the nursery-school sounds of a lot of rock and roll. They've *got* to grow out of it. And that goes for their parents too. I mean the kind of parents who try to pretend they love rock so that their kids won't think they're old fogies. You can only maintain that stance so long—unless, in musical terms, you're retarded."

As more young white listeners begin to evolve out of rock, another, earlier development—the rise of black consciousness—has also begun to enlarge the audience for jazz. In the "Soul and Collard Greens" section of *The Jazz Life*, I had touched on that phenomenon but had underestimated its potential strength through the 1960's and beyond.

Black consciousness meant, among other things, a searching for black roots in the American experience. This involved intensified research in, and sometimes revisions of Afro-American history. In the process, the jazz heritage was plumbed not only by black social and music historians but also by black poets and educators. One of those poets, Sterling A. Brown, had been mining the blues, among other basic elements of Afro-American music, for many years as an extraordinarily influential professor at Howard University. For a long time, however, Brown had tried unsuccessfully to have jazz "legitimated" at Howard through its official inclusion in the university's curriculum. Brown has incorporated aspects of black music into his literature and social history courses, but there was no department (or division of a department) devoted wholly to jazz, the blues, and other forms of black music.

This long-time official resistance to jazz was not limited to only Howard University. For decades, jazz has not been considered "respectable" enough to be taught as such in most black colleges and universities, let alone white institutions of higher learning.

With the rise of black consciousness during the 1960's, however, courses in jazz—and black music in general—started to proliferate in both black and predominantly white colleges and universities. An index of the bipolar attitudes toward jazz that still, though decreasingly, exists among black educators is a story told by Dr. Donald Byrd, a trumpeter-educator, who became head of the first jazz studies division in the history of Howard University.

Byrd travels frequently to other campuses as a consultant and lecturer. During one such engagement at a black college, he was greeted by a senior professor of music who was bewailing the fact that, as he put it, "I can't get my students to listen to *good* music."

"What exactly do you mean?" Donald Byrd asked.

"You understand," the professor said, "Bach, Beethoven, Brahms."

Byrd stared coldly at the faculty member. "I wasn't quite sure what I was going to lecture about tonight," Byrd said, "but now I know. *You* are going to be the subject of my lecture. Your narrow, uptight, European-based limitations on what's 'good' in music. Wake up, man, there are all kinds of *good* music in this country, music that grew up right here! And I particularly mean black music."

Max Roach, a key drummer in the history of modern jazz, has also become an educator—at the University of Massachusetts at Amherst. Roach stresses that jazz is America's "classical music" as he adds pointedly that all the major innovators in the music have been black.

Not only college students, however, are learning the scope and depth of black contributions to the American grain. Increasingly, in secondary schools, youngsters, through concerts and workshops by visiting musicians, are being exposed to jazz as the product of our indigenous culture with by far the most world-wide influence.

Furthermore, in what may be an augury of jazz being recognized in some schools as an integral part of the context of black American history, students of the Arthur A. Schomburg Intermediate School in East Harlem —during graduation ceremonies in the early 1970's—were presented with such honors as: the Gwendolyn Brooks-Arna Bontemps Award for Creative Writing, the Sterling A. Brown and Langston Hughes Award for Scholarship in Language Arts, the Frederick Douglass Award for Excellence and Dynamic Leadership as it Relates to the School, *and* the Bessie Smith Award for Excellence in Vocal Music.

The Arthur Schomburg School, as you might expect, is largely black. But as a new generation of music educators and other teachers—themselves having grown up in the ecumenicism of rock—move into policy-making positions in the schools, it is very likely that, in all kinds of classrooms, greater emphasis is going to be placed on the full spectrum of authentically American music—from Charles Ives to Duke Ellington.

It has to be noted, however, that although the audience for jazz is certainly going to remain heterogeneous, there are black musicians who see the future of the music as being primarily separatist in that its seminal creators will continue to be black and will consider themselves to be communicating principally with black audiences. And those audiences, the prophecy goes, will be shaped in large part by the ineluctable continued growth of black consciousness so long as this remains a predominantly segregated country.

Simultaneously, though, there is a strong trend toward erasing most of the boundary lines that now separate diverse musical idioms. As Miles Davis, one of the new ecumenicists, puts it, "Jazz is a white man's word. And rock is a white man's word. It's all just music. It's just being out there. André Watts plays a good piano; so do Herbie Hancock and Bill Evans. Puccini is great, and so is Jimi Hendrix. Everyone who's out there is connected, not pigeonholed according to some label."

Larry Coryell, a white guitarist who started as a jazz player and then moved into rock while retaining much of his jazz conception, agrees with Miles Davis: "Contemporary music has absorbed the whole thing called rock or rock and roll, and what's coming out now is a wide variety of creative efforts by people with both jazz and rock backgrounds. It's not classifiable as either jazz or rock, it's just music that is as good as the people doing it."

If Miles Davis and Larry Coryell are correct in their appraisals, eventually there will no longer be a body of current music that can be unmistakably defined as jazz. And then, the jazz life, as such, will have become an historical artifact.

In my view, what is much more apt to happen is that there will be audiences both for the separatists and the new ecumenicists as well as a substantial number of listeners for the "mainstream" jazz that is explored, along with its makers, in this book.

(The term, "mainstream," as first coined by critic Stanley Dance, was meant to apply to the kinds of jazz that developed out of the late 1920's and through the 1930's and early 1940's. Among its examplars, by Dance's initial definition, were Count Basie, Earl Hines, Lester Young, Teddy Wilson, Billie Holiday, and in his own uncategorizably protean way, Duke Ellington. It seems time to me to extend the meaning of "mainstream jazz" to apply as well to such of the creators of post-swing-era jazz as Charlie Parker, Dizzy Gillespie, and in this book, Charles Mingus and Thelonious Monk.)

In any event, the jazz life—broadened to also encompass separatism and the new ecumenicism—continues. Now, as when this book was written, it is composed, at its best and most resonant, of strikingly individualistic improvisers whose roots go back to field hollers and blues and whose imagination will continue to create the unexpected, thereby continually challenging its listeners to grow along with it.

— Nat Hentoff
New York, 1974

T<small>HE</small> J<small>AZZ</small> L<small>IFE</small>

Books edited by Nat Hentoff

Hear Me Talkin' To Ya (*with Nat Shapiro*)
The Jazz Makers (*with Nat Shapiro*)
Jazz (*with Albert J. McCarthy*)

T_{HE} J^{AZZ} L_{IFE}

by
NAT HENTOFF

LONDON: PETER DAVIES

Printed in Great Britain for Peter Davies Limited
by Lowe & Brydone (Printers) Limited, London

To MARGOT

Acknowledgments

My primary sources have been the musicians. They have provided many different kinds of guidance through the years—blunt, confused, angry, abrasively honest and mockingly dishonest. The jazz world is not an entirely open society. Although at times there seem to be no locks whatever on the door, you're seldom really inside at all.

I am particularly indebted for such insights as I may have developed to Jo Jones, the late Frankie Newton, Pee Wee Russell, Miles Davis and Charles Mingus.

The book itself is partly due to Murray Kempton of the *New York Post*. After I had co-edited three books on jazz, Kempton asked me whether I was ever going to *write* one.

The Jazz Life is neither a history nor a technical analysis of the music. It is an attempt to explore several of the social, economic and psychological elements that make up the context of modern jazz.

Part of an earlier version of *Soul and Collard Greens* appeared in *Harper's* as *Race Prejudice in Jazz*. Sections of *Bringing Dignity to Jazz* were printed as *Requiem for*

7

a Jazz Festival in *Commonweal.* An outline of the economic conditions detailed in *The Apprenticeship* was first prepared for *Dissent.* Part of the material on Thelonious Monk, Ornette Coleman, and Miles Davis appeared in *Esquire* articles I've written about them in a somewhat different form, and the descriptions of the recording sessions in *Studio Time* are from *Hifi/Stereo Review.* I appreciate the permission of these magazines to make use of the material for this book.

I am grateful to Gilbert Millstein for allowing me to include part of his transcript of an interview with Mrs. Lucille Armstrong and to Dr. Charles Winick for permission to quote from his papers on drug addiction.

The book has been written for the non-specialist reader, although I hope those who already consider themselves informed may also find this appraisal of the jazz life a stimulus to further explorations of their own.

Contents

I Backgrounds

1. Night School at the Savoy   15
2. The Changes   29
3. The Apprenticeship and the Accounting   46
4. Soul and Collard Greens   60
5. Junk   75
6. Bringing Dignity to Jazz   98

II The Foreground

7. Studio Time   117
8. A Brief Note on the Romance of
   "The White Negro"   138
9. Count Basie   143
10. Charles Mingus   157
11. Three Ways of Making It:
    John Lewis, Miles Davis, Thelonious Monk   170
12. Ornette Coleman   222
    Epilogue   249

W. H. Auden says of music (*In Praise of Limestone*) that it "can be made anywhere, is invisible, and does not smell." But music is made by men who are insistently visible, especially, as in jazz, when the players *are* their music. This book is about several of those players. Through telling something of where they came from and how they live, I hope their music too has become less disembodied.

Backgrounds

"This revolution, or whatever you want to call it, in the 1940's took place for many reasons, and not only for musical reasons. . . . For the younger musicians this was the way to react against the attitude that Negroes were supposed to entertain people. The new attitude of these young Negroes was: 'Either you listen to me on the basis of what I actually do or forget it.'"

—John Lewis

Night School at the Savoy

My own introduction to the jazz life began with a record of Artie Shaw's *Nightmare*. I came from a home where any overt expression of emotion was calculated and measured lest it roar out of control. Standing in a record store one afternoon, however, I shocked myself by yelling in pleasure at the first bars of *Nightmare*. Pianist Red Garland recently reminded me of that day by describing his reaction to first hearing Charlie Parker on a jukebox in Dallas. "I just laughed aloud," Red recalls. "He made me feel so good."

Jazz stays with many of us because, as Whitney Balliett has noted, it is "the sound of surprise." When you walk into a jazz club, you never know what combinations of emotions, some perhaps long dormant, will be reawakened and reset before the night is out. I've seen rigidly introverted listeners begin tapping their feet, rocking their bodies, and suddenly break into an uncontrollable "Yeah!".

From Shaw I went to Duke Ellington, Louis Armstrong, Fats Waller, blues singer Peetie Wheatstraw ("The Devil's Son-in-Law"), and I was hooked. I knew how irretrievably lost I had become when, at thirteen, I went to see a Count Basie stage show on the afternoon of one of the high holidays, and never made it to the syna-

15

gogue at all. Neither God nor my father struck me dead,
though the latter thundered for weeks. In any case, my
record collection continued to grow.

Records, however, can only provide a small insight
into the jazz life as a whole. I know critics who avoid
going to jazz clubs and getting to know the musicians because they feel the resulting personal relationships,
friendly and otherwise, would inevitably affect their
judgment of the men's music. Yet records are not enough
to provide a full understanding of a jazzman's work.
There is an added physical and emotional impact in seeing a man play. The music is so personal that with the
best players, their instruments have become extensions of
themselves. Furthermore, the musicians feel much freer
in a night club than in a recording studio and most take
many more chances in a week of club work than in a year
of recording.

Sidney Bechet is the first jazz musician I remember
seeing. I was twelve, and had evaded the bouncer's eye at
a Boston night club. I'd heard Bechet's throaty, swooping
soprano saxophone on recordings, but I wasn't prepared
for the visual power of the man. Chunky, with a deceptively benign face and a soft, Creole-drawl voice, Bechet
changed into a demonic top sergeant when he raised his
long, straight soprano sax, stomped out the beat, and
hurled his band as if with his fist into the music.

My night school in jazz was the Savoy Café in
Boston. I attended it for thirteen years, and left to go to
New York as an editor of *Down Beat*. Nearly all of my
first impressions of the jazz life were from what I saw
and heard at the Savoy or from people I first met there.

The Savoy was just across the tracks that separated
the Negro section of the Back Bay from the white. It was
a long, narrow room with the bandstand crammed against
the center of the wall on the right. At first, its patrons
were mainly Negroes with a small, prideful nucleus of
white jazz buffs that included amateur and professional

musicians, a bank guard and a bank official, a cab driver, a physicist, and assorted intellectuals, lesbians, and pre-beats.

The manager was a remarkably even-tempered, beer-bloated Irishman who never quite recovered from having changed his base from a predictable neighborhood bar to a room where the sound climbed in volume through the night as the personal relationships of the regulars became more jangled and the drunks multiplied. Steve, who had no visible racial prejudices and was equally polite to the lesbians and the policy runners, was often made a confidant, mainly because he was the only one present who didn't seem interested in telling his own story. He never knew quite what to make of what he heard and what he saw; but years later, after the Savoy closed and he retired to Florida, Steve told a former regular how much he missed the place. "It sure was lively there, wasn't it?"

Steve did come to recognize a number of automatic reactions in the jazz life of the Savoy. Negro trumpeter Frankie Newton, a tall, gentle man, was standing at the bar when a white photographer pressed him for payment of a long-due bill. Newton sighed and gave him two dollars. The photographer, disappointed, grunted, "That's mighty white of you." Newton grabbed the man by the collar and lifted him until his eyes were on a level with Newton's. "You mean," Newton whispered, "that's mighty black of me." Steve continued wiping the beer glasses.

Some months later, I was in trouble with a local Negro plain-clothes detective because I was dating a Negro singer. Newton appointed himself our bodyguard. When we left the club after closing, Newton marched a block behind us. He was criticized by several Negroes on the block for volunteering his protection. "Hell," he answered, "they're not hiding."

From the bouncers, waiters and musicians I heard through the years an anthology of Jim Crow in America. A young, incisively intelligent trumpet player, Stix, was telling me one night of his boyhood in Florida. "I had to have a pass after dark, just like in South Africa." Stix had a hospital day job that started at nine in the morning. From eight at night until one the next morning, he worked under scale in a windowless clip joint downtown. The room was crushingly noisy, stifling and depressing. Actually, no music was required for what usually happened on the dance floor. From both jobs Stix may have earned $70 a week with which he supported a wife and two children. He kept hoping for an opening in one of the bands that played the Savoy, but he wasn't a good enough musician. He wanted no other life than jazz, however, and kept practicing although I couldn't imagine when he had the time. Stix worked his double shift for several years and eventually was also elected treasurer of the Negro musicians' local. (Although more and more American Federation of Musicians locals throughout the country are being integrated, many remain separate and distinctly unequal.)

I lost track of Stix when I left Boston, but heard later that he had embezzled the local's funds and soon after, as my informant put it, "he flipped."

At the Savoy, I learned, I think, to recognize the "put on." A Negro musician who was originally from New Orleans was cornered by one of those white record collectors (none of them were ever Negro) who burned with a religious sense of mission. Their grail was to collect the definitive jazz discographies of all players ever involved in a jazz record session. The courteous, white-haired musician accepted the offer of a drink and then several more while inventing a series of ancient, all-star recording dates that drove the collector into a frenzy of self-congratulation at his private-eye perseverance. No gold prospector could ever have been happier with a strike.

Years later, Louis Armstrong was more candid in a British interview. "All I was interested in was doing the sessions and getting paid." Similarly, there was a night when Duke Ellington, hounded by a collector, turned in uncharacteristic public exasperation and pointed to his men returning to the stand. "Look, what you see there is just sixteen men earning their living."

Steve was put on regularly. The cellar of the Savoy was coat room, rehearsal quarters, and private drinking club for the musicians. There were no windows and no door other than the one leading up to the club. In the mid-forties, Coleman Hawkins brought a group to the Savoy. The pianist was an impregnably reserved young man named Thelonious Monk. I had waited until after closing one night while Steve and his bouncer locked up. When we were on the sidewalk, Steve remembered that he hadn't seen Monk leave. "Go down and look for him," he told the bouncer. The bouncer came up from the cellar and reported there was no trace of Monk. Steve scratched his head and stood indecisively in front of the door. Suddenly there were steps on the cellar stairs, and Monk appeared.

"Where were you?" asked Steve.

Monk looked at him as if from a great distance and answered with slow, calm dignity. "I was walking on the ceiling."

Occasionally, in its early years, the Savoy was visited by college boys curious to investigate the lower depths. One of the regulars was a white girl, Miriam, who was friendly with many of the musicians and had been married to a drummer. Two undergraduates, majoring in sociology, noticed that Miriam was obviously one of the in-group, and invited her to join them for a drink. They asked her to point out the marijuana-sellers and other local celebrities. Miriam made the room turn into one of the most dangerous hangouts in the history of Western man. The amiable cook, whose only major avocation was seducing stray college girls, became an arm of the Syndicate. Steve, trying to soothe a tearful drunk, was identi-

fied as a receiver of all manner of dangerously "hot"
goods. And Miriam herself created fables of her own
grimly existential life as a prostitute. The investigators
had begun taking notes when Junior Raglin, a huge, bear-
like Negro musician of perennial good humor walked by.
Miriam summoned him to the table, improvising, "I want
you to meet my husband, but please try not to make
him angry. You know how they are when they lose control." The boys hastily gripped Junior's hand, and left.

Years later in Pittsburgh, Miles Davis was set upon
by two indomitable psychologists on the faculty of the
University of Pittsburgh. They were doing a paper, they
explained, on the private lives of jazz musicians. Miles
drew a detailed, uninhibitedly fictional portrait of his
daily sex life that made Humbert Humbert appear to be
deprived. The information was duly written down; and
for all Miles knows or cares, it may well have already
appeared in a professional journal.

Although Miriam had known enough musicians and
enough Negroes to judge each one on his own, there were
"band chicks" at the Savoy, as at nearly every club where
jazz is played. Often white, the girls bring with them
their fantasies of the jazz life and the mythical prowess of
the Negro in bed. There are always musicians willing to
add to the girls' experience. Some of the band chicks eventually become call girls. Others marry accountants, and
a few cannot brake their passion for self-destruction. One
such at the Savoy was an extraordinarily attractive girl
whose family, Bostonians for many generations, lived in
that part of the Back Bay that was as exotic to a Savoy
regular as a Vermont farm. She said little, dressed with
flawless taste, and seemed to be consumed by an insatiable need to give affection. She moved in with a Negro
trombonist in his forties. Once a featured sideman with
the major big bands, he was on his way down, primarily
because he was an alcoholic but also because his imagination had shriveled. His solos had become as predictable

as his recitals of past conquests, musical and sexual. He had no other skill than jazz, and so worked at it wherever he could.

The trombonist was too involved with his own frustrations to pay much attention to the girl. He accepted her love, her money, and at first didn't beat her too often. As his anger with himself grew, so did his rage at the whites who, he became convinced, were now freezing him out and profiting from the music he and other Negroes had created. The girl, affectionate or not, was white, and the beatings increased. She finally left him, but stayed in the neighborhood, and when I left Boston, was living with a bookie. She dressed carelessly, and her eyes were constantly glazed, somewhat like the heroine in the last pages of a Dreiser novel.

Although quite different, girls like Miriam and the "society chick" complicated life for Steve. He paid regular tribute so that he had no routine trouble with the police, but there were captains who would sooner have accepted the Savoy as a front for drug traffic than allow the fact that it was one of the few places in Boston where mixed couples could relax. Plain-clothes men would swarm in, bark at a Negro-white couple for proof of age and then order them to leave, even if they had evidence of being over twenty-one.

Much has been written about the "inner democracy" of jazz insofar as the alleged absence of racial prejudice among musicians is concerned; but actually, much of what the music has done to blur and, in many cases, erase racial lines has happened within its audiences. The musicans have not, as I'll indicate later, been as free of color bias as the jazz writers, particularly the Europeans, have believed. What jazz has created, however, is one of the very few areas in American life where whites and Negroes, otherwise residentially segregated, have been able to form relatively casual friendships. Even full-time white liberals still seldom know Negroes apart from their

roles in committees or Negro organizations. As for the
average American, I expect a wide sampling might indicate that a revealingly huge majority have never had a
Negro, other than a domestic, inside their homes.

Jazz clubs, however, have become islands of at least
acquaintanceship between Negroes and whites. It is instructive to see how in most cities this unintentional function of a jazz room alarms police. The Savoy finally solved
its problem by deciding in the late 1940's that Dixieland
was more commercial than swing and modern jazz. With
Dixieland on the stand, hardly any Negroes came any
more, and the police were relieved.

Since the Savoy was in a Negro neighborhood, I saw
many terrifying examples of willful police brutality
through the years. In any major city, North as well as
South, the Negro is aware that a cop will hit him quicker
and harder than he will a white suspect. Fear and hatred
of the "fuzz" is, therefore, thoroughly ingrained in most
Negroes from the time they first play in the streets. In
that respect, the bitterness at "the captain" that courses
hotly though many spirituals and work songs has not left
jazz by any means. In recent years, with jazz identified in
the public and police mind as largely synonymous with
narcotics, in certain cities "fuzz" looking for shakedowns
prey on visiting jazzmen, particularly Negroes. In Philadelphia, where a musician may be stripped if anyone in
the band is suspected of being an addict, a prominent
Negro trumpet player broke precedent a couple of years
ago and shocked the narcotics detectives by saying with
pointed politeness, "If you're going to search me, I want
to call my lawyer." He wasn't searched.

There was at times a hatred in the musician at the
Savoy that had nothing to do with the police or even with
whites. Several leaders were so fiercely conscientious and
so jealous of their own reputations that they would glare
with rage if a sideman continued to make mistakes or
play sloppily. Sidney Bechet once had a poor band at the

Savoy. By the end of his engagement, he looked and acted like a headmaster about to expel the entire student body and close the school. On the last night, Bechet didn't show up for the first set. He finally arrived in the middle of the second, sat down in front of the stand, and began to request some of the more difficult tunes in the book. Until asked to leave, Bechet threw shot glasses at the stand each time a musician made a mistake.

In the best players, there is a stubbornness in finding and pursuing one's own way, although the search is anxiety-producing at first if your way is alien to the current orthodoxy. Billie Holiday once told Willis Conover on a *Voice of America* interview of Lester Young's early difficulties:

> "Everyone, when he first started, thought: This man, his *tone* is too *thin*, you know? A tenor sax! Everybody thinks it has to be real big; and Lester used to go out of his mind getting reeds, to sound *big* like Chu Berry, and—he was very popular in those days—and I told him, 'It doesn't *matter*, because,' I said, 'you have a *beautiful* tone and *you watch*. After a while *everybody's* going to be *copying* you.' And it came to *be*."

Jazz is not so casual a vocation as it has often been described. The standards of most of the professionals are demandingly high. To achieve their most basic satisfaction, jazzmen try to impress other musicians. Whether the audience or the critics have caught a clinker, the musician knows that his colleagues have, and usually he's ashamed. The jazzman can be irresponsible in his personal life, but he generally retains considerable pride in keeping his music up to the level he's set for it. The man who coasts too long may retain the admiration of the critics long after he's lost the respect of other musicians. "He's not blowing *nothing*" is one of the most damning judgments a musician can deliver on one of his contemporaries. A jazzman will, on the other hand, excuse much boorish behavior from a colleague who otherwise is a superior player. A brilliant drummer, drunk, hit an alto saxophonist hard in the mouth at a New York club one night. "I didn't hit him back because he was high," said the altoist. "Besides, I love him for what he plays, not for what he is."

The saxophonist's nonviolent resistance is an exception. Most musicians would have hit back, but his attitude does reflect the degree of admiration a particularly original player achieves in the field despite the relentlessly competitive nature of the music. Several musicians loaned Charlie Parker money, gave him a place to sleep, and otherwise tried to help him through his many self-imposed difficulties in the last years of his life. They all felt indebted to him for what he had opened up for them musically. "God knows," said one player after Parker's death, "we all owed him so much. He'd come to my place and stay for a time, and I'd share whatever I had with him. But eventually, if I wasn't getting many gigs, I'd run out of resources myself, and he'd go somewhere else. Who could afford him? I mean that literally. And I mean it the other way too. Which of us could pay him what he owed him?"

The man I've met who most glows with the pride of being a professional jazzman is Jo Jones. The former Basie drummer has a nearly religious feeling about what he considers a gift that he has somehow received. Jo has been a lay preacher through the years to the younger players, the "kiddies" he calls them. He advises them on personal problems and gives them leads to jobs. And he keeps reminding them, as I heard one night at the Savoy, "You're a musician. Don't ever forget that. You can do what very few other people can do. You can reach people; but to move them, you have to be all open. You have to let everything in you out. And you have to be in condition to play what you hear."

In addition to their professional pride, I was also impressed during the Savoy years by the flexible intelligence of many jazzmen. The theory has long been that jazz musicians, if not dumb, are inarticulate; but I've interviewed several hundred and most of them make lucid and often vividly graphic sense about their music and their lives.

What probably distorts the image of the jazzman most is that many players do "put on" casual questioners or often are simply uncommunicative. The jazz musician, Negro and white, is generally on the defensive against the day people. He is not sure that even the fan really understands what he's playing, and he is convinced that the average "square" certainly does not. Many jazzmen besides have had to cope with enough hostility and misunderstanding in their choice of vocation—from childhood on—to be suspicious of strangers. Furthermore, being part of the urban night life eventually leads many players to adopt a façade of toughness, an external impassivity.

I remember as a teenager attending a dance at which the Duke Ellington band was playing. There was a scuffle in front of the stand and a man was knifed. As he fell, the band continued playing without the slightest break. Only a few of the musicians showed moderately open interest, and I can still see alto saxophonist Johnny Hodges, who was in the middle of a solo when the knife came out, not indicating by so much as a change of expression that anything untoward was happening. "You see so much in a night club over the years," one player explains, "and after a while, it takes a lot to surprise or startle you."

Yet, beneath the professional toughness, there is a wide-ranging diversity of temperament among the players. There is the shy, ironic clarinetist, Pee Wee Russell, whose playing is among the most unsentimentally lyrical and introspective in jazz. The widely read, sharply questioning Rex Stewart plays with the cutting force and restless intensity that mark his speech. The deadly serious John Coltrane, groping for as many possibilities as he can think of and combine in each chord that rushes by, performs with a hugely emotional "cry" of desire that has been at the center of jazz since the first field hollers. And I remember the late "Big Sid" Catlett, a drummer, spending hours patiently advising young apprentices, showing them figures and devices it had taken him years to develop. Conversely, I've seen an established Negro drummer brutally refuse a compliment from an apprentice white admirer. "Haven't you people stolen enough already?"

A jazzman can also be as sentimental as anyone who has been exposed, however mockingly, to the "American dream." Louis Armstrong's wife, for example, describes one Christmas eve with Armstrong:

"I got a little small Christmas tree and I got all the decorations for it, and set it up in the hotel room while Louis was at work. I didn't say anything to him about it. So when he came in about three o'clock, this tree was up with the blinking lights, you know? And he took one look at it and he just clammed up, you know? Louis isn't very emotional; he doesn't say much when he's overwhelmed, you know? So, we talked around a while; I gave him his Christmas present—had all the Christmas presents under the tree, and gave him his, and those that I had for a few special friends in the band.

"We finally went to bed. And Louis was still laying up in the bed watching the tree; his eyes just like a baby's eyes would watch something. So Louis was watching this tree, you know? So finally I asked him—I said, 'Well, I'll turn the lights out now on the tree.' He said, 'No, don't turn them out. I have to just keep looking at it.' He said, 'You know, that's the first tree I ever had.'

"Well, I hadn't realized that, you know? Louis was forty years old, and it seems to me that in forty years a person would have at least one tree. I was all swollen up inside when he told me that. We were to leave the next day for Kansas City. I figured Christmas is over; today's the 26th now; I'll leave the tree. So Louis said, 'No, don't leave the tree; take the tree with you.' And he had me take that tree on those one-nighters. Before I even unpacked a bag I had to set that tree up, his Christmas tree. And I've had one for him every year. Louis hasn't been home too often for Christmas, but whenever he has been home, he's had a tree the length of the room.

"I kept that first little tree until way after New Year's, putting it up every night and taking it down every morning, in a dozen hotels. And then when I did take it down for its last time, Louis wanted me to mail it home. It was a real tree, not an artificial one, and I had to convince him—I really had to convince him—that the tree would dry up."

From Louis Armstrong to Thelonious Monk, jazz musicians are as unpredictable as their music. One possible generalization about them is that a basic reason the music attracted and holds them is that jazz offers its players more freedom to express who they are—at any moment—than any other form of Western music. The classical composer has another and considerably more reflective genre of freedom, of course; but as for playing musicians, even the most individualistic and imaginative of classical instrumentalists must interpret within limitations which jazzmen find intolerable.

To some jazz players this freedom and the skills they've developed to utilize it are the most valued assets they have. Late one night, the big tenor saxophonist Ben Webster was about to swing on a man who'd been annoying him. "No," Webster dropped his arm and lectured himself. "I'm getting old; I've got to save all that fire for the horn."

This kind of insight was the most useful result of my classes at the Savoy, but I began to learn much more about the jazz life and its pressures when I came to New York as a full-time reporter of the jazz scene. It was, I learned, harder than I had supposed to make it as a jazz-man. Also, I had not been so fully aware in Boston as I later became of how radically the music itself was changing, and of how those changes were reflected in the players and the jazz audience.

2

The Changes

"Paying dues" is the jazz musician's term for the years of learning and searching for an individual sound and style while the pay is small and irregular. Sometimes there isn't enough work in jazz to live on, and the apprentice is forced into paying the hardest dues of all—the taking of a day job.

In the earliest years of jazz, however, few of the players took the music that seriously. The "musicianers" of the South and Southwest at the beginning of the century regarded the need to work at another trade during the day as a matter of course. In the country, many were sharecroppers or independent farmers who taught themselves whatever instruments were available and played for their own amusement or at local dances and picnics in their spare time. They formed raw unorthodox brass bands and string groups, but hardly regarded themselves as "artists." For them, music was self-expression and also served a community purpose that brought them added status and income.

Later, in the cities, men who played in brass bands for parades and worked dances at night were often also barbers, cigar makers, longshoremen, bricklayers, carpenters, or roofers. Some—particularly the wandering blues pianists and singers—worked on the periphery of the law, supporting themselves partly by gambling, pimping, or becoming professional pool sharks. The majority of the early jazzmen, however, were relatively responsible citizens who, in their roles as musicians, were playing a thoroughly functional music.

Jazz (or "ragtime" as the music was loosely called in the South) was played for dances, parades, intermissions at brothels, and to complement the joy, rage, or sorrow of whiskey in the blood. The music worked if it made its listeners feel better. The early jazz musician measured his success by how far ahead he was hired. The only critics were the dancers and the drinkers.

Gradually, in the second decade of the century, it became possible for more players to make the music a full-time career. But none of the early travelers was ever allowed to forget that he was primarily an "entertainer." The first waves of jazz professionals worked carnivals and tent shows; made the vaudeville circuit; and accompanied blues singers and comedians, sometimes taking part in the latter's sketches.

The jazzmen who gained their basic experience in the 1920's and 1930's operated under the same contract. Many still doubled in vaudeville, and when they did play at dance halls or in small combos at bars, they worried if the audience remained motionless. Usually they had to include enough "novelty songs" and even some visual comedy to keep the drinkers amused.

It was worst for Negro musicians playing to white audiences, particularly, of course, in the South. Texas pianist Sam Price recalls: "If a man hired you to work someplace, you had to act a fool in order to hold a job. The drummer had to do all these stick deals, and put the stick in his mouth. If you were a pianist, it helped to be able to Charleston at the same time." In playing for Negro audiences and in some white rooms in the North and Midwest, there were occasionally musical kicks on

the job, to be sure, but the major pleasure and challenges
of the music-making itself were often reserved for the
after-hours sessions where musicians were the only audience.

When British bandleader-critic Humphrey Lyttelton defended Louis Armstrong's commercialism a few
years ago, his main argument was that Louis had known
no other possibilities in the formative years of his career.
Lyttelton cited the mid-twenties, during the period when
the Hot Five recordings were made, which contained
some of Armstrong's most brilliantly daring work. But
outside the recording studio, conditions were different.
Lyttelton asked how present-day critics of Armstrong
would "react to the Reverend Satchelmouth, to the 'boy
and girl' dance routine which he used to do with Zutty
Singelton, or to the version of *Heebie Jeebies* in which,
according to an eye-witness, he sang not words but 'a
guttural mouthing of incoherent nonsense, supplemented
with unearthly grimaces'?"

"They might go even back further," Lyttelton continued, "to the Good Old Days in New Orleans, 1918,
when, with Kid Ory's band, he worked out 'a little jive
routine with dancing and fooling around between numbers to get laughs.' And if they want to know who taught
him such deplorable goings-on, they needn't look to publicity men or agents or commercial bigshots. Let them
ask Kid Ory, himself a master of New Orleans hokum; or
Joe Oliver, who specialized in . . . muted 'effects' like the
horse-laugh, the baby-cry and the talking cornet, using
glasses, bottles, tin mugs and anything else that came to
hand."

Inexorably, however, the standards of musicianship
rose, because jazz *had* become a profession, if not yet an
acknowledged "art." One sign of the departure from the
folk practices of jazz's infancy was the fact that by the
1920's nearly all apprentices learned their trade from
the beginning on regular instruments. Two decades before,

it was still not uncommon for a youngster to begin on makeshifts of his own invention. Kid Ory's first instrument was a home-made banjo; Jelly Roll Morton put together his own percussion set from two chair-rounds and a tin pan; clarinetist Johnny Dodds first developed an embouchure on a penny whistle while his brother, Baby Dodds, accompanied him on a pile of tin cans. Many of the early jazzmen then graduated to instruments of varying and vulnerable condition that an older member of the family had discarded or that could be bought cheaply in a pawn shop. Some of the first jazzmen waited a long time before they had a really adequate instrument. The next generation, however, usually started on a higher grade of instrument, and quickly became conscious of brand names. Today, most young players will ration their food rather than compromise on the quality of their horns. Some jazzmen, once they achieve renown, insist that companies make up new instruments to their specifications.

There was soon less and less room for semi-amateurs in jazz. For all the romance that has been interwoven with the early history of jazz, criteria of intonation and technique were spotty at first. Old New Orleans musicians insist, for example, that many bands had only one or two superior soloists. The other musicians were relatively competent, but often were better cigar makers than trombonists or drummers. Vaudeville performers and night club singers were more demanding, however, in their requirements of musicians than were picnic-goers or neighborhood dancers. A jazz professional had to be at ease in more than just a few keys, and especially as the big bands developed, he had to be able to read if he wanted steady work. Lester Young was fired from his own father's band—which played carnivals and tent shows—because he had learned his horn entirely by ear. His father wouldn't let Lester back until he had learned to read. "That hurt me real bad," Young remembered, "I practiced every day and was back in the band in about six months."

Among the musicians, a hierarchy of excellence had been established long before there were music magazines and polls. Buddy Bolden and, later, King Oliver had enjoyed acknowledged pre-eminence in New Orleans; Louis Armstrong dominated Chicago and New York in the 1920's and well into the 1930's; pianists "Luckey" Roberts, James P. Johnson and Willie "the Lion" Smith were the criteria for such younger pianists in New York in the 1920's as Duke Ellington, Count Basie and Fats Waller. In every city along the seaboard and throughout the South, Southwest and Midwest, there were local style-setters. Some never recorded, or weren't recorded in the right context, but they are still referred to with awe by musicians who learned from them.

The increased traveling of jazz musicians soon made the hierarchies of jazz less localized. Coleman Hawkins and Louis Armstrong were demonstrating in each town they played that jazz was evolving into a virtuoso discipline, and they usually replaced the local experts as models for the apprentices. Moreover, through the popularization of phonograph records, the beginning player in Wisconsin or Florida had, by the end of the 1920's, a wide selection of major influences to study. As the challenges increased from within the music, new jazzmen were driven to achieve greater command of their instruments and to be able to play more than a dance date or vaudeville engagement required.

Before the first critic wrote that a jazzman was developing a "significant contribution" to the language, the players held their own seminars at after-hour sessions where the musicians themselves were faculty, student body, and critics. New ideas were exchanged and tested; new players were pitted against the established stylists.

B

"We used to call them cuttin' contests," Coleman
Hawkins, the patriarch of the jazz tenor saxophone, recalls. "Like you'd hear about a very good tenor in some
night spot, and I'd have to go down there and cut him."
"We weren't out to change the world musically," Duke
Ellington adds. "We wanted to make a living and get as
much self-satisfaction out of our work as we could."

Another stimulus to self-consciousness arrived with
the specialist magazines. The historians and discog-
raphers of the "new art" already existed in Europe in the
1920's, but only those relatively few jazzmen who traveled
abroad in those years were aware of them. The jazz cult
began to grow on native grounds in the early 1930's. First
were the collectors who began to analyze recordings that
had been originally made, for the most part, to entertain
and had often been released by companies primarily for
the Negro market. As trade magazines such as *Down Beat*
began to grow in the middle and late 1930's, musicians
were able to read acidulous debates about their styles.
They also followed the popularity polls that *Down Beat*
and similar journals instituted.

For all the clamor in the jazz press, however, the
musicians knew that the large majority of the audience
they faced each night was merrily ignorant of the aesthet-
ics of jazz. They still came to hear music that made them
feel good, music that was usually accompaniment for
dancing and drinking. The true jazz public was still small
in the 1930's, and its representatives could be easily identified as those few customers who listened intently over a
night-long beer in preoccupied contrast to the happy
imbibers all around. At dances, the *aficionados* stood im-
movable in front of the bandstand and tried to draw the
musicians into discographical discussions at intermission.

Not only was the majority of the audience that came
to listen indifferent to jazz as "art," but throughout the
1930's, sections of the general populace were actively op-

posed to the music and regarded its players darkly. There were whites who recoiled from jazz because it had been created by Negroes or had been associated with places where inhibitions were quickly lost.

As recently as 1960, Sol Hurok thundered in a British TV debate, "I know cases, murder cases, committed after a wild jazz session and a couple of drinks, . . . Jazz fans lose their sentiment for the parents, for the people, for the community. There's no morality exists any more after this terrible jazz."

There were also many middle-class and upper-middle-class Negroes who objected furiously to jazz because the music reminded them of the past, of the South and slavery. They also feared that the emotional freedom and passion of jazz would reinforce the caricature of the "natural" Negro drawn by the white majority. Ragtime pianist Luckey Roberts recalls that by the early 1900's, the blues were not allowed to be played in the parlors of many "decent" Negro homes. Ralph Ellison, growing up in Oklahoma City in the 1920's, remembers that "jazz was regarded by most of the respectable Negroes of the town as a backward, low-class form of expression,. and there was a marked difference between those who accepted and lived close to their folk experience and those whose status strivings led them to reject and deny it." Ellison himself was later forbidden to play jazz at Tuskegee under threat of expulsion.

Sterling Brown, a professor at Howard University, struggled for years to introduce a knowledge and appreciation of jazz to the "official" precincts of the campus. "I did get to the point," he once said drily, "of being able to play a Milhaud recording in the library and point out that the composition had been influenced by jazz. I think though that I'm still suspect among some of my colleagues because I like and write about the blues."

Pianist Billy Taylor, whose interest in jazz was regarded coldly by the faculty at Virginia State College, wrote in an article for the now defunct Negro magazine, *Duke*, titled *Negroes Don't Know Anything About Jazz*: "Classes in jazz appreciation and jazz technique have long been conducted in many major U.S. colleges and universities, but I haven't heard of any such courses being even mentioned in our Negro institutions of higher learning. Negro high schools and colleges which could do much to make promising young jazz musicians aware of their potential aren't doing it and haven't even tried! They could show these budding players the achievements of their predecessors in the field and offer them encouragement and guidance instead of, as in too many instances, treating such students as offbeat characters and putting them on the defensive by frustrating their attempts to practice and perform for their fellow students. . . . Where are the Negro priests and ministers who could take an active part in showing the good that jazz has done?"

As recently as 1960, a group of young Negro intellectuals were deciding on the policies of a new weekly Harlem paper. The editor, who enjoyed jazz, suggested that the paper give the music and musicians wide coverage in contrast to the avoidance of jazz by most of the Negro press. "It was one of the hardest battles I had," he said later. "Nearly all the other staff members opposed giving jazz more than a little space even though every one of them spent at least one night a week in a jazz club and collected records. They didn't think jazz was 'respectable' enough for a paper as important as we wanted ours to become."

Whatever their reasons for rejecting jazz, few opponents of the music in the 1920's and 1930's, Negro or white, could claim it was particularly difficult to understand. While there was increasing subtlety in the way the rhythms were shaped by the soloists, the rhythmic base of a jazz group's performance was infectiously pulsating

and sturdily regular. While the harmonies of the music
had grown more complex, the improvised variations remained reasonably easy to follow in the case of most
musicians. And the players continued to classify themselves as entertainers. What happened after hours was,
they felt, of interest only to themselves.

It was the modern jazz of Charlie Parker, Thelonious
Monk, Bud Powell, and Dizzy Gillespie that accomplished
the major shift in the attitude of the jazzman toward
his music and his public. Parker and Gillespie had both
grown up in big bands and were all too aware of the
relationship between jazz and show business. (Gillespie
still is; but his clowning, although it disturbs some of the
more austere of the younger musicians and critics, is
considerably more sophisticated and "inside" than the
more openly vaudevillian turns of an older generation of
jazzmen such as Louis Armstrong.) The young modernists of the early 1940's were also heirs of the pride that
jazzmen had been taking in their expanding capacities.
They felt, however, that jazz up to that point no longer
sufficiently challenged them. Accordingly, they evolved a
musical language that required closer attention than the
jazz that preceded them. It could be danced to only by
resiliently creative improvisers, such as the regulars at the
Savoy Ballroom in Harlem. The pulse of the music remained constant but it was persistently overlaid by the
drummer's complex polyrhythms which involved multiple
subtle accents and displacements of the beat. ("Dropping
bombs" became a graphic term for the disturbing "new"
drumming.)

Harmonically, the modernists became so intrigued
by the challenging, expanded chordal possibilities of improvisation advanced by Charlie Parker and his colleagues
that until recently, most players "ran changes" (improvised on the chords of a tune) instead of developing
melodic variations on the theme. The modernists often
played new lines that were based on the chords—but

not the melody—of a standard tune. The casual listeners groped for the tantalizing, implied melody, and many gave up jazz itself as well as the search in frustration.

By the 1950's, however, the concept of jazz as an object in itself, a non-functional music in the sense that it is no longer designed for dancing or background listening, had attracted a sizable new audience for the music. The listeners, or most of them, accepted the music on the players' terms and went to Birdland as if it were Town Hall. Older musicians who have occasionally played modern jazz clubs in recent years are often made nervous by the seeming passivity and stern concentration of contemporary "serious" listeners. Anita O'Day, who is temperamentally of the jazz-as-entertainment tradition, speaks for most of the pre-modernists in insisting: "I feel better when the audience is balling it up a little; then I can relax too." Several of the modernists agree with her, but most expect silence and sustained attention from the customers.

A large part of the contemporary jazz audience, however, is apt to be more "serious" in its mien than in its comprehension of the music. Much of the audience, as has been true in every jazz generation so far, is young and more compulsive about being "hip" to the newest innovations in the music than it is concerned with the content of those innovations. Most of the more febrile enthusiasts, however, abandon the music in their twenties. They may play the recordings of their adolescent years in brief bouts of nostalgia; but like those of their parents who waited in line to see a Benny Goodman stage show, they gradually lose touch with jazz. These are youngsters who find in jazz a surface corollary of their own safely transitory "rebellion" of adolescence. They become attracted to jazz partly because their parents and teachers generally don't "dig" the music. In the early 1950's they were titillated by the bombastic dissonances of Stan Kenton's otherwise largely empty music, but found Thelonious

Monk too "far out." In the late 1930's, their predecessors
bought all the new records of Artie Shaw, but had barely
heard of Lester Young.

An increasing percentage of listeners are staying,
however, through their twenties, thirties, and beyond.
To the musicians, the turnover is still unsettlingly huge
in each generation, and any knowledgable jazzman who
has been around for more than a few years knows that
he can decline in popularity precipitously. Yet he also
knows that there are more listeners in the clubs and at
concerts who are eager to invest the same amount of care
and time in understanding his work as their equally
committed counterparts in classical music. Jazz, in short,
is slowly beginning to acquire a durable audience. Included are listeners who have overcome the initial difficulties of modern jazz and are now willing to cope with
the further challenges of John Coltrane and Ornette
Coleman. Through study and listening, more of them
know and enjoy the entire scope of jazz history—the
Afro-American folk base, early blues and ragtime, the
raw collective improvisation of the New Orleans march-
ing-and-dance bands; the tangy, pre-swing-era, riff-built
drive of the southwestern and midwestern territory units;
and such of the first waves of solo virtuosi as Louis Armstrong, Earl Hines, Roy Eldridge, Coleman Hawkins, Art
Tatum, and Duke Ellington. They recognize that jazz
had a complex, strongly expressive tradition before
Charlie Parker; and that as of 1961, it is beginning what
should be its most unpredictable, daringly exploratory
decade.

The contemporary jazz audience, both its majority
of instantly intoxicated adolescents and its smaller but
significantly growing "serious" segment, is in any case
radically different from the customers that jazz musicians
had to please for the first forty years of the music's history. Except for ragged remnants of parade bands in
New Orleans, the music hasn't been played for funerals

or store openings for a long time—although it is still occasionally enlisted for political rallies. As for contemporary brothels, the preference there, I expect, would be for Mantovani. Jazz is now seldom even played for dancing, except for occasional dates by such big bands as Basie's and Ellington's.

Jazz concert opportunities have accordingly expanded, but the music is still most often heard in night clubs where many jazzmen are more comfortable despite the obbligato of drinks being served and consumed.

"How," asks Miles Davis, "are you going to feel free at a jazz *concert?* And feeling free, after all, is the whole act of jazz. There ain't but two things you can do at a concert—go there and play or go there and sit down. You can't drink; you can't move around." When a friend insisted that the future of jazz was on the concert circuit, Miles snorted. "All right. You listen to what the musicians say *after* a concert. Every time, backstage, someone will say, 'Now, where are you gonna *blow?*' You can't stretch out and really play at a concert and you can't make everybody sit still and feel the same way."

The modern jazzman, as truculently aloof as he may sometimes appear, still wants to reach and move his listeners. Miles Davis retreats into gloomy reappraisal of his work if a room is cold. Thelonious Monk, though he will not dilute his music for more widespread approval, is delighted if the audience is large and enthusiastic. What have been altered are the *terms* on which the jazz musician communicates with his listeners.

The jazzman, no matter how commercially inclined —and not all modern jazzmen are paragons of musical integrity—has inevitably become self-conscious about his work. The modern jazz combo, for example, is much more carefully integrated than the average small group of the 1930's and tries for as distinctively identifiable a repertory and group style as the musicians' imaginations allow.

In more and more clubs, the audience expects the experimenting and "stretching" out to be done during working hours for *them,* and not later for musicians only. As Miles Davis, Thelonious Monk and Ornette Coleman have proved, it has become "commercial" (in the denotative sense of that word) to be as uncompromising in public as one wants to be.

Not all contemporary jazz leaders are interested in further searching, publicly or privately. Some, such as Erroll Garner, have found and stay with a safe formula, but even these formulas are based on more substantial jazz content than previous "commercial" (using the term connotatively) routines such as George Shearing's emasculated modern jazz or Lionel Hampton's sweaty showboating.

It is still far from easy for an unknown player with a strikingly original approach to win acceptance in contemporary jazz; but he is now, as the chapter on Ornette Coleman will indicate, more apt to find the stiffest initial resistance from the established jazz musicians rather than from the audience. A constricting side-effect of many modern jazzmen's increased self-consciousness has been a fear of anything too disruptively "new." Having won attention for their music, they are suspicious of any developments that may suddenly make them sound dated. Thelonious Monk waited for years for large-scale acceptance among musicians, partly because most of the latter were afraid they couldn't play his music. In 1960, Ornette Coleman found more support from non-professionals than he did at first from all but a few musicians.

An irony of the current jazz scene, then, is that much of the audience is more open to the unexpected than many of the musicians. As noted, part of that audience may be receptive mainly for superficial reasons based on a desire to belong to the innermost circle of hipsters. At least, however, it *is* much more attuned to experimentation than the jazz public of any preceding generation.

If the established modern jazz musician is not always fully aware of how much the jazz public is now willing to try to understand, the older jazzman—with his long-term, fiercely pragmatic experience of jazz as a subdivision of popular show business—finds it hard to realize that a basic change has taken place. An example is Duke Ellington. Now in his sixties, Ellington remains the most original composer in jazz, but he is unable to abandon his fragmentized view of the jazz public. For a time, he tried to, but his optimism was premature. From 1943 to 1950, Ellington prepared an annual Carnegie Hall program of new and at least hopefully major works. He usually repeated the concert at Boston's Symphony Hall and similar locations. The initial reaction was encouraging—though not from the critics—but Ellington eventually became discouraged and decided that there was not a large enough "serious" jazz audience to support such ventures.

Ellington continues to compose, but his musicians complain that they get to perform only a small percentage of his new material. In fact, most of Ellington's more remarkable early originals are no longer played by him. The band concentrates on the more familiar Ellington standards and on those of his new recordings that appear to have the most commercial potential. Ellington hires mediocre singers to appeal to what he expects will be the square element in any audience. Even in his concert programs, he invariably mixes only a small amount of provocative new material with medleys of "old favorites" and slight pieces aimed primarily at the type of non-jazz night club-goers to whom he still occasionally plays in such locations as Las Vegas.

In the summer of 1956, Ellington was presented in two concerts as part of the jazz series of the Stratford, Ontario, Shakespeare Festival. He selected a characteristic program that included a few challenging numbers, a lengthy, banal drum exhibition and several flimsy vocal novelties. The audience, which had come both for the plays and to learn more about jazz, was visibly disappointed. Ellington admitted after the first night that he had underestimated the listeners, but his ingrained habit of "entertaining" the broadest possible audience to keep his band and himself solvent led him to repeat exactly the same program for his second Stratford concert.

Three years later, in Europe, Ellington disappointed audiences in Britain and on the continent by seldom changing his programs and by scheduling only a few of his more challenging works. When the tour's promoter, Norman Granz, criticized him bitterly one evening for his conservatism, Ellington answered with equal heat that he knew what the audiences had come for and he intended to give them what they wanted. Ellington was wrong. European jazz audiences, in fact, have generally been more demanding musically than those in America for some time.

From the 1920's on, the European public for jazz, as Francis Newton has noted in his book, *The Jazz Scene* (The Monthly Review Press), "has been markedly middle-class and intellectual. . . . On the Continent, jazz had the advantage of fitting smoothly into the ordinary pattern of *avant-garde* intellectualism." In America, until comparatively recently, most American intellectuals ignored jazz or excoriated it along with nearly all popular culture. Most of those comparatively few intellectuals who adopted jazz did so because they viewed it with bellicose romanticism as one of the last vestiges of a folk-rooted "purer" popular art. As the music, no longer a functional folk expression, inevitably became more sophisticated, many of the intellectuals left it in anger, keening that jazz had become corrupted by European influences and by the very fact that it had turned professional.

James Agee mourned that it used to be possible to hear "true lyric jazz at the point when the deep-country and the town have first fertilized each other, and before imitation, ambition and the possibility of earning much of anything . . . destroyed it." More recently, Nelson Algren complained that jazz was losing its vitality and "should be kept in the kitchen." Ralph Ellison, who has been a musician and has written excellent appreciations of Charlie Christian and Jimmy Rushing for the *Saturday Review,* also looks back at the older, less technically complicated players as having been among the last extensions of John Henry. "The older jazzmen," he says, "were even bigger in size. They *looked* as if they had more to say."

Yet by the late 1950's, more of the younger American intellectuals, even including some Negro writers and educators, had become intrigued by jazz and joined the small but multiplying adult section of the jazz audience. The quarterlies are still largely ignorant of jazz and its subculture, but the music now has its own "serious" journals in America as well as abroad. Among the critics for these magazines are several of the musicians themselves, another index of the changing intellectual climate of jazz.

Most of the younger players now approach jazz as a career with as much seriousness as apprentices in classical music. More are coming from middle- and upper-class homes. Jazz has always had some children of skilled workers, businessmen, and professionals; and the percentage rose during the 1920's as more Negro children of solid bourgeois families (Coleman Hawkins, Don Redman, Duke Ellington, Fletcher Henderson) began to find in jazz an expanding area for their ambitions. Particularly in the past decade, however, many white and Negro children, whose families have the resources to support schooling for more conventional careers, are choosing jazz as a life's work.

The young jazzman today often does attend an established music school because of the increasingly demanding requirements of jazz; but once he is trained, he still must—as has been true throughout jazz history—find his own way.

When Sahib Shihab, a reedman, told Thelonious Monk a few years ago that he was returning to Juilliard for additional courses, Monk cautioned him: "Well, I hope you don't come out any worse than you sound now." "I know what he meant," said Shihab. "He was referring to what has happened to several jazz musicians who go to school, and then, when they get out, are scared to play certain things that don't fit with what they've been taught. They lose that urgency of personal discovery that's jazz."

For all the changes that have taken place in the nature of the music, the musicians and the audience for jazz, the goal of the jazz musician still remains that proclaimed by Charles Mingus, a bristlingly serious modern jazzman: "I play or write *me*, the way I feel, through jazz, or whatever, whether it's hip or not. Music is a language of the emotions. If someone has been escaping reality, I don't expect him to dig my music . . . my music is alive and it's about the living and the dead, about good and evil. It's angry, and it's real because it *knows* it's angry."

3

The Apprenticeship and the Accounting

Whether he comes from Juilliard or is largely self-taught, the young jazz musician usually finds the period of apprenticeship difficult and lonely. Many Negro players work in rhythm-and-blues bands until they can find a place in a jazz combo. Other beginners pay the rent through jobs in strip joints and commercial bands until they're accepted by the established jazzmen.

To indicate the "dues" the apprentice usually has to pay, I've focused on the hardest town of all, New York. Certainly there have been jazzmen who have first made their reputations in other cities, but for most, the final tournament takes place in New York. Here the jazzman from Detroit or Houston or Paris is tested. The judges who are initially most vital to him are the other musicians. He is interested economically in being noticed by the critics, but with very rare exceptions, the young musician's self-respect rides on what the established players say. So do his chances of getting more and more challenging work.

"This place," says patriarch Coleman Hawkins, "makes *all* musicians sound kind of funny when they come around. When they first come *here*, I don't care what they were in their home towns, when they come

here, they get cut. . . . They have to come here and learn
all over again, practically. Then when they come back
they are all right. Or, if they stay around they can develop to be all right."

Hawkins cited the case of Florida alto saxophonist
Julian "Cannonball" Adderley and his brother, Nat, a
trumpet player. They arrived in the summer of 1955,
made an initial impression, but according to Hawkins,
"the boys were talking. . . . 'His brother plays a nice trumpet, but man, he's *nothing!*' . . . Well, Cannonball left—
he came back . . . he's blowin' now."

Now a successful combo leader, Adderley agrees
with Hawkins about New York: "No matter how much
talent and experience a player brings here, there are
things to learn when he sits down with a seasoned band.
. . . No matter what they bring here, New York shakes
them. A young tenor player was complaining to me that
Coleman Hawkins made him nervous. Man, I told him
Hawkins was *supposed* to make him nervous. Hawkins
has been making other sax players nervous for 40 years.
. . . This town is like a world governing body of jazz."

The key testing grounds used to be jam sessions, but
these informal after-hours debates have become less frequent. One reason for their decline is involved with the
increased compartmentalization of jazz. Nearly any jazz
player could "sit-in" nearly anywhere twenty-five years
ago. But now there are more generic styles than there
were in the 1920's and 1930's—although not as many individual styles—and as a result, cliques have developed.
There are also racial divisions. The older men have become separated from the younger. The "hard boppers"
and "soul brothers" seldom associate with the practitioners of softer, more melodic jazz. The experimentalists are
divided from the neo-orthodox followers of Charlie
Parker. The old-style, free-for-all sessions are therefore
difficult to assemble. And furthermore, since most established players are now grouped into their own combos,

their need for jamming is not nearly so compelling as in
the 1930's when many of the better players were limited
to brief solos in big bands during working hours and
needed room to stretch out musically before they went
home.

With infrequent jam sessions and so few big bands
left in which to gain experience, the newcomer to New
York, white or Negro, finds the pressure of getting training and acceptance more immediately productive of
acute anxiety than his predecessors did. The apprentice
has to catch on as best he can, and nearly all forms of
work, including jazz, are scarce. Of the 30,000 members
of New York's Local 802, American Federation of Musicians, perhaps 3000 work fairly regularly.

If the apprentice has no contacts to begin with, he
must somehow become known to the regularly working
players. No notices of auditions are published anywhere.
If a leader makes a change or a sideman quits, hiring and
recommendations for hiring are all by word-of-mouth.
"It's the same thing in the studios, and the Broadway
shows," says one Negro musician. "That's why it took us
so long to get in there. If you can't live in the same part
of the city with the other guys, if you don't hang around
with them, you don't hear about the jobs." A complete
loner in New York music, of whatever color, is apt to
starve if he thinks talent alone will feed him.

Most of the younger players, however, know someone when they arrive. There has been, for example, a
large number of Detroit emigrants to New York in the
past seven years. The earlier adventurers are now part of
"the establishment" so that the newer wave at least has a
chance to be heard and considered for jobs. A similar
geographically oriented hiring-hall exists for most of the
other players in a latter-day equivalent of Jewish *lands-
men* organizations.

An out-of-towner is not fully admitted to Local 802,

American Federation of Musicians, for six months. For the first three months, he can only play one-nighters in the area, although he can begin working regularly after those three months. There are ways around the regulations. A card has been given a player after three months if he has a job with a band that will be spending most of its time out of town for the next three months. And if a booking agency has a particular interest in getting a man a card immediately, a certain amount of "persuasion" will usually work.

While waiting for jazz employment, the Negro player especially finds it harder to get other kinds of jobs, although conditions are improving in New York where the racial discrimination that existed in the networks, Broadway pit bands and classical orchestras has been somewhat modified as a result of a 1958 Urban League report that embarrassed symphony orchestras, Broadway producers, and network officials. The union still countenances an extraordinary procedure by which contractors —hiring agents—are both union members and hirelings of employers. These powerful figures build up their own factions and few of them will voluntarily hire Negroes.

In addition to waiting for a union card, the newcomer also has to apply for a police permit. New York is the only major city which requires anyone who works for more than three days where liquor is sold to be approved by the division of licenses of the police department. A musician or waiter has to be fingerprinted and mugged, and pay $2 for his cabaret card. The card has to be renewed at the same fee every two years. The money finds its way—with no statutory authority—into the police pension fund.

There is strong indication that this requirement is unconstitutional but no musician or other night club employee had the money to fight a denial of his card through the courts, until a test case was instituted in late

1960. The case has been lost in the state courts, and there is no indication, as of this writing, that funds exist to try an appeal to the Supreme Court. Permits have often been denied on whim. A card has been refused because a musician has been arrested—not convicted—in the past. A card has been denied because a player was arrested ten years before for having a gun in his car. A previous arrest for possession of marijuana or narcotics usually means automatic denial unless the musician has heard of Maxwell T. Cohen, a tough lawyer who consistently fights card cases, and sometimes wins them.

One of Cohen's clients summoned an impressive collection of character witnesses for a hearing a couple of years ago—writers, recording officials, even a priest. The card was denied a few weeks later. When the musician asked for permission to buy a transcript of his hearing, he was told that the minutes hadn't been transcribed yet.

If a player has ever been convicted previously of a felony or certain specified misdemeanors (such as possession of narcotics or "lewdness"), he may not be able to work even if he somehow gets a police card, since a musician also needs a work permit from the State Liquor Authority which has its own quixotic criteria. It does appear, however, that if a booking agency or another interested party has strong economic reasons for wanting a man to have a card, the card can somehow be obtained.

Having been mugged, printed, granted a police card and a union card, the player then begins the obstacle course. If he acquires enough of a reputation to draw the interest of a record company, he may well be cozened into signing a contract by which the firm has so much the upper accounting hand that at the end of the contract the musician will owe the label money. Options usually are entirely at the firm's discretion and generally run for two additional one-year-options after the contract's first year. Costs of a session, album covers and liners and "promotion" are usually charged against the leader of a date, and some strange bills have been included under "promotion." Sometimes the man in charge of recording has a *sub rosa* publishing firm and insists that several of the songs he controls be included on a session, or the leader will not be allowed to play the tunes *he* wants to. Not all companies are dishonest and the musicians' grapevine eventually warns a player about those he should avoid.

Few jazz leaders derive much income from recordings—except, of course, for the major figures in the field. Accordingly, most jazzmen try to get as large advances against royalties as they can because they expect to see hardly any royalties. Sidemen get paid only for the date, no matter how much their improvisations contribute to the eventual success of the record. Grace notes—such as sending a sideman a copy of the record on which he's played—are practically unknown in the record business.

Club work is not especially well paid. In some of the Greenwich Village jazz clubs, scale is as low as $76 for a six-day week (Local 802 is seldom militant for its jazz constituents). Birdland in midtown pays about $130 for a six-day week, as does the Roundtable with hours from 8:15 to 2:30 or 9:45 to 3:45. A sideman can get all of $154 for a six-night week at the Embers on the East Side, but he has to work from 7:30 P.M. to 3:45 A.M.

With some exceptions, club owners are not especially fond of jazz and hardly regard the musicians as "artists." Dressing rooms are tiny or non-existent and about the only refuge a player can find between sets is a neighboring bar. Normally querulous, the owners are further harassed by insistent police graft. There are not only the Christmas payoffs but there is the week-to-week greed. A cop who is overlooked can palm the soap in the men's room and issue a summons to the club owner for not having a cake there. He can find the club's illumination wanting or he can otherwise maintain pressure until he gets on the gift list.

The gall of some keepers of the peace is awesome. I
was talking one evening about nine with a jazz club
owner when a man in street clothes came in and tried to
mooch five dollars. I moved away, assuming the man to
be a friend or relative of the owner. The visitor became
louder and increasingly importunate. Finally, the owner
went to the register and gave him the five.

"That," the owner said in disgust after the solicitor
left, "was a clerk at the local precinct. He doesn't even
walk the beat, but he makes the gravy rounds like the
rest of them. He was bugging me so much because this
was his first call of the evening, and he's superstitious. He
figured if he didn't make out here, he wouldn't have a
good night."

Some cops, notably in Greenwich Village, are actively
displeased when a room begins to attract Negro-white
couples. When Charles Mingus played one club, he drew
a considerable number of mixed couples, and the local
constabulary told the owner not to book Mingus again.
"That guy encourages miscegenation."

New York obviously isn't Birmingham, but a Negro
musician with a white girl often finds the evening hazard-
ous. Several have been beaten up, again especially in the
Village, and it is not uncommon for a taxi to pass by
mixed couples. "Why," asked one young lady after two
cabs had whizzed by, "don't they stop?"

"Because you're Jewish," her Negro pianist friend
assured her.

Though hoods don't own all the jazz clubs, they own
some. One owner assigned a bodyguard to a vocalist who
wanted to leave his club and his record company. "Be a
nice girl, sweetie," he soothed her, "or I'll break your
arm." One owner somehow manages to persuade nearly
everyone who appears regularly at his club to sign with
his record company. The same label was one of the leading disbursers of payola to disc jockeys, according to
belated FCC statistics.

The jungle hardly ends at the city limits. Musicians playing some of the summer festivals found in 1960 that a new combine which controlled several of the outdoor packages had forced prices down so that if a man wanted to work any of their cultural events, he had to take their price or be frozen out. The booking agencies are run, some musicians complain, "like plantations." If a player doesn't like the way he's being treated, he can move on to another "plantation"—if he can get his release. When a leader becomes a valuable enough property, the office is solicitous of his desires; but so long as the commissions a leader brings in are small, he "co-operates" and takes whatever work is given him at whatever fee, or he's ignored. Moves to start a co-operative, musician-directed agency have so far failed because most of the players fear being blacklisted by the large agencies. If the booking offices are against them, most of the clubs will follow. Several agencies "block-book." If a club owner wants to buy a group he knows will draw, the agency handling the combo may make clear that the club owner can have the unit only if he'll take one or more lesser combos. If an owner were to deal with an agency directed by musicians, he might not be offered any of the other offices' more desirable properties.

A few bookers at the agencies are concerned with developing a musician's career for other reasons besides the amount of commissions they can collect. For example, Jack Whittemore of the Shaw Artists Corporation works exceedingly long hours, visits his clients in the clubs to hear their complaints, and often becomes involved in their personal problems.

For some musicians—Miles Davis, particularly—Whittemore has worked even harder. He understands Davis, respects Davis' desire not to work constantly, and tries to arrange a schedule that will allow Davis long spaces at home during which Davis can just rest or un-

hurriedly prepare his record dates. Whittemore serves
as an interpreter of Davis to club owners and concert
promoters and gets Davis—with astute coaching from
Davis himself—the maximum possible prices. Davis has
received as high as $3500 for one set at a summer fes-
tival. He receives at least $2500 for a one-nighter, and
sometimes is paid $3500 a night if he has to play two
concerts. On a weekly basis, Miles usually works for
$3500 to $4000.

Whittemore's favorite story of Davis' own bargaining
acumen concerns a Town Hall concert a few years ago at
a time when Davis' normal price for a one-show concert
was $1000. The Town Hall contract was for two per-
formances in the same night—an evening and a midnight
show. Whittemore told Davis he might be able to get the
price up to $1500 for the two shows. Davis suggested a
solution. "I'll take $1000 for the first show and $500 for
the second, but you tell the promoter to rope off half the
house for the second show and sell tickets for just the
half that's left." Davis was paid $2000 for the two
performances.

Davis is rare among musicians, however, in his stubborn skill at bargaining. One player, a major jazzman, has
had to remain with the same record label for many years
even though he has received considerably more lucrative
offers from other firms who would also spend much more
money promoting him than his present label does. The
musician is in thrall because he cannot break himself of
the habit of asking for advances against royalties. The
owner of the label eventually will get the loans back
from the record sales. At the end of each contract period,
however, the musician owes so much money at that point,
he feels he *has* to continue with the label. Booking offices
have occasionally also played cat-and-mouse in advancing
money to a musician so that he is never free to leave the
office. The musician can switch to another agency, of

course, if he is able to pay his debt; but the musician who keeps asking for loans is generally never in a financial position to buy his freedom.

Nor are all booking agents honest. Charles Mingus tells the not uncommon story of a combo being booked for $2000 a week, of which the leader only received $1750. The leader finally learned of the arrangement, but never did get back his money.

More competent personal managers would help prevent musicians from setting their own traps and falling into others, but there are very few who know the business thoroughly, have the tenacity to fight for their clients' rights with booking agencies and club owners, and are honest. One player, for example, received a statement from a record company charging him $500 for work on his date by the company's own a&r (artists and repertory) director. The a&r man is paid by the record label, and charging his fee against the artist's royalties was palpable fraud. The musician had a personal manager who protested to the owner of the firm, and the $500 "debt" was erased. The same manager, John Levy, a former musician, extricated a client, Julian "Cannonball" Adderley, from a seven-year contract with a company. The union only allows three-year pacts; but Adderley, who signed with the firm shortly after he came north from Florida, didn't know the rules. Another performer— with a poor personal manager—signed a contract which allowed the company to stop her royalties if she ever left the company although the firm could continue to sell her records indefinitely.

Without a personal manager, the jazz leader finds that having to worry simultaneously about business affairs and his playing is too exhausting a burden. He usually ends up concentrating on the music. Art Blakey, for instance, had no manager until recently. His group in 1960 was getting between $1500 and $1750 a week, filling

nearly every club they played, but receiving no increase
the next time around. "I'm out on the road when the contracts come in," he explains, "and it's hard to bargain
from that far away and keep on top of the music too. So
I generally take what they offer."

When the CBS radio network broadcasts from the
summer jazz festivals, the musicians are usually offered
flat scale even though the programs are sponsored. Those
with personal managers, however, generally succeed in
holding out for a fairer rate.

By union rule a manager gets a five per cent commission. Usually, however, he has a personal contract with
the player for an additional five per cent. An agency
receives ten per cent commission on location dates and
fifteen per cent for one-nighters. The bookers concentrate
on their best-paying properties; lesser names and com-
parative unknowns find it difficult to get steady work
without a personal manager. A disgruntled leader can get
a release from an agency if he can prove that he has been
out of work for six consecutive weeks and has received no
offer of any job from the agency within that period. The
clause is seldom invoked, because any office that wants
to hold a client (in case he may eventually become successful) can dredge up an offer of at least a one-nighter
every six weeks. The musician without a major reputation and without a personal manager signs with an office
even though he knows he can't expect much encouragement or work from the booker. He signs, because he has
no place else to go.

Even with a superior manager, a leader who is not
yet established finds that trying to keep a band together
on the road is usually a harrowing experience. "Cannonball" Adderley has given an account of his experiences
in 1956, and the situation he describes has not changed.
As a matter of fact, when Ornette Coleman first went on
the road at the beginning of 1960, he had to pay his side-

men's salaries, traveling expenses, union taxes, and booking office commissions out of $800 a week for four men.

"Cannonball," during his first expeditions as a
leader, was getting $1000 a week for five men. As he re-
calls, "Out of that came $150 commission for my manager
and booking office, $75 in union taxes (a third of which
we eventually got back), about $125 in Federal with-
holding taxes, and maybe another $15 in social security
taxes. Now we should have deposited the money due the
government in a separate account every week. But after
a while, we began spending that money because we also
had gasoline bills, hotel bills (for my brother and myself). We were paying the sidemen $125 out of which
they had to pay their hotel bills.

"By September of the next year, 1957, although we
had been working steadily, we were about $9000 in
debt. We had no royalties from our recordings and had
only made scale for making them. Besides, a lot of recording costs were charged against us which shouldn't have
been. The band had not been particularly successful in
that we had done about the same amount of business all
the time. Very few clubs lost money on us, but they didn't
make a hell of a lot either.

"We finally broke up that first band. After twenty
months, we still couldn't get more than $1000 a week."

Adderley then spent two years as a featured sideman with Miles Davis, became better known, and started
a band again in 1959. His quintet now gets a minimum of
$1000 for a one-nighter, averages $1500 to $2000 a week,
and is gradually moving into the $2500-a-week category.
These fees will last, of course, only so long as Adderley is
"hot"; and since the jazz life is still very much a part of
show business economically, there are absolutely no
guarantees.

There are signs that a number of the younger established musicians are becoming somewhat more sophis-

ticated about the business aspects of jazz, and are trying
to make sure they get their full share of the profits while
they're on the ascendant. They read contracts more carefully than most of the older jazzmen did, and are much
more suspicious of the booking offices, club owners, and
record companies. The suspicion often verges on paranoia,
but many have been so exploited in the past that their
current bitterness is at least understandable. It would be
almost impossible for a record company today to persuade a new bandleader—as Decca did Count Basie in
1936—to sign a contract providing for no royalties at all.
Nor is a young composer now likely to be pressured, as
Duke Ellington was in the 1930's, to split his royalties
with "co-writers" who can't read, let alone compose
music.

In fact, as original compositions become a more
important factor in jazz, several young writers have
formed their own publishing firms. They hope that if
enough of their tunes become jazz standards, they may at
least derive a small income from their publishing as well
as their writing royalties in the autumnal years.

Unfortunately, musicians can still only find out from
each other what new sleight-of-hand stratagems have
been developed by the more amoral businessmen in the
trade. The jazz press is weak on reporting skills, and
except for syndicated columnist Ralph Gleason, seldom
hints at the more questionable practices of several of the
major enterpreneurs. Competent personal managers remain scarce; booking agents are usually distrusted; the
union is regarded as disinterested; and there is no professional organization of jazz musicians which could serve as
a clearing house of information and as a pressure group.
Accordingly, most jazzmen continue to think of themselves as loners, exploited or ignored by the day people.
The few attempts made to organize a guild of working
jazz musicians have failed because the itinerant lives of
most jazzmen make regular meetings difficult or because

there is such uncontrolled suspicion among some players that they no longer trust anyone, including their colleagues.

For many reasons, some due to the temperaments of the players themselves, the jazz life is not usually best suited for those who are gregarious or guileless.

4

Soul and Collard Greens

One of the first and most unpleasant surprises for the more guileless white apprentices is the realization that despite the legend of jazz as an ideal democracy where only musicianship, not pigmentation, counts, there is prejudice in jazz. And often it is reverse prejudice.

A few years ago, the wife of the Negro leader of a jazz trio finally discovered that the reason several of her friends had begun to seem distant was that her husband had hired a white bassist. "There are enough of ours looking for work," she was told, "without his giving a job to one of *them*."

In the same city, Los Angeles, a Negro bass player joined the trio of a white leader and was severely criticized by his friends in the Negro community. "That combo wouldn't swing at all if you weren't there," he was lectured. "Why do you go with them and make those whites sound good?"

In New York, a white pianist said recently, "I'd prefer not to work in an all-white band, at least not with an all-white rhythm section, because there aren't that many white guys who can really swing."

A white trombonist-leader had been explaining to the same pianist a few hours earlier why he would hire no Negroes. "There are still places I can't get booked into with a mixed group; and besides, it's much less trouble in other ways too. Listen, I'm not prejudiced, but I'm in this to make a living."

Backstage at a Town Hall jazz concert, an angry Negro bassist, waving a copy of a jazz magazine, shouted, "They tell us we're the best jazz musicians and that we invented the music. So how come they get most of the work?"

These not atypical incidents reflect dissonances of the jazz life which are seldom discussed, but which eventually reach nearly everyone involved in the music. There is, it should be re-emphasized, more interracial social equality in jazz than in any other area of American society because more whites and Negroes actually come to know each other as individuals in jazz than they are yet likely to in their business or social lives.

It is also true that for several years, mixed small units—and to a lesser extent, mixed big bands—have managed to exist in jazz, though the first major break-through didn't take place until late 1935 when Benny Goodman hired Teddy Wilson. There had been a few mixed record dates before then, but Goodman was the first white leader to hire a Negro as a regular member of his unit and, as a matter of fact, Wilson began his associa-tion with Goodman only as a member of a trio with the orchestra rather than as the regular band pianist.

The difference in patterns of segregation between the jazz world and American society in general, however, is that in jazz there are Negro musicians who are not yet ready to extend full musical and social equality to whites.

One reason why many Negroes are reluctant to accept white jazzmen is economic. From the beginning, Negro musicians have resented the fact that white jazz-men, by and large, have had a wider choice of better-paying jobs, more publicity, and more credit from the public. Even fifty years ago in New Orleans, the fear existed that whites might copy what the Negro had originated.

New Orleans trumpeter Freddie Keppard rejected a 1916 Victor invitation to make the first of all jazz phonograph records because he was afraid that his music would be easier to steal if it were ubiquitously available. As a result, the white Original Dixieland Jazz Band was the first jazz group to record.

In the 1930's, when the large jazz bands were in the ascendant, the Goodmans and Dorseys and Shaws were the most consistent money-makers while the musically superior Negro bands of Duke Ellington, Count Basie, and Jimmie Lunceford (all of whom had vitally influenced the white bands) were usually restricted to less lucrative engagements and more grueling road trips, many of them through the South.

"Some of those people," recalls bassist Milt Hinton, who traveled the South for years with Cab Calloway, "came and paid their money just to heckle the Negro bands, like some people like to tease an animal, and we had no recourse."

A characteristic experience of the Duke Ellington band was described in 1944 by Richard O. Boyer in a *New Yorker* profile of Ellington. He was telling of a trip to St. Louis:

> ". . . when the colored members of the band went out for lunch after the first performance, they couldn't find a restaurant in the neighborhood that would serve them. They didn't have time to go over to the segregated district before they were due onstage again. They returned to the theater and arranged for a white man to go out and buy sandwiches at a drugstore. When the proprietor of the store, making inquiry, found that the sandwiches were for a Negro band, he refused to fill the order. A few minutes later the men went back to work, hungry, the curtain rose, and from the white audience out front there came a burst of applause. The crowd

cheered, whistled, and stamped its feet. As the curtain was going up, the dejection on the faces of the players vanished, and as swiftly as an electric light is switched on, it was replaced by a look of joy. The music blared, Duke smiled, threw back his head, and shouted 'Ah-h-h!' Rex Stewart took off on a solo that was greeted with fervor, and as he bowed, the musician next to him muttered out of the side of his mouth, 'Bend, you hungry fathead. Bend!' "

Even in the North, a Negro with a Negro band wasn't safe from humiliation. When the late Billie Holiday played the Fox Theater in Detroit with Count Basie, she recalls in her autobiography, *Lady Sings the Blues*, "they told Basie I was too yellow to sing with all the black men in his band. Somebody might think I was white if the light didn't hit me just right. So they got special dark grease paint and told me to put it on. . . . It's like they say, there's no damn business like show business."

Later, Billie traveled with the white Artie Shaw band. She endured the predictable hurts of traveling through the South as a Negro with a white orchestra and was supported emotionally to some degree by the sympathy of the musicians, but she couldn't withstand the bitter disappointment in the North when she was no longer allowed to sing with the band on its coast-to-coast wire from the Lincoln Hotel in New York. The Southerners, she noted, had at least been honest about their bigotry.

One of literally innumerable examples of incidents that refuel Negro jazzmen's anger is the 1960 case of a Pacific Jazz album cover. The leader of the combo on the record was Joe Newman, a Negro trumpet player with Count Basie. The album was recorded in Sweden, and the cover portrait was of Newman and his white Swedish fiancee.

Several weeks after its American release, the album

was withdrawn from sale because of its cover. The owner
of Pacific Jazz, Richard Bock, explained: "Dealers and
distributors in all parts of the country have refused to
display and promote the album because it shows a Negro
man with a white girl. I have decided to change the
cover in order to make it less objectionable. I don't want
the album to die and I can't force record dealers to take
the album as it now stands. I regret this very much, but
it is necessary."

Toward the end of the 1930's and the beginning of
the 1940's, several of the younger Negro musicians became restless, not only with the language of jazz up to
that point but also with the externally polite behavior of
most Negro musicians to white players and audiences.
The "boppers" at the beginning of modern jazz, states
Mary Lou Williams, "deliberately worked out a music
they thought would be hard to steal." And the seemingly
bored, distant, on-stand behavior of some of them in night
clubs seemed to defy the audiences to want to relate to
the "new" music.

As before, however, white musicians quickly moved
in on modern jazz and many, in fact, contributed importantly to its development. Yet by the 1950's, when the
white pianist Dave Brubeck and his unit achieved unprecedented publicity and commercial success for a
modern jazz group, he was bitterly resented by a number
of Negro musicians, not on personal grounds but because
he was another white who had, they felt, harvested huge
rewards from what Negroes had largely started.

"I was on the same bill with Brubeck," a prominent
Negro trumpet player-leader has said, "and his combo
got nearly all the attention even though they were playing nothing. It's like the people took it for granted that we
could swing because we were Negroes, but thought it
was something to make a fuss about when whites do it."

A corollary source for the anger of Negro jazzmen is

the fact that for nearly all of them, no matter how thorough their training or diverse their goals, work opportunities are limited to jazz or rock 'n' roll. Modern jazzmen, Negro and white, have had to become unusually skilled technically in order to meet the increasingly complex challenges of jazz; but most TV and film studio work remains closed to Negroes. The Negro who is fully qualified for work in a symphony orchestra is even more likely to be frustrated. Though a very few symphony orchestras have admitted an isolated Negro or two in the past few years, most are all-white, an area of Jim Crow that for years has escaped the attention of even the most "liberal" concertgoers.

Among the few Negroes who have been auditioned for studio and other "institutional" engagements, several have been made to feel excessively conscious of their race by the straw bosses. In 1956 Roy Eldridge auditioned for a job in the orchestra of a late night network television show. "Because I was a jazz musician and because I was a Negro," says Roy, "the music director came on with warnings that I'd better not be drunk and with questions about how well I could really read. I've been a professional for thirty years, and I have to prove myself now?"

Furthermore, there is less socializing off the stand between most white and Negro jazz musicians than an idealistic jazz listener might imagine. Close interracial friendships and visiting between families do exist, but most white jazzmen tend to hang out with other whites and Negroes with Negroes. One factor that works against frequent casual socializing everywhere in the country, of course, is that most Negroes are forced by housing discrimination to live in different neighborhoods—as in the Los Angeles area, for example—that are often a considerable distance from each other.

The pressures are initiated, therefore, in the surrounding society. It is because Negroes are denied full

c

acceptance as individuals outside jazz that they take such
fierce pride in the fact that at least jazz is theirs, that it
began as Afro-American music, and that the majority of
its most internationally applauded figures are Negro.
Since the whites outside fight their entrance into homes
and schools and jobs, many Negro musicians are all the
more determined to fight to keep jazz for themselves, or
as much of it as they can. Added to this is the further
irony, as I've noted, that many locals of the American
Federation of Musicians, the union they must join to get
work of any quality, have for years been Jim Crowed into
white and Negro divisions.

Accordingly, jazz has come to symbolize for many
Negro musicians a secret society to which American whites
have to pay heavily to be admitted. In the plantation
days, another kind of musical secret society existed. Field
hollers and work songs often doubled as codes to allow
the slaves to communicate plans for rebellion or their
hatred and scorn for their overseers, or just to warm
themselves with the knowledge that they had something
of their own, if only a language, that the whites couldn't
control. Later, after the Civil War, many of the blues had
double meanings, as did some of the language that
Negroes began to develop among themselves.

The development of a Negro argot was in part a protest against the very language as well as behavior of the
whites. In *Phylon: The Atlanta University Review of
Race and Culture,* Simon Podair has indicated just one
subspecies of "white" language whose connotations many
Negroes resent—black magic, blackball, blacken, black-
guard, blacklist, blackmail, and black sheep. Negro code
language, on the other hand, has developed words and
implications that reversed the negative. "Ofay," once a
Negro term for a white, is said by some theorists to be
pig Latin for "foe;" but whatever its etymology, the usual
connotation of the now passé word was at best neutral
and usually hostile. Once, in a night club in Detroit, a

Negro modern jazz player cursed one of his sidemen loudly for playing "too white."

Years before, when Roy Eldridge first came to New York, he had been strongly influenced by Red Nichols. Lips Page heard him and said, "Man, how come you play like an ofay trumpet player?" Page took Eldridge to hear Louis Armstrong, and Eldridge's soul was saved. Eldridge in turn carried the message. Long after he had become established, Eldridge was invited to play at Jefferson High School in Los Angeles with accompaniment by the school band. In that band was Charles Mingus. "One of the guys in the band, a Negro," Mingus recalls, "was putting down the older players like Roy. He said they couldn't play in tune, couldn't play in a section, and that they weren't trained at all. He was impressed by white technicians. He'd written a little thing for Roy to play, and Roy preferred not to. I mentioned something to Roy along the line this guy had said, and then Roy told me: 'You see this horn. I play what I feel on it. That's jazz. You'd better find out about the music of your people. Someday you're going to thank me for talking to you like this.'"

Despite this strong racial proprietary feeling, there has also been much warm rapport between jazzmen of different races. Though Negro musicians have been innovators in all the various stages of jazz, several influential Negro jazzmen fully credit white players for having helped shape their own careers. Both the late Lester Young and Benny Carter, for example, have expressed their debt to the late Frank Trumbauer; and at one time in his career, Rex Stewart, though Joe Smith and Louis Armstrong were the trumpeters he most admired, could play several Bix Beiderbecke solos by heart.

There has also been a continuing tradition in jazz of older Negro musicians helping and advising young whites. The late Baby Dodds, for instance, supplied Gene Krupa and George Wettling with many tips when he was with King Oliver on the South Side of Chicago in the 1920's.

During the same era, Louis Armstrong befriended Muggsy Spanier, and in more recent times Charlie Parker encouraged Gerry Mulligan.

But in the past ten years or so, this tradition has not been quite as evident. There is the experience of the young Negro trombonist from Detroit who came close to starvation during several months of trying to establish himself in New York, but nourished himself on the belief that his jazz at least had the authenticity that many white musicians lacked. His playing had "soul," and, as he once explained the term warily to a white jazz critic, "that soul only comes from certain kinds of experiences, and only we—you know who I mean—go through what you need to have the kind of soul that makes real jazz."

The use of the words "soul" and "funk" among many young Negro modern jazzmen sometimes differs from the use of those words by jazz critics. Both groups intend the terms to indicate approbation, but the Negro musicians often add the connotation that "soul" and "funk" are exclusively Negro qualities. "Funk" or "funky," in fact, has had its meaning almost entirely reversed in Negro usage, having originally meant something egregiously dirty or smelly. Now, to the embarrassment of some older Negro musicians, the word has come to mean basic, earthy, blues-based jazz.

The frequency with which "soul" has entered into the conversation of young Negro jazzmen is allied to the fact that many of the young Negro modernists have in the past few years taken reawakened pride in the Negro origins of jazz, the folk blues, and gospel music. A number of players whose size of "soul" is admired especially by their Negro contemporaries would agree with Quincy Jones, who told a French jazz magazine that "le style 'funky' est né à l'église"; and several of them have written quasi-gospel jazz pieces like The Preacher, Sermonette, The Congregation, and This Here.

In a way, glorification of gospel and blues is similar

in motivation to the Negro intellectuals' discovery forty
and more years ago that the Negro *did* have a pre-slavery
history that included several complex, creative civiliza-
tions. Aligned with this motivation for finding the "roots"
of jazz is the need of the young-in-power to authenticate
the music itself. Men like Julian "Cannonball" Adderley
and his brother, Nat, are proud of their knowledge of
South Side Chicago blues singers and trace part of their
approach to jazz to this awareness of the "soul" of the
blues. When Memphis Slim, a Chicago-based blues singer
and pianist, was working the downstairs room of Storyville
in Boston a couple of years ago, a member of Duke Ellington's band—which was in the main room—rushed down to
hear Slim between sets every night. "That man is authentic!" he proclaimed to a friend, and the implication was
that he was too since he was able to appreciate Memphis
Slim's "down home" playing.

This renewed reverence for "church" feeling and
"funky" blues by Negro musicians has turned into one of
the most commercial jazz commodities in the past fifteen
years, judging by the record sales and club appearances
of the neo-gospel boppers. "I think most of that 'soul'
music is now being manufactured rather than felt," said
a Harlem record store owner, "but at least this is one time
in jazz history when the Negroes are popularizing their
own music. It would take a lot of courage for Stan Kenton
or Shorty Rogers to call one of their albums *The Soul
Brothers*."

Some Negro jazzmen have meanwhile turned from
the shouting Christianity of their boyhood to Islam, but
retain love and respect for gospel music. The move to
Mecca is less often motivated by new theological insights
than it is a seeking of identity with non-whites throughout
the world. One new Mohammedan answered a white who
had asked him what had caused his conversion with the
rhetorical taunt, "Did you ever see a Negro Jesus Christ?"

Though these roots in blues and gospel music are

now celebrated by many young Negroes, there is much traditional jazz that has been excommunicated by the modern militants. Most Dixieland, for example, connotes to them the second-class citizenship of the South. It is significant that no young Negro jazz musician of ability takes to Dixieland. A number of young whites have tried to make a career out of reviving the old New Orleans styles, but no young Negroes belong to these groups or are likely to buy their records.

If a Negro jazzman, no matter how important his contribution, has achieved a reputation as an Uncle Tom, the attitude of younger musicians to him is pitiless, as in this dialogue from James Baldwin's short story, *Sonny's Blues*, when Sonny tells his square older brother that he must make jazz his career: " 'You mean—like Louis Armstrong?' His face closed as though I'd struck him. 'No. I'm not talking about none of that old-time, down home crap.' " Armstrong regained some favor among some young Negroes, however, after his sudden and unexpected criticism of President Eisenhower over the handling of integration in Little Rock.

The conviction that jazz is Negro property has been encouraged for many years by a majority of the European jazz critics who believe, for the most part, that a Negro jazzman must be superior to a white musician if only because he *is* a Negro. Frenchman Hugues Panassié, author of the section on jazz in Grove's *Dictionary of Music and Musicians*, writes therein that clarinetist Milton Mezzrow was "of all white musicians the one who most perfectly assimilated the Negro spirit, and therefore of true jazz." The German critic, Joachim-Ernst Berendt in *Das Jazzbuch* has constructed tables of influence for each jazz instrument, and frequently sketches a *schwarz* line and a *weiss* line. British critics often use "Negro jazz" and "white jazz" as distinguishing terms, with the latter often applied pejoratively.

Many American white musicians might subconsciously agree with Mezzrow about the "innate" superiority of Negroes in jazz since the whites have been made insistently aware that their roots do not include the gospel music, the centuries of field hollers that led to the blues, and the general social and musical environment as youngsters that some Negro jazzmen believe to be necessary for authentication as a jazz player. European white jazzmen are even more self-conscious, since their early musical environment is not likely to have included jazz at all. Belgian jazzman Jean "Toots" Thielemans, a George Shearing alumnus, has been playing in America for almost ten years but did not feel until recently that he had been graduated into being a "real" jazzman.

"The main thing I learned in this country," Thielemans believes, "was the meaning of the blues. That was one experience I couldn't know from listening to records in Europe. I learned how important a single, simple phrase can be. It can be a phrase that looks like nothing technically, but is an expression of the life of an American Negro. It can be just a long, simple note played on the beat, but it's more than a note." And predictably, Thielemans was particularly heartened by Negro drummer Oliver Jackson's approval of his current work: "I haven't heard harmonica played with that kind of feeling since the fish fries at house rent parties in Detroit when I was growing up."

It has been a new experience for many Negro musicians to visit Europe—and some have stayed—because they are beguiled for a while at least by the experience of having European *aficionados* regard them as "naturally" superior to a white jazz player. In time, however, this prejudice in reverse, which still treats the Negro as a collective abstract, eventually irritates some of the Negro jazzmen who travel abroad frequently. "When they get to like everything we do," notes Miles Davis, "even the mistakes, that gets to be too much."

Nor are all Negro musicians as convinced as the

"soul brothers" that they can tell by ear alone whether a white or Negro musician is playing. Not all by any means exclude whites from the possibility of playing authentic jazz. There are musicians like John Lewis, pianist and music director of the Modern Jazz Quartet, who not only doesn't limit his appreciation of jazzmen by race but—unlike most of his American contemporaries of whatever race—doesn't even assess jazz musicians by country. Though most American jazz players feel that non-Americans are by definition derivative unless perhaps they emigrate here and absorb the roots of the music firsthand, Lewis is convinced that a growing number of jazz musicians in Europe are developing fresh, individual contributions to the language.

Miles Davis reacts to reverse prejudice by noting: "I haven't time to learn to Jim Crow. I've been busy since I was thirteen years old, and I've known enough Crow myself. I wouldn't want to take the next thirty-three years to learn to be prejudiced myself. When I first hired Lee Konitz years ago, some guys said, 'Why do you want an ofay in your band?' I asked them if they knew anybody who could play with a tone like Lee's. If I had to worry about nonsense like that, I wouldn't have a band. I wouldn't care if a cat was green and had red breath—if he could play."

Another non-chauvinist is pianist Hampton Hawes, whose father was a minister, whose own playing is characterized by earthy blues power and fully authenticated "funk," but who refuses to pre-empt jazz for Negroes alone. When Hawes was in the Army and stationed in Japan a few years ago, he met Toshiko Akiyoshi, a gentle, ingenuous pianist with a consuming desire to express herself in jazz. She has since come to the United States and has acquired a respectable reputation as a jazz musician. But when she first met Hawes in Tokyo, Toshiko asked him guilelessly, "How do you play the blues that way? How can I learn to play them so authentically?"

Hawes told her, "I play the blues right because I eat collard greens and black-eyed peas and corn pone and clabber."

"Where," sighed Toshiko, "can I find that food? Do I have to go to the United States to get it?"

Hawes finally laughed and told the girl, "All you need is the feeling. If you have the feeling, you could eat Skippy peanut butter and play the blues right. And if you don't have that feeling, you could eat collard greens and all that so-called Negro food all the time and sound corny."

"At one time," Hawes says, "everybody thought if you were a Negro, you could just naturally sing and tap and play the blues. But that's as much a caricature as other forms of prejudice. If I say that all colored people can play blues better than all whites, that would fit into the white racists' argument that 'all colored are alike.' To play the blues, to play jazz, you have to have the feeling. You can't study up on it. Some Negroes and whites have it, and some don't. Yes, at one time, the differences in environment were such that only Negroes knew the blues, in the musical terms that I mean, but the experience of the blues is a lot broader in the kinds of people it reaches now."

Similarly, a white musician, describing a British lady pianist who has been trying for years to become "funky," pointed out as an index of her progress toward her goal that "the exposure she's had to players with melodic conceptions rooted more in the blues, the Jewish wails, and the Slavic music (more of a minor inflection and open phrasing) has influenced what she hears or looks for in her own playing." And John Lewis welcomes the Irish background of Gerry Mulligan, whose jazz authenticity he admires, as an indication that jazz is not alien to any race or nationality.

Empiricists such as Hawes and Lewis are gaining more adherents among young Negro jazzmen as integration in American life as a whole increases. The less bitterness a Negro is forced to experience simply because he is a Negro in his life off the stand, the less bitterness he will bring to his music. And even in the harshest, most hating jazz, there is an undercurrent of affection among the players themselves; because jazz, to exist at all, has to be created collectively. It has to depend on the rapport of a group, and even if the group is annealed by its collective hatred of the outside, sometime in the night the experience of sharing even the hate becomes mellowed. Though jazz has been used for many generations to express— among other emotions—pain and sorrow that can't be verbalized, it is difficult for even the "hardest" modernists to hate all night on their horns. A man swings most deeply and self-satisfyingly when he's feeling good, not lacerated.

Some years ago, a quartet had just completed a particularly exhilarating set, and its young Negro drummer came off the stand grinning with satisfaction.

"You guys sounded good," said a listener.

"Yeah," said the drummer, "there was a lot of loving going on up there."

5

Junk

The reasons for the racial tensions and reversals of prejudice within jazz are considerably clearer than the factors that have caused the sizable problem of narcotics addiction among jazzmen of all shades during the past twenty years.

I don't know exactly how many jazz musicians are now or have been addicted to narcotics. Nor does anyone else. There has been surprisingly little research in the field as a whole; and except for the work of psychologist Charles Winick, practically no systematic study has been made of jazz addicts.

For a time, jazz writers reacted to the specter of the junky by gossiping avidly about who was "on" but ignoring the problem in their magazines until an incident—such as Stan Getz ineffectually holding up a drug store—made the wire services. There are still editors and musicians whose considered answer to questions about addiction in jazz is: "Look how many more doctors are on than musicians!" (A valuable exception is Gene Lees, editor of *Down Beat*.)

In 1957, I arranged a symposium on addiction for the Newport Festival. Several attempts were made to dissuade me. One of the most widely published of all jazz writers neared apoplexy in the process of assuring me that

75

the symposium would harm jazz grievously. Jazz survived.
So did the junkies.

Three years later I was discussing the junk scene
with a combo leader. "You know," he said, "if I wanted
to organize a big band, I'd have trouble hiring men of the
caliber I'd want without at least some of them having
their problems with narcotics." Later, on a panel discussion of addiction, the same leader swore he personally
knew of only five addicts in jazz. The other two musicians
on the panel also knew, they said, only five apiece. But
the various incidents all three cited concerning musicians
who were hooked gave the impression that the fifteen
weary addicts traveled constantly, and besides, carried a
trunkful of disguises.

There is, then, understandable defensiveness among
the musicians. They are resentful, for one thing, at the
automatic association tabloid newspapers make between
jazz and addiction. A couple of days before the panel discussion that uncovered the peripatetic fifteen addicts, a
Washington, D.C., part-time musician was accused of
murder. The man had absolutely no reputation in the
jazz world and, as I recall, was more of a "general business" pianist than a jazz player. The headlines predictably
informed the populace that a "jazzman" was the prime
suspect. The musicians are also probably correct in assuming that the general public does not realize that other vo-
cational groups, notably physicians, contain more than a
few users, though none has more proportionately than
jazz.

There *is* a narcotics problem in jazz and I don't believe the situation is at all improved by simply keeping
score of addicts in other fields. The first excess generally
attributed to jazzmen was a heavy dependence on liquor.
Like the doctor and drugs, the musician works in places
where liquor is immediately accessible. There were heavy
drinkers among the early players, and there still are some
among the modernists. The hours are long, careers are

erratic, and if a man has a psychological and/or physiological propensity to drink, the jazz life provides the set-up he needs. While there is some mythology that marijuana and heroin clarify one's playing, even the lushes agree that too much liquor can only lead to clinkers.

For at least thirty years and probably longer, marijuana has been not unfamiliar to many jazzmen. I know several older players who have smoked marijuana most of their lives. They usually limit their indulgence to a regular amount, and are discreet in its use. Technically marijuana is non-addictive. Technically, it does not inexorably lead to experimentation with heroin. But actually, as record executive Gary Kramer notes in his essay on narcotics and jazz in *The Jazz World* (Ballantine): "The truth seems to be that many people who smoke marijuana, while not physically dependent on it, are 'hooked' by circumstances in life to feel a need for the escape that it can give. The more this becomes the habitual way of facing up to problems, the more the marijuana user is conditioned to identify with the drug subculture. Being 'hooked' in that sense establishes a basis for experimenting with the addicting drugs—and becoming 'hooked' in a very real psychological sense."

The older jazz players who are experienced in marijuana seldom do, however, turn to heroin. Nor do they often abandon marijuana, because it has indeed become their "habitual way of facing up to problems." The same is true of the heavy drinkers in jazz. Some of the latter have been warned by doctors that further drinking is dangerous, but only a few have been able to stop, and those usually with the help of Alcoholics Anonymous. Some drug addicts have also been able to kick, but almost invariably by themselves. Neither Narcotics Anonymous nor the United States Public Health Service Hospitals at Lexington and Fort Worth has been of much help so far. The latter course is usually ineffectual because, among other reasons, there are no provisions for follow-up therapy.

The long-term usefulness of psychiatric and psycho-analytic techniques on heroin addicts is still largely unknown. Statistics are slim, and besides, many private psychiatrists and psychoanalysts will not accept a drug addict for treatment because the process is so long and unpredictable and there are so many other patients.

The one major research project is the Musicians' Clinic in New York, established "to provide a psychiatric resource for addicted jazz musicians" in 1957 on a grant from the Newport Festival with Dr. Charles Winick as executive director. As expected, several of the musician addicts who applied for treatment eventually dropped out, but some have remained, and while it is too soon to make any significant generalizations from the clinic's experience, a considerable amount of data is being collected and more is being learned about the most effective methods of treating the musician-addict.

Winick and Dr. Marie Nyswander have presented a paper, based on the experience of the Musicians' Clinic. Called *Psychotherapy of Successful Musicians Who Are Drug Addicts,* it was presented at the 1960 annual meeting of the American Orthopsychiatric Association. The paper follows fifteen full-time jazz musicians addicted to heroin—eleven Negro and four white—who applied to the clinic in its first year. Of the fifteen, two completed the psychotherapy, and eight as of the writing of the paper were still in contact with their therapists. The other five left for various reasons.

The paper explains:

"For each of the fifteen musicians who made initial contact with and were seen at the Clinic, a control group of an equal number of musicians in the New York area was selected. The members of the control group were also addicts and played the same instruments as the patients with whom they were matched. This control group of non-patients was matched in the dimensions of race, marital status, approximate age and approximate degree of success and creativity as a musician."

Significantly:

"All of the patients who stayed in therapy have been off drugs for a mean period of thirty months. Of the patients who applied for therapy and for one reason or another did not continue, all have been off drugs for an average of twenty-nine months. All of the members of the control group are still using drugs regularly. . . . All but one of the ten active patients and four of the five dropout patients have improved their standing in the profession and have gotten better jobs since their contact with the Clinic; several current patients have more than doubled their incomes. Three of the members of the control group are faring better musically than they did when they were first contacted, and most of the rest are at roughly the same level. Two have deteriorated in their work situation."

Charles Winick has a theory that in jazz, the kind of stimulant or depressant chosen by an addictive personality has been connected with the kind of music he plays. New Orleans jazz, for example, "was generally outgoing and aggressive" and "alcohol has the effect of facilitating aggressive tendencies." The alcohol basis of Winick's thesis could also include such celebrated jazz imbibers as the "Chicago jazz" musicians whose playing was also "outgoing and aggressive."

When "jazz moved north and became more light and swinging," Winick continues, "alcohol began to give way to marijuana. . . . The post-World War II development of a more detached and cool jazz was simultaneous with the great increase in musicians' use of heroin, a drug which usually helps make the user more cool and detached."

Winick also believes that a jazzman's selection of alcohol, marijuana or heroin may be partly determined by the degree to which his music is accepted by the over-all society. New Orleans and Chicago jazz and its equivalents elsewhere in the country forty and fifty years ago connoted "good time" music and its audience drank as much as the players. By the swing era of the 1930's, jazz had become less totally regarded by its practitioners as primarily background for entertainment. Some jazzmen were taking themselves more seriously, although hardly any yet thought in terms of jazz as an "art" music. "This was a transitional period in jazz, when its exact role was not clear," Winick points out. "Similarly, marijuana was a kind of marginal drug, which was not finally brought under Federal law until the Marijuana Tax Act of 1937."

Finally, modern jazz in its early stages was met with unmistakable hostility by most audiences. Accordingly, Winick continues a number of these "far-out" musicians reacted by indulging in "far-out" behavior, including the use of a definitely illegal drug, heroin.

They were so at odds with the majority of what had been the jazz audience that they chose a significantly anti-social route to extra kicks.

The Winick thesis is intriguing, but I have some reservations. For one thing, I doubt if there was any significant diminution of drinking among jazzmen during the swing era. Marijuana became an ancillary route to relaxation for those who preferred it, but hardly replaced liquor.

There probably was a relationship between increased heroin usage and the initial non-acceptance of modern jazz in that heroin is a dangerous drug, which a square would be least likely to try. Jazzmen have always been an "in" group—with many additional "in" and "out" subdivisions among them according to race, age, and musical style—and never more so than in the first years of modern jazz.

I am not convinced, however, that the choice of heroin was primarily determined by the music itself having become more "detached" and less "aggressive." First of all, many interpreters of the searingly "hot" modern jazz of musicians such as Charlie Parker in the early 1940's were hooked on heroin. (The allegedly more detached "cool" jazz was not in vogue until the late 1940's and early 1950's). The jazz of Parker, Gillespie (a non-addict), Fats Navarro (who died largely because of his habit) and others of their contemporaries was more bitingly aggressive than much of the preceding swing. It became even angrier because it *was* misunderstood.

The "cool" jazz style that was largely introduced by such recordings as those by the Miles Davis units on Capitol in 1949 and 1950 was not as detached as the term connoted. It was lighter in texture both in ensemble and solo passages, and the rhythm sections were subtler. But for all the audience-be-damned, limp stance of many of its players, the music they produced was often bitterly intense and aggressive. Miles Davis, for example, has never been emotionally "detached" in his work, nor has Gerry Mulligan, who was largely identified at first with the "cool" nucleus. In fact, the "cool" jazzmen generally distilled all the emotional strength they could muster *for* their music. While it is true that the effect of heroin on the "cool" addicts was to lower their emotional commitment to nearly everything but jazz, they didn't consciously use junk to separate themselves from their music. Many were, on the contrary, under the illusion that they could play more "purely" if they were "high."

Heroin, in short, became the "in" drug more because it was so defiantly anti-square than because of any relationship between the music as such and the effects of the drug.

As for whether marijuana and heroin generally help a musician's playing, introspective or otherwise, the usual flat answer by writers on jazz is that they do not. I'm not

sure that the answer is in fact so decidedly negative for
marijuana in relation to certain types of personalities. I
prefer the more cautious answer of Dr. Winick: "Studies
by the United States Public Health Service on a very
small number of subjects found that some subjects, after
marijuana, often thought they had done better on a
standard test of musical aptitudes, but actually had done
worse than when they were not on the drug, illustrating
that being alert and feeling alert are not the same." But
Winick continued: "A performance score on an objective
test does not approximate the conditions of mutual group
facilitation and relaxation of an ongoing jazz performance
so that the effect of the drug or non-drug status of the
other members of the band must be considered in deter-
mining the effect of drug use on any individual."

As a matter of fact, in one of the two tests, only two
of the twelve subjects were professional musicians. And,
as Winick added in an article in *Social Problems* on *The
Use of Drugs by Jazz Musicians*, ". . . a test in which non-
musicians are given objective questions on matters like
the consonance of pitch between two sounds can hardly
be compared to the musical creativity and expertise required of the jazz musician playing in a group situation
which is based on mutual reinforcement and in which improvisation may be extremely important."

Nor need heroin automatically lead to deterioration
of playing. Gerry Mulligan, who was addicted to heroin
in the late 1940's, does claim that "heroin eventually has
a degenerative effect, and in my case, I finally couldn't
finish an arrangement." Heroin does indeed have a fairly
quick degenerative effect if an addict has to scrounge for
supplies, often gets adulterated drugs, and is not on a
regular, medically controlled dosage. Under other conditions, however, it does not in all cases.

Obviously there is no disputing the multiple dangers
of heroin; but the point is that once a man is addicted,
until such time as he can break himself of the habit or be

withdrawn (and some, it would seem so far, cannot be permanently withdrawn), he may be able to function quite well so long as he receives his regular dosage. In Britain, where an addict can be treated by a doctor in whose discretion drugs can continue to be administered, some men who have not been able to withdraw have functioned for many years with consistent competence in such highly demanding skills as the practice of medicine. In his report, *Drug Addiction in America and England* (*Commentary*, September, 1960), Edwin Schur observes further: "While it is true that with increasing tolerance to his drug the addict usually wants more and more of it, the British experience indicates that some addicts can, under favorable circumstances, get along reasonably well on legally prescribed limited doses. Certainly we have everything to gain and nothing to lose by instituting at least an experimental clinic through which to test the British approach."

That approach, in Schur's summary, is that "narcotics may properly be administered to addicts after prolonged attempt at cure if 'the drug cannot be safely discontinued entirely, on account of the severity of the withdrawal symptoms produced' or if the patient, 'while capable of leading a useful and relatively normal life when a certain minimal dose is regularly administered, becomes incapable of this when the drug is entirely discontinued.'"

It is true, as Dr. Winick notes, that "there is absolutely no reason to believe that heroin use improves anyone's playing, although it may help a musician to function at all. Without the drug, the addict is unable to do anything, so that the drug helps him to reach his minimal level of functioning. There has never been any demonstration that any 'plus' factor is added to a musician by his heroin use. There has, however, been ample proof from the experience of the Musicians' Clinic . . . that a heroin user who *stops* taking drugs, with appropriate psychotherapeutic help, improves in his musicianship."

Until there are enough hospital facilities and there
is enough "appropriate psychotherapeutic help," however,
there can be no radical improvement in the narcotics
problem in America until doctors are allowed to treat
addicts, as in Britain. A man who cannot break his habit
with presently available techniques can function better
as a person—and in his craft—if he can legally be given
a regular dosage of drugs under medical supervision. In
this way also, the non-pusher addict will no longer be
made to feel he is a criminal by the very fact of his addiction. A further corollary of reintroducing medical treatment of addicts would be a major reduction of illegal
traffic in drugs and all its attendant abuses. The addict
would not be forced into crime, and the elimination of
most of their clientele would largely stop pushers from
trying to get potential new customers hooked.

One of many indices of the present absurd lack of
medical facilities for addicts is this excerpt from a report
on musician addicts who applied in 1957 to the Musicians'
Clinic in New York for psychotherapy: "All were withdrawn at home . . . because of the total lack in New York
of municipal hospital facilities to accomplish withdrawal."

Given a chance to kick, and with after-care available,
two-thirds of the fifteen jazzmen who first applied to the
Musicians' Clinic remained in therapy, a much higher
percentage than has been reported in the few other published records of psychotherapy in relation to addiction.

As Gerry Mulligan has observed: "I feel strongly
that my problems and those of my group with drugs came
in part from the way we were introduced to them. If
there had only been some sort of oriented introduction
available and a method of understanding what was taking
place in our bodies, instead of our having had to search
for drugs furtively and illegally. We all started to feel
like criminals, and had to hide our addiction. After a
while, our whole way of life became involved in our habit
and we were thrown in contact with people whom we'd

usually go out of our way to avoid. Instead, we had to cultivate them as friends."

The question of what in the jazz life itself has led so many of its players to addiction is complex. For one thing, for all the various kinds (and occasionally, depths) of expression of which jazz is capable, it has attracted a sizable percentage of emotional adolescents. In *The Drug Addict As Patient* (Grune & Stratton), Dr. Marie Nyswander observes of the personality pattern of the addict: "So great is his need for immediate recognition, for *being*, that he does not allow himself a period of *becoming*. . . . He cannot take present deprivation in the hope of building toward security in the indefinite future but must continually bolster his self-esteem with immediate proof of present success."

It's true that much of the freshness and unpredictability of jazz has been due to the fact that, from its beginnings, its players set their own pragmatic musical standards. Music school rules of "legitimacy" of tone, for example, were ignored. A man was judged by the quality of his ear, his capacity to improvise, and the personal texture of his sound and style. But these flexible criteria also made it possible for musicians with considerable "natural" talent but limited powers of self-discipline (in music or anything else) to make a place for themselves fairly quickly in the jazz life. Some blew well, but remained quasi-children all their lives.

In the aftermath of Charlie Parker, for example, there were scores of musicians around the country who knew enough about their horns to copy several Parker choruses from records and then presented themselves in jazz clubs as professional jazzmen, so great was their "need for immediate recognition." This kind of personality can also fantasize, much like a savage who eats a lion's heart to be brave, that if a superior jazz musician is an addict, the neophyte may somehow play better if he too is "on."

Particularly in the 1940's, when heroin addiction among jazzmen was highest, emulation-by-needle was frequent. So was the contributory social pressure of the "in-group." A couple of years ago, I was reminded of the adolescent modern jazz outcasts of the 1940's by two teenage addicts in East Harlem who said, "We were the only holdouts in the gang, the only ones not on. But finally, we had to start using if we were going to be accepted. And up here, if you don't belong, you might as well be dead."

While "high," many infantile addicts also feel that by their daring they've finally proved their superiority to the squares. Such an addict was the protagonist in Clarence Cooper's accurate novel of addiction, *The Scene* (Crown). Even after "cold turkey" (sudden and complete withdrawal) and a life term for murder, the addict-unhero mumbles in his cell:

"They better leave me alone, they better remember me. . . . They don't know about stuff, they don't know about the *feelin,* the *good* feelin, they don't know about speedin with stuff, when the cocain and heroin seems like it's a man and woman inside you, twistin on a big bed. . . . The stiff, no-livin bastards! They're dead, they're just dead bodies!"

For some musicians, addiction, aside from proving how much hipper they were than the squares, also provided a rationalization for failure. Norman O'Connor, a Catholic priest who was in New York in the late 1940's and knew several jazzmen, has pointed out: "It works like this. 'It's too bad. He's a creative person; and if he'd only been able to get off that kick, he'd have done tremendous things.' It's a way of copping out, of not creating, of knowing you're not that good a musician, but of being unwilling to admit it."

Other addicts and observers of addicts in the late 1940's provide fragmentary insights into why pushers for a jazz clientele especially prospered then. Pianist Billy Taylor recalls:

"1948 was the peak of getting on. One thing that may have made narcotics traffic easier in New York then was that everyone was concentrated in one area. In the mid-'40's, it was 52nd Street with eight or ten clubs in two blocks, at least two quartets in each club or trios or five-piece groups and sometimes three units in each club. It became easier for guys pushing chicks or dope or whatever to find their easy marks. Later, around 1948, everything was concentrated on the Royal Roost. I'd come back from Europe in 1947. I thought I was sophisticated, but I stood there with my mouth open. All you had to do was walk behind the bandstand and guys were doing whatever they wanted to."

Gerry Mulligan remembers:

"In the late 1940's, just making a living was rough. I had my first hard stuff, heroin, in 1947 or 1948. It was a one or two time affair. A friend of mine thought I'd like to try it. The first time somebody tried to inject a needle in me, I jumped ten feet and felt that was the end of that. The next time was a muscle shot and I liked it pretty much. These were the days of widespread general use of junk around town. I knew there were guys in bad shape, but I didn't associate their conditions with junk. I figured they were in bad shape anyway. There was a frustration everywhere with us. Nobody really seemed to know what they were doing or where they were going. Junk could provide a dream world. The daily process of living was dull, and you had to scrounge for an income when you just wanted to play your horn. Junk seemed to help in a bad time."

According to pianist George Wallington:

"Maybe in some cases, it was a matter of getting on to show you weren't a square, and it's possible some got on just because they wanted to imitate Bird that much. Another way some started was from the strain of being up all night, taking bennies and other things. I guess it's true that some of us had knowledge in front of us of what the hard stuff could do to you, but you still don't really know what it's about until you're on yourself. I suppose it's a matter of taking a gamble, of saying to yourself: 'Well, they claimed you couldn't stop smoking pot and that didn't turn out to be habit-forming."

Jimmy Guiffre theorizes:

"There is something in all of us that defies reason and logic. In many ways, often little ways, we sacrifice the future for momentary pleasure. Some of us can't wait and overeat or smoke too much. Junk was a little like that for some people. There were those who were so depressed from bad luck, from not being financially successful, from not being able to blow when they wanted to. Somebody got hold of them and told them this was the answer to life, that this led to the real world, and if they were in a very gullible state of mind, they'd get on. When I was in Woody Herman's band, eight were on at one time. They thought it was hip and they were putting on the squares. It's like when you're very young and smoke cigarettes and drink coffee to be hip. Junk was a strong force around that time. I remember opening at the Clique Club, now Birdland, with Buddy Rich's band. He fired half his men for being on."

Trombonist Bob Brookmeyer adds:

"Another consideration is that jazz is the most ecstatic form of creativity. No form of music is as intense emotionally for the men making it as jazz. It is an immediate, sensate emotion that does not last. With a painter or sculptor, creation is a slower building process. In these and other arts, you reach a pitch but only at certain times. In jazz, when you're playing with the right people, you can hit that pitch frequently in a night, and when you do, it's a thrill exceeded only by making love. Reaching that high a pitch intensifies everything else. Suppose you're in Cleveland. If it's been any kind of good night, you're roaring by the time you have to stop playing. Where do you go afterwards? There's no pub or similar place to relax in. It's an arrested orgasm.

"Some guys," Brookmeyer continues, "try to prolong that feeling of ecstasy. Others want to cut it off, and a lot of drugs are designed to cool you down. There's also a fraternity among some of those who are addicted that satisfies a need for 'togetherness.' Life can be pretty purposeless for a jazz musician. You lose a feeling of being an accepted part of society. There's a need to be one at least with your own group."

Drummer Jo Jones, who is of an earlier generation of jazzmen, agrees in part with Norman O'Connor about the "cop-out" aspects of addiction by lesser musicians and with Brookmeyer about the enormous intensity involved in the act of jazz. In the book, *Hear Me Talkin' to Ya* (Rinehart), he related both factors to the frequent stretches of unemployment for the young modernists in the 1940's:

"I know how frustrating it is for me, as long as I've been playing, when I'm not able to play. I want to play twenty-six hours a day, even though I know I need sleep. I don't want to go near music when I can't play it. I sit there and the palms of my hands are perspiring. It's a real feeling of frustration. And when the young kids don't get a chance to play, that's one of the things that happens. And so, one of the things that got the kids into dope was to get something to bolster their courage. Also, there were some of them doubly demoralized because they had gotten so far into music before the realization set in that they weren't the musicians they thought they were in the beginning."

The explanations of Brookmeyer and Jones, while accurate, unwittingly underline the degree of immaturity that exists in jazz and that sometimes leads those who have to wait or those who experience failure to substitute a needle for a security blanket. Yet personalities with large areas of infantile reaction have demonstrated in all

the arts that they can produce strikingly creative and
emotionally powerful work, possibly because they are
more in touch with their unconscious feelings than are
most of the more "responsible, adult" members of society.
I mean this not as a moral value judgment but as an
attempted antidote to the wishful assertion of the moral-
ists that responsible people invariably do the best work.
It depends on the work. Even if addiction ceases to be a
problem of the jazz musician, the field is likely to have
a sizable share of neurotics.

In fairness to the jazz addict, a study of Musicians'
Clinic patients by Drs. Nyswander and Winick points out
what may be several revealing differences between typical non-musician and jazz addicts. The differences would
seem to indicate that the jazzman who becomes hooked
does so for somewhat less infantile reasons than the
average addict. According to the paper, *Psychotherapy of
Successful Musicians Who Are Drug Addicts:*

"The typical addict is not married. Over half the
Clinic patients had fairly stable marriages to non-addicts,
and most of the marriages had resulted in children. The
typical drug addict does not have the ability to take himself off drugs, by and large. Although the Clinic patients
were regular heroin users, most of them had relative
degree of control over the drug, and almost all had taken
themselves off drugs in the past. . . . The typical addict
who started taking heroin in the late 1940's and early
1950's in New York was about 17, whereas the Clinic
patients began taking heroin when they were at an
average age of 24—*after their careers had begun.* (Italics
mine—N.H.)

". . . In the case of most drug addicts, the threat of
arrest traditionally serves as a motivating factor in seeking psychiatric help. For our Clinic patients, neither
arrest nor jail were motivating factors in getting them into
treatment. It was largely the realistic problems with the
successful resolution of which drug use interfered, like

marriage, which did contribute to their motivation for getting into treatment. . . .

"The typical addict may begin taking heroin to help cope with the problems associated with puberty, whereas the musicians began their addiction, like addict physicians, when their professional careers were launched and in order to help them meet relatively adult problems, like those connected with their marriage and career. They took drugs to help them master a problem area, rather than to help them run away from it. . . . The musician addicts differed from the typical addict, and resembled many physician addicts, in the single-mindedness with which they pursued their careers. Drug addiction made sustenance in their profession much more difficult and sometimes required them to take non-musical jobs, but they all remained in the profession. In contrast, the typical addict is likely to have a different job each month."

In an earlier paper, *The Use of Drugs by Jazz Musicians* (*Social Problems,* Vol. VII, No. 3, Winter, 1959-60), Dr. Winick made several other observations based on interviews with 357 jazz musicians from 18 to 54 years old, of whom sixty-nine per cent were white and thirty-one per cent Negro. The resulting statistics can only be tenuous guides because although the sampling is larger than many on which statistics are often based, it is just that— a sampling—and I would have wished that the percentage of Negroes interviewed were higher. In any case, a number of the results are provocative:

". . . In terms of individual musicians, eighty-two per cent were reported as having tried marijuana at least once, fifty-four per cent were occasional users, and twenty-three per cent were regular users. A smaller degree of heroin use was reported among band colleagues. Fifty-three per cent were said to have used heroin at least once, twenty-four per cent were seen as occasional users, and sixteen per cent as regular users. There tended to be more certainty about identifying the

more regular than the more infrequent users. . . . It could
be speculated that one reason for the frequently found
subjective feeling that the musician is playing better
when on drugs is perhaps that the kind of dependent
person who takes the drug is having his dependency
affirmed every time he takes it. Thus having again re-
established and satisfied his dependency, he feels relatively
free to 'let go' and express himself in music. . . . An
example of the kind of rationalization employed by some
heroin users was a comment by one very successful
musician, who compared taking heroin to '. . . going into
a closet. It lets you concentrate and takes you away from
everything. Heroin is a working drug, like the doctor who
took it because he had a full schedule so he could work
better. It lets me concentrate on my sound.' "

Winick found that:

". . . There were disproportionately large numbers of
marijuana users reported up to the age of twenty-six,
after which age the use of marijuana appeared to be
almost evenly distributed to age forty-eight, beyond
which no users were reported. Heroin use was concentrated in the age group from twenty-five to thirty-nine,
after which it fell off to very little. . . . One possible theory
to explain the cessation of heroin addiction among musician addicts in their late thirties is that those who began
taking heroin in their late teens or early twenties as response to the problems of early adulthood, mature out of
addiction by the time they are in their late thirties, for
reasons which are not known but possibly because the
stresses and strains of life are becoming stabilized for
them and because the major challenges of adulthood have
passed. This cycle is perhaps analogous to that of the
prototypical delinquent whose delinquency increases during his teens and remains constant till he reaches his
late twenties, when it declines. . . . It is possible that addict musicians see life as less likely to require aggressive
action by the time they reach their late thirties, and

problems like those involving the expression of sex and aggression which drug use has helped them to evade or solve or mask, have become less urgent."

As modern jazz itself grew older and more accepted—while young musicians saw brilliant players die or increasingly stumble musically because of drugs—heroin addiction became somewhat less brave a declaration of hipness. Some players with more than ordinary will power broke the habit by themselves. Miles Davis was one. "I got hooked," he says, "after I got back from the Paris Jazz Festival in 1949. I got bored and was around cats that were hung. So I wound up with a habit that took me over four years to break. I broke it because it was too damn much trouble." During those four years, Davis worked infrequently, and supported himself and his habit mostly by recording and by transcribing music from records for lead sheets. "I'd take the $30 for the transcribing, go uptown, and get high." Much of what Davis recorded in those years he regards as inferior. He didn't object then when the records were released, but is angry now. "When I had a habit, I didn't care. I do now."

Davis is pragmatic in his advice on how to lead an addict to relinquish his habit. "I just tell them if they work for me to regulate their habit. When they're tired of the trouble it takes to support a habit, they'll stop it if they have the strength. You can't *talk* a man out of a habit until he really *wants* to stop."

Others who broke the habit did so because they could more easily stand the considerable pain of withdrawal than they could endure their loss of self-respect. One, Gerry Mulligan, credits his breakthrough to psychotherapy. Another gives his unusually understanding and supportive wife much of the credit.

Some of the young and a few of the old still get hooked. I believe—but cannot prove—that the percentage of addicts in jazz is smaller now than it was a decade and more ago, but it is not inconsiderable. The connections are still accessible; many of the old pressures remain as do those who react to pressure in panic. And theories as to why addiction is more prevalent in jazz continue. One such, a psychoanalytic one, comes from Charles Winick:

> "It is possible that some orally inclined persons who had some interest in using drugs selected the occupation of jazz musician, perhaps unconsciously, because of their feeling that a musician drug user is somehow regarded differently and more favorably than a non-musician drug user and because of their feeling that jazz music offered a favorable climate for drug use. It is also possible that some white musicians drifted into drug use, on an unconscious level, in order to help express their identification with what they regard as the double debasement of the Negro musician drug user—double because of his being both a Negro and a drug user. Such reasons for drug use are not, of course, generally accessible to the musicians' conscious reasoning process, but have emerged as possibly relevant in psychoanalytic investigation of musician addicts."

There is also the more frequent theory that addiction—among other retreats from reality—takes place in the most frustrating contexts. It is most frustrating in America to be a Negro (and now, a Puerto Rican) in a slum. Therefore, slum-reared Negro children who become musicians are among those who introduce addiction into jazz. The equation is oversimplified and does not take into account middle-class and upper-middle-class addicts of both races, but as part of the over-all fabric of explanation, it has some relevance.

The factors, as I've tried to indicate, are multiple, and at base there is the individual character structure of each addict and the complex influences that have shaped him to the stage at which he becomes susceptible to addiction. As Winick explains:

"There are some people who are exposed who do and some who do not succumb. Thus, although pharmacists have easier access to narcotics than do physicians, there are practically no pharmacists who take drugs, while there are many physicians who do. It would appear that the kind of person who becomes a physician is more likely to become an addict than the kind of person who becomes a pharmacist. Similarly, just as policemen represent the occupational group most likely to commit suicide, this is not because they have access to guns but because of the characteristics of the kind of policemen who commit suicide. For the same reason, there is no reason to assume that there are many addicts among jazz musicians merely because there are many jazz musicians who are Negroes and there are many Negroes who use drugs; this is a logical fallacy. Negro jazz musicians have no inherent predilections for drug use any more than they are intrinsically more subject to any other chronic illness."

In his article in *Social Problems*, Winick observed further: "It might be speculated . . . that Negroes are not over-represented among musician drug users. Negroes are disproportionately present in the general addict population because they represent the kind of low status and low income group in which drug use is concentrated. . . . The working Negro jazz musician [however] is highly trained, generally enjoys high status and income, and represents a proud group which has given rise to most of the innovations in the whole jazz field."

As indicated elsewhere in this book, the income and status of the jazz musician, white and Negro, are not usually as high as Winick believes, but both are indeed higher than those of the average American Negro.

There is also in the climate of the jazz life—particularly its equation of protest with cryptic argot and inner musical expression rather than action—a quality that does draw a certain personality type who, under

certain conditions, may become addicted. Although actors, writers and other artists have become active politi-
cally, practically no major jazzman has. Some were caught
up in the Camp Unity-type of "popular front" of the 1930's
and 1940's, but nearly always as rather guileless followers,
not as originators of ideas or actions. I think you could
hire practically any jazz musician today to play for *any*
political rally (except for a Communist conclave, because most jazzmen don't want to take that much of a
chance, particularly for a cause in which they have no
conviction).

The jazzman, by and large, is narrow in interests and
scope of protest, when he does protest. Admittedly there
are exceptions. But I think Francis Newton is quite right
(with space for the usual exceptions), when he writes in
The Jazz Scene:

> "What jazz is *against* may be reasonably clear in
> theory, though it may find only a rather passive, evasive
> and individualist expression outside music. (There is no
> reason why we should expect anything else of an art,
> considered in isolation.) What jazz is *for* is much less
> clear. No doubt, liberty, equality, fraternity and a chicken
> in the pot every Sunday, or every day, allowing for the
> American standard of living. . . . And this has always
> beset the protest of jazz, like a good many other individ-
> ualist and spontaneous protests, with a great temptation:
> that of settling for very small positive gains—for official
> recognition, for personal satisfaction. Or, to be more
> precise, of oscillating between a discontent which can
> never be satisfied because, like the 'blue flower' of the
> German romantics or the crock of gold at the foot of the
> rainbow, it is so defined as to be beyond satisfaction, and
> one which can rather be rather easily satisfied, by grow-
> ing up, by being sent on a tour as 'cultural ambassador'
> for the U.S. Government, by playing with the New York
> Philharmonic, or earning a lot of money."

Complementing Newton's comments are those of Charles Winick:

> "It is impossible to talk to either jazz musicians or addicts without becoming aware of the extent to which they share a special language of fantasy and alienation, in which values are reversed and in which 'terrible' is a description of excellence."

What keeps jazz most challengingly alive is the fact that players keep arriving who will not yield easily to fantasy or be that "easily satisfied" by such "acceptance" as by a cultural ambassadorship or increasing sums of money. However neurotic they may be, they are pursued by more insatiable demons. These are the driven ones like Charles Mingus, John Coltrane, Sonny Rollins, Cecil Taylor, Miles Davis. Some get on drugs for a time, but usually they get off, because the furious and infuriating urge to make the sound right and the emotion clear takes up too much energy to waste on staying high.

There has never been a single satisfactory definition of jazz or the jazz musician. But young soprano saxophonist Steve Lacy has made a provocative attempt to indicate verbally something of the confusions involved in properly defining the latter. He feels that "a jazz musician is a combination orator, dialectician, mathematician, athlete, entertainer, poet, singer, dancer, diplomat, educator, student, comedian, artist, seducer, public masturbator and general all-around good fellow. . . . No matter what you do, some people are going to like it, and other people not. Therefore, all you can do is try to satisfy yourself, by trusting the man inside."

Sometimes the man inside becomes a junky, and more and more often, he does not.

D

6

Bringing Dignity to Jazz

More pervasive than addiction to heroin—and for many, more difficult to "kick"—is the drive to "success" and "acceptance." Nearly everyone in the arts—and increasingly, in the sciences as well—is drawn by such lodestones as wide public recognition and accelerating income. Some resist these definitions of achievement; others gradually accept them in part. Jazz musicians are no more immune than any of the others. A few, such as George Shearing, have yielded entirely to the guarantee of a large, predictable income in return for formularizing a soothing, predictable "pop-jazz." Others have made various compromises on occasion, diluting their music in anxious attempts at broader public acceptance. I am still astonished, in a lingering naïveté about jazz, at the number of musicians—including some fierce experimenters—who would falsify their styles on a record if they could be guaranteed that record would be a "hit." There are, to be sure, forces of the Establishment—record company executives, booking agents, night club owners, etc.—who are perfectly willing to encourage jazzmen to "compromise." But there are also many jazz musicians who are perfectly willing to be encouraged.

The Newport Jazz Festival has become the bleary

symbol of how "success" and "acceptance" can eventually corrode the "image" of jazz more effectively than intermittent Sunday supplement stories about jazz and junk. For several years, the promoters of the Festival had been programming the concerts as if they were vaudeville shows, and had been generally lowering the musical standards of their celebrations of America's "only indigenous art form" until by 1959 the Festival had become the backdrop for a weekend of drinking by as many teenagers as could fit into the town.

Most musicians were privately contemptuous of the commercial rites; but they came for the money and the "exposure," even though they knew they were being used as "acts" before crowds that would have been even more enthusiastic if Elizabeth Taylor had been scheduled to sing with the Count Basie band. Several jazzmen threatened to boycott the Festival as a matter of principle and artistic integrity, but until 1960, the most vehement rebels kept returning—at higher fees.

Independence Day weekend of 1960 at Newport is worth detailing as the most mephitic event yet in the usually inglorious campaigns to win wider "recognition" for jazz. Several observers had predicted the explosion. The year before, an unusually imperturbable night-club-owning hood had made his first visit to Newport. "Jeez," he said. "It's revolting." The big man and his bodyguard left, never to return.

For those who did return, "The world's leading jazz ritual," wrote Ben Bagdikian in the Providence *Journal* on Friday, July 1, 1960, "opened at Newport last night as a mature international institution complete with foreign coverage, lawsuits and bitter competition."

By Sunday, July 3, the Seventh Annual Newport Jazz Festival had burst in its "maturity," having been canceled by Newport officials as the aftermath of ugly Saturday-night rioting involving 12,000 teenagers and post-graduate adolescents. The Festival expired in unprecedentedly extensive and vivid foreign and domestic coverage. Tass, in fact, offered a *Journal* photographer a sizable sum for his riot pictures; but the cameraman, a staunch patriot, sold the negatives instead to *Life*.

Izvestia covered the riots with relish, noting that "the savage beat of the drum and the howl of the trumpet" so often used in recent years as "a cold war propaganda weapon" in support of "Western Civilization" had been decisively unmasked.

There was even an added lawsuit by Monday, July 4. The Festival had already been coping with one legal action, involving $100,000, by Mrs. Elaine Lorillard, divorced wife of Louis Lorillard, who largely underwrites the Festival. Mrs. Lorillard had been cashiered from the Board of Directors during her marital wars and now claimed she deserved compensation for having originally thought up the idea of bringing dignity to jazz by importing it to Newport.

The second pre-riot lawsuit, for $75,000, concerned a New York producer of fashion shows who claimed she had not been paid for expenses connected with a fashion "festival" she had arranged for the Jazz Festival in 1959. The third, *post-riot* suit was one instituted by the Festival producers themselves for a wildly optimistic $4,000,000 after the dam broke. (It was later scaled down to $750,000.) They sued the city of Newport for canceling the Festival and for having taken insufficient precautions to avert the Saturday-night violence.

As one who wearily attended all but one of the Newport Jazz Festivals, I was not surprised at the denouement nor did I feel sorrow for either the Festival promoters or the city merchants who with so little conscience benefited from the Festival. Both sides, equally motivated by greed, received their just tear gas.

The "bitter competition" cited by Bagdikian in his Friday morning lead was still alive Sunday night after the overblown official Festival had been punctured. A small, rival musicians' festival had been organized, staffed, and produced by the jazzmen themselves at Cliff Walk Manor, a few blocks from vast Freebody Park where the official Festival was being held. The rebels, protesting the venality of the Newport chariot races, had been holding concerts, starting June 30, in direct competition with each of the NJF events. The rump group had started poorly, but attendance continued to grow, and by Sunday night—with the big Festival and all the bars in Newport closed down—some 500 paid $5 a head at Cliff Walk Manor to drink Coke and just listen to jazz for four hours.

The musicians—among them Charles Mingus and the widely influential modern drummer Max Roach, the leaders of the rebellion—were protesting the hypocrisy of the Newport Festival. Although still technically "non-profit" as a cultural event dedicated to the encouragement of "America's only indigenous art form," the NJF had become increasingly concerned through the years with amassing the largest possible gate receipts—"jazz as an art form" be damned. The NJF still scheduled a few experimental units and historical lectures during the poorly attended-—and poorly promoted—afternoon concerts, but at night crammed as many big names as they could find into almost every concert and sometimes cared not at all whether the "names" had much to do with jazz or not. Eartha Kitt, the Kingston Trio and Pat Suzuki had been among previous "jazz personalities" at the NJF.

The Festival, in essence, was largely to blame for its own cancellation because in grabbing for more and more receipts each year, it had encouraged the conviction among thousands of teenagers that Newport had become a carnival town over the July 4 weekend. Neither the beer-drinkers nor the musicians had any illusions left that the NJF had anything basically to do with "art." It had become a money-grubbing enterprise of the same

category as any giant midway staffed with shell games,
taffy candy, freak shows, and thrill rides.

By moving into Freebody Park, several years before,
the NJF had further advertised its primary concern with
mass audiences and mass tastes. The park has all the intimacy of Yankee Stadium, and the only listeners who can
get an adequate perspective of the proceedings are the
box-holding socialites and the press who are sufficiently
near the stage. Some of the ticket-buyers can absorb some
of what's going on if they listen hard enough, but most
spend the evening guzzling beer and nuzzling friends.
As a part of its apologia following the rioting, the NJF
pointed out with virtuous indignation that there had
been no violence inside the park during the street battles
outside. The NJF neglected to note that for the first time
in Festival history, the Newport police chief had closed
down the beer stands inside the park that night before the
concert started. It's true that in previous years, only
sporadic fighting broke out inside the park itself, but the
condition of many of the teenagers in the bleachers and
at the beer booths by the end of each night was, in any
case, too limp to do battle.

Unsatiated, the NJF even *added* to the seating capacity of Freebody Park in 1960, making 16,500 places available to music-lovers. In fairness, it should be noted that
the NJF finally did yield in the year of the tear gas to
criticism of its programming policies. There were fewer
groups on each program so that each had sufficient time
to build a balanced program; and no Suzukis or Kitts
were hired. But the NJF's repentance was too late.

Another cumulative grievance among musicians—
and a basic reason for the rebellion at Cliff Walk—was
the NJF's cavalier financial attitude toward jazzmen who
lacked mass name appeal but who were recognized by
their colleagues as among the most important of current
contributors to the language. A Louis Armstrong or a
Benny Goodman had the box-office appeal and a suffi-

ciently tough booking office to get top fees from the NJF,
but the less widely renowned jazzmen were often pressured into coming to Newport for smaller sums than they
deserved, particularly since the announced goal of the
weekend was to advance jazz as an "art form." Ordinary
box-office laws, one might have thought, did not have to
be applied so stringently by a non-profit, tax-exempt institution.

The arguments that were employed to persuade
musicians who had to bargain for themselves were multiple. Newport, they were told, is a "cultural, non-profit"
event that benefits "jazz" so that any musician who refused to come for a nominal fee was being disloyal to his
art form. If that line didn't work, the musicians were reminded that anyone who appeared at Newport received
publicity in the mass media, while conversely, if someone
was not invited, it might appear that his career was de-
clining.

Young jazzmen who had not yet attained a broad
reputation and older players who had few work opportunities anyway usually came for the fee offered them.
A particular irony in the way the NJF exploited the
older players was that although it cited its use of the
jazz elders as proof of the festival's recognition that jazz
had a history which should be respected, the older players were never allowed enough rehearsal time or enough
care in planning their appearances so that they could be
heard at their best.

Few of these causes for many musicians' anger at
the NJF have ever been covered in the jazz trade press.
The widely printed Leonard Feather wrote in the 1959
NJF program, for example, that "the initiation in this
country of the large, spectacular, outdoor jazz event has
been both cause and effect of a maturing interest in jazz
as a whole. The American attitude toward jazz as an art
form has improved measurably" since the NJF began July
17, 1954.

The day before the 1960 riots, I was lectured in a similar vein by a Newport Festival official. Ignoring the beer cans strewn along the streets and the teenagers high at noon, he said, "You keep forgetting how much dignity the Festival has brought to jazz."

I saw him the morning after the National Guard had been called out, and noted that if the NJF brought a little more dignity to the town, it would blow up.

In the 1960 program, jazz writer Ira Gitler also apologized for the Festival. Among other proofs of its virtue, he cited the fact "that two-thirds of the money from refreshment sales (inside the park) goes to the Kiwanis Club of Newport and the Newport Boys Club, who put it to worthy uses." The fact that these stands always sold as much beer as any teenager, no matter how young, could drink was apparently more than compensated for by the fact that the money was funneled into an irreproachable cause.

A more realistic observer of the NJF has been Murray Kempton of the New York *Post*. In January, 1960, he wrote of "the gentry in the front row with their Martini shakers, the sailors squatting in the back, their heads between their knees, upchucking their beer. . . . Was ever anything in America at once so fashionable and squalid?"

On the Friday before the rioting, Kempton covered the musicians' rebellion at Cliff Walk and approved their activism: ". . . the issue here is the dignity of a trade. It had to begin somewhere in this country, and there could be no better place to draw the issue than Newport, which has been for many years a place unendurable for any civilized man. . . . What did the reality of Newport ever have to do with its myth? Do you think any sober man could honestly say that he enjoyed himself there? Jazz has been so vogued and Kerouacked as to be almost unheard in any case, and nowhere was its presentation more nauseating than at Newport. The washrooms were a crime against nature . . . the atmosphere stank of spilt beer and the sweat peculiar to people not enjoying themselves. . . . And, whenever either a musician or a sensitive observer complained about these conditions, Newport's sponsors answered in tones of personal righteousness that sounded like the letter Woolworth's sends people who want to know why a Negro can't get a cup of coffee at its lunch counter.

Kempton, in fact, might also have mentioned the occasional Jim Crow at Newport. Not all restaurants there have served Negroes attending the jazz festival, and in 1959 several Negroes who had been assured rooms by mail—through a central clearing office organized by the Festival and the Chamber of Commerce—found on their arrival that the rooms were for whites only. Despite exposure of the situation, the NJF had never publicly demanded that the town not discriminate. The lame automatic response by Festival officials to criticism of Jim Crow in Newport was, "Well, there'd be Jim Crow anywhere we went. Besides, our musical director is married to a Negro." In 1960, Charles Mingus, a musical director of the rival musicians' festival, was refused a room at a Newport motel that he had confirmed by telephone.

Since the NJF brought in about a million dollars worth of business to Newport each year, it would not have been difficult for the Festival to make an anti-discrimination policy clear and make it stick. Greed had superseded the Newport burghers' concern with drinking by minors; it could also have transcended—for one weekend a year—Jim Crow in the town.

As for the riots, Newport city officials were indeed as responsible for the inevitable explosion as the NJF. It was all too evident in 1959 that the streets were unsafe at night during the Festival, and one police official, several months later, still wondered how a riot had been averted the previous year. It is also true that the NJF added more Pinkertons to its staff policing Freebody Park and asked the Newport city manager for more police

throughout the town before the festival began. The city
manager regarded the request as insulting. His present
force, he barked, was adequate. Why run up additional
expenses? But on June 16, the Rhode Island Public Safety
Commissioner warned: "It's a tough situation down there
and they're asking for trouble if they close their eyes to it."

By Friday afternoon, it was evident there would be
serious trouble. Although there were signs in the street
warning that drinking on the street and littering the side-
walks would not be permitted, the police made practically
no moves to stop either practice. On Friday night, thirty-
nine revelers were arrested; there were scores of fights in
the town and on the beach where the police allowed
hundreds of potential spenders to sleep all night. At the
Viking Hotel, four youngsters flooded the second-floor
corridor and the atmosphere in the hotel was such that
a room clerk, pretending to be the manager, literally
broke into my room at three A.M. demanding to know
whether I was married to my wife.

The Newport *Daily News* on Saturday morning gave
a "sampling" of the previous night's incidents: "Eight
youths jumped onto a car being driven along Pelham
Street and smashed two of its windows. A sailor was held
for ripping the radio microphone off a police cruiser. . . .
As usual, the bulk of the trouble took part outside Freebody Park. Inside, control was easier in the illuminated
area. But the park itself was not exactly a Sunday-school
picnic grounds. Boys and girls looking as young as fourteen or fifteen were drinking beer and feeling its effects.
. . . This morning jazz fans were waiting outside the cafes
and barrooms for the opening hour."

It had rained torrentially Friday night. The hundreds on the beach and those who had slept in their cars
were bleary-eyed and disgruntled. A Providence *Bulletin*
reporter wrote as part of a post-mortem the next week
that by 10 o'clock Saturday morning ". . . it was common-
place on Bellevue Avenue . . . to see a driver with a can

of beer in one hand while his other held on to the wheel. A few of these fellows yanked from behind the wheel and carted off to the pokey to face charges would have improved the situation. . . . The beer tents at Freebody Park bore bold signs stating 'Minors Not Served.' But I happened to see one girl who couldn't have been more than fifteen standing at the counter gnawing on a chocolate-flavored ice cream popsicle in one hand and accepting a freshly-opened can of beer with the other."

All for the Kiwanis.

The Saturday-night rioting started near Freebody Park, but the violence spread rapidly. The police, who had not been tough enough during the previous two days, were being treated with contempt by the teenagers. Jack Williams observed in the Providence *Journal:* "I have experienced genuine fear twice in my life. Once was in combat in Europe during World War II; the other was Saturday night in Newport." Police and military police were bloodied—some were knocked unconscious—by full cans of beer hurled by the teenagers. Youngsters urged other teenagers on to attack the police. "Reeling youths," said Williams, "kept rallying their forces for new assaults on the police. 'Kill the cops,' one youth cried as he tossed a full can of beer at a car. . . . More cried out defiantly at the weary troopers. 'Get the stinkin', lousy cops,' one youth yelled as he tossed a half-filled bottle of beer at the troopers."

The Providence *Journal* described the scene before the tear gas arrived: ". . . hundreds of cans and bottles came flying through the night to the men pinned down in the center of the block and troopers, many of them with bloody faces, kept asking, 'When are they going to fire that gas?' "

A *Journal* reporter tried to find a phone. Walking up the stairs of a house, he was confronted by "a grim young man who stretched his arm across the stairs in front of me. A small club was in his hand. I showed him

my identification and asked if I could use the phone.
For a moment he considered. Then he shook his head,
'No, I've got children trying to sleep in there.'"

In significant contrast to the chaos in the streets,
the "musicians' festival" at Cliff Walk was continuing in
complete calm. The musicians had handled everything
from the beginning—tickets, press, promotion. They had
set up the chairs, stitched the canvas for the tents in
which they slept. They did their own programming and
their own announcing. Some even passed the hat among
free-loaders who were listening to the music outside the
fence.

The musicians who had been contracted for the main
festival were sympathetic to the dissidents. A few came
to visit; others were afraid, lest the Establishment re-
taliate economically. Pressure, in fact, had been placed on
Cliff Walk by the city, and several musicians were convinced that the NJF had been behind some of it. The
day before both festivals began, the city council, without a hearing, had banned outside amplification at Cliff
Walk and had complained about its sanitary facilities (a
particularly outrageous irony in view of the sanitation facilities at Freebody Park, where musicians were allotted
two pails behind the stage). The owner of the Cliff
Walk Manor, a blustering, successful businessman, refused to be intimidated. He ordered the outside amplification continued, and the police, who were feuding with
the city council anyway, yielded.

"I hear," said one drummer at Freebody Park, "that
they're really cooking over at Cliff Walk. Well, you play
better when you're mad."

Yet the music at Cliff Walk, while intense, was also
subtle. During part of the worst street warfare Saturday
night, trumpeter Roy Eldridge was blowing a softly
muted solo as drummer Jo Jones accompanied him in
complex, polyrhythmic patterns shaped just with his fingers and palms, no sticks or brushes. Eldridge had earlier

decided not to play for the rebels. "My fighting days are over," he sighed. But, seeing that patriarch Coleman Hawkins was one of the more determined dissidents, Eldridge finally also joined in.

A *Time* correspondent present was becoming cumulatively frustrated—before the rioting—at his inability to convince the New York office that the story of the rump festival was important enough to get into the music section. "Actually, it belongs in National Affairs," he was insisting. "This is like an extension of the sit-ins. I called it a sit-out."

Bassist Charles Mingus, who had earlier been pounding a tent stake with a huge rock, was now prowling around the entrance, trying to stop multiple use of single tickets. "It's tough to play, man, while you've got all this on your mind. But somebody had to do it." Jo Jones, a father figure to many young jazz players, was meanwhile explaining to a newspaperman: "The big festival forgot about music, but these little kiddies," he pointed to several modernists on the stand, "have got to have a chance to be heard. That's one reason we did this."

"Now this," Mingus pointed at the musicians playing with the sea and the beach as a backdrop, "is what Newport jazz was supposed to be. But I think we started this too late to save the town for the music."

The NJF was ordered to cease all music on Sunday afternoon, July 4. Although the Sunday and Monday night and Monday afternoon concerts were cancelled, the city allowed the Sunday "educational" daylight session to go on in the knowledge that it would attract few people. It was a blues afternoon—one of the best in the Festival's history. There were no big names. The passion of the players and singers reminded one musician, "That's the way this festival started. Music was its reason for being. Then it began to get hungry."

Soon after the Newport breakdown, Bill Coss, then

editor of the jazz magazine, *Metronome*, sent a letter to "over eight hundred persons in all forms of media"—and many printed and broadcast it—claiming that the culpability was entirely the town's. His was a characteristic example of the trade press protecting its own. "If there is fault to be found it is not with jazz, or with festivals, but with the city management which had not properly geared its enforcement agency to be able to stop the unlawful drinking in the first place, the massing together in the second."

On the Mutual Network after the brawl, Pegeen Fitzgerald revealed that the riots had not been spontaneous, but like those in Japan, Korea and Turkey, had been Communist-inspired. Someone apparently had forgotten to alert *Tass* to have its own photographer in readiness.

A more accurate assessment of the rioters was made by Phyllis Battelle in the New York *Journal American:* "The Newport rioters were definitely not delinquents with holes in their pockets. These were 'good' boys and girls from 'better' families and colleges." Present at the festival had been Father Norman J. O'Connor, chaplain of the Newman Club at Boston University, and more widely known as the "jazz priest." O'Connor wrote in the Boston *Globe:* "It was a college crowd . . . with a good sprinkling of juniors and seniors from high schools. It was a crowd that had money because the great share of them were travelling the streets in . . . sports cars . . . and convertibles. . . . Parents must not care if sons and daughters sleep out all night on beaches, in cars, or not at all. Parents no longer care if teenagers come home at night or not. Parents no longer care about the drinking habits of their children."

"A can of beer," continued the Providence *Evening Bulletin*, "was just the prop they needed. It was something they could use to attract attention to themselves. It wasn't quite as good as a crazy hat, or a fur coat in the damp heat, or going barefoot, or a real nutty costume,

but it could be used impressively. It could catch onlookers' eyes. And that was what these youngsters wanted
most of all. They wanted to be both 'of' the crowd and
somehow to stand 'out' from it. Being of it gave them a
sense of mass security; standing out from it gave them a
sense of individual importance."

It was a similar crowd, mostly composed of college
students, in Grand Lake, Colorado, on the night of July 3
which, according to UPI: ". . . rioted . . . after tavern
operators shut down bars ahead of the regular eight
o'clock Sunday closing time. The mob charged the Grand
Lake fire department with clubs, set fire to gasoline in
the street and chopped fire hoses with axes which they
took from a fire truck. The bars were closed after holiday
weekend patrons exploded fireworks inside the buildings."

The New York *Herald Tribune* editorialized: "Perhaps the most discouraging aspect of the whole sorry
mess was the emptiness and futility of it all. American
youth hit some sort of a new low in Newport this week
end. Here was mass violence—vicious violence, poten-
tially lethal missiles hurled at total strangers—with
neither point nor reason, done by several thousand of
those bright college students who supposedly are our
hope for tomorrow. In capitals around the world, desperately earnest students have lately been demonstrating,
often rioting, for causes. Some of these have been good
causes, some bad; it is as if a contagion of violent fervor
were overleaping national boundaries and spreading from
university to university. But these young Americans had
no cause. They were rioting for nothing but the perverse
pleasure of violence. Theirs was hedonism gone wild, and
an irresponsible animal self-indulgence that reflects dis-
credit on their generation."

Although there were many Negro college students
in town, I saw none engaged in the rioting nor did any
of the reporters to whom I talked. Perhaps their disinclination for the purposeless violence was caused in part

by their knowledge of what non-violent direct action during the southern sit-ins had accomplished both for those taking part and—involuntarily—for the country as a whole.

Newport had been quieted by Sunday. Most of those fined were over twenty-one, thereby proving, said one newspaperman sardonically, "that liquor wasn't sold to minors." At the rival festival, several dissidents told reporters they were sorry the NJF had ended. All, that is, but Charles Mingus, an unyieldingly honest man who said: "That's the way it should be. They deserve it because . . . they lost their true identity with jazz."

There was already grumbling among the town merchants about the loss of business in 1961 and the mayor, James L. Maher, who had voted against canceling the festival, proclaimed: "I'd like to see it back next year; if given a chance, it can develop enough." Ward Harvey, president of the Community Hotel Corporation and owner of the expanding Viking Hotel, which has a considerable financial stake in whether the Festival continues in Newport, said he expected there would be an attempt to hold the Festival in Newport the next year. And, added this lover of jazz: "I'm 100 per cent in favor of such a movement."

There were counter-rumors. George Wein, Newport's musical director, was quoted as saying the NJF might take place in Yankee Stadium next year, a notable showcase for the arts. Father O'Connor wrote with surprising ingenuousness: "Strangely, cities and towns with reputations similar to Newport have already bid for the festival to come to them, regardless of the problems."

On one train back from Newport, Miff Mole, an elderly jazzman who had been a major figure in the 1920's but is now practically unknown, was depressed. He had been ill for some time, but had gathered up what he could of his strength to make an appearance at the Sunday-night Festival. The concert had been canceled, and he might not get such an invitation again. Some college students on the train began mocking him as "a broken-down jazz musician." When he didn't respond, they began talking about the "counterattack" they'd mount against the cops next year.

A reporter meanwhile was reading a New York *Post* interview with Alfred Kazin. "Kazin," said the interviewer, "also visited the Soviet Union last year as part of a State Department exchange. He found that Soviet life confirmed his lifelong criticism of communism: the leadership is dishonest and as a result, the entire society corrupts itself by practicing deceit and falsehood, even though materially the society has advanced by leaps and bounds."

Newport certainly did not represent all of America in the summer of 1960, but what happened there was the result of many more basic factors than the playing of jazz —factors, however, that have affected more and more of the music. In that respect, the publicity men for Newport have been quite current. Jazz does indeed reflect American life.

The Foreground

"You know, there's this mood about the music, a kind of need to be moving. You just can't set it down and hold it. Those Dixieland musicianers, they tried to do that; they tried to write the music down and kind of freeze it. Even when they didn't arrange it to death, they didn't have any place to send it; that's why they lost it. You just can't keep the music unless you move with it."

—Sidney Bechet

7

Studio Time

Another part of the background for jazz is the recording studio. Records are still the basic self-instruction tools for the musician, and they are the quickest way his reputation is made with the jazz audience, here and abroad. To provide some indication of the way jazz recordings are made, I've selected two sessions—an informal Dixieland date with Louis Armstrong and a complex, carefully rehearsed modern jazz experiment with Miles Davis. In both, as in all record dates, there are intersecting pressures on and by the musicians, the a&r (artists and repertory) director, and the silently critical engineers.

The Armstrong record, made in the spring of 1960, was issued as *Louis and the Dukes of Dixieland* (Audio Fidelity 1924/ AFSD 5924). The Davis album, recorded toward the end of 1959, is *Sketches of Spain* (Columbia CL-1480; stereo CS-8271).

I—*"Place It Where You Want, Dolling!"*

Louis Armstrong was forty-five minutes late for the first session of an album he was to make with the Dukes of Dixieland for Audio Fidelity. Sid Frey, the label's voluble, intense owner, was not disturbed at Louis' tardiness. "It takes him half a day to get up," Frey explained

to a bystander while waving at Armstrong. "Then it takes
him a couple of hours for the lip salves and checking the
horn. He lives his life for that horn."

When he arrived, Louis, who had gained some weight
in recent months, was in buoyant spirits. He greeted the
Dukes, a white Dixieland combo, warmly, and they
treated him with marked deference. Louis was in sport
shirt and slacks, as were the other players and Mr. Frey.
The latter prowled the studio, checking microphones.

Frey moved in on Louis, who was gently unpacking
his horn. "Louis, have you decided whether you'll do that
Bert Williams tune, *Nobody?*"

Louis looked up, grinned, and shook his head nega-
tively. "Well, Mr. Glaser thinks the NAACP wouldn't like
that."

Mr. Glaser is the shrewd, apopleptic Joe Glaser,
Louis' personal manager and head of the Associated
Booking Corporation, the most powerful agency in the
jazz field. Glaser has the final veto over Armstrong's personnel, repertory, and nearly everything else concerning
the band.

Frey shook his head disgruntledly and walked away.
"I don't believe it," he muttered. "I think Glaser is sav-
ing that song for an all-Bert Williams album for another
label."

The huge Webster Hall studio meanwhile was clang-
ingly alive in a jangle of trombone blasts, shouts from
Frey in the control room to "turn that mike a little," a
spiraling trumpet, and general disjointed noise. Webster
Hall, on New York's lower East Side, occasionally doubles
as a site for local neighborhood functions but is most
often in use for RCA-Victor's pop recordings. When time
is available, a number of independent entrepreneurs such
as Frey use the hall and generally also employ RCA staff
engineers.

By three o'clock, an hour and a half after the session

had been scheduled to start, Frey was moderately satisfied with the way he had set up his forces. The Dukes
and Louis were arranged as a large triangle. To the
right of the control room, young trumpeter Frank Assunto and tuba player Rich Mateson were stationed. To
the left of the booth were Frank's brother, Fred, on
trombone, and clarinetist Jerry Fuller who had joined
the Dukes after five years with Jack Teagarden. In the
center of the triangle's base was Louis Armstrong.

At the apex of the triangle sat drummer Mo Mahoney. Between Mahoney and the trumpet-tuba corner
was pianist Stan Mendelson. Between Mahoney and the
trombone-clarinet position was Jac Assunto, father of
Frank and Fred. Jac doubles on banjo and trombone.

Armstrong's wife, Lucille, a woman of great charm
and total devotion to her husband, brought Louis a cup
of coffee. In the control room, RCA staff engineer Ray
Hall, a young man for whom New York jazz musicians
have particular respect, was saying softly to Frey, "We
should spend some time with the clarinet. It's the only
instrument that's peaking."

Frey agreed. The stocky, bustling Frey is the man
who stampeded the record business into stereo by first
releasing a "Stereodisc" to the industry in November,
1957, and then making stereo recordings available to
the public the following February. A compulsive lecturer,
Frey was vehemently indoctrinating a visitor as Armstrong continued warming up. "We record with very little
reverberation," Frey declared. "There's already enough in
the room. Maybe a little bit too much. And we get all
the presence, intimacy and warmth of sound we can so
that the listener can identify with what's going on. Louis,
for example, leaves me emotionally exhausted; but until
we cut him, he hadn't been recorded right so that record
buyers could get his full impact."

Audio Fidelity had already released *Satchmo Plays*

King Oliver (stereo, ASFD 5930; monophonic, AFLP 1930) and had recorded but not released a June, 1959, meeting between Armstrong and the Dukes of Dixieland. The latter was being held up because Louis used some tunes in it that he had recorded for Decca a few years ago and was not supposed to record again for five years. For both last year's session and the new album with the Dukes, Frey had paid Armstrong $40,000.

Louis meanwhile was producing vibrantly full, round tones in his warmup. Now sixty, Armstrong continues to play with the most richly plangent tone in jazz; and at his best, his solos are still models of economy and passionate order.

"Pops," Frey spoke into the control room microphone in his customary roar, "could you stand more in front of the mike?"

Louis did, and decided to warm up the band as well as himself in *Indiana,* a tune he usually plays at the beginning of a night club or concert date.

Added to the high command in the control room was Joe Delaney, manager of the Dukes of Dixieland. A Louisiana lawyer with extensive experience in the record business, Delaney is tall, relaxed, and alert. Although his crew-cut hair is greying, Delaney has a perennial innocence of mien.

As *Indiana* ended, the restless Frey said to no one in particular, "This is a typical Audio Fidelity session. They're doing a number we're not going to record."

"Pops," Frey shouted, "will you want to face in any particular direction?"

Louis turned toward the control room. "No, you place it where you want, dolling," and broke into laughter.

"Pops, I want you to be comfortable," Frey persisted.

"No," Louis said seriously, "you fix it. I don't know anything about microphones. You put it where you want, and I'll play there."

Louis and the Dukes began to discuss the routining of *Avalon*, the first number to be actually recorded for the album.

Louis looked at the control room and grinned. "Anyone in there know the lyrics to *Avalon?*"

No one did. Louis began to sing what he remembered:

> "I found my love in Avalon
> Beside the bay . . ."

He stopped, "Well, there's no sense telling them all we did there," and chuckled.

"Want to let them run it down once?" asked Ray Hall, "before we make it?"

"No," said Delaney, "let's try our luck."

"We're rolling," Frey's voice shot out into the hall. "Take one!"

The take broke down when Louis slipped: "I left . . . I mean I found my girl . . ."

"Louis," said Frey, "sing into the same mike you play into. And take it easy on the drums behind the vocal."

"All right," Frey turned to Hall. "Rewind the tape."

"We can't erase today," said Hall.

"That's nice," Frey grimaced. "I'd like to have the tape concession here."

The next try worked out well. Louis improvised on the lyrics:

> "I found my girl in Avalon,
> Beside the bay.
> Oh, she was so nice in Avalon,
> Hmmmmmmmm, I'll say.
> But now we up in Harlem,
> And oh boy, hey, hey,

> She's not down in Avalon, folks,
> She's right here in the studio—
> Today!"

Frey decided to ask for another take, and went out into the hall to adjust Armstrong's microphone. "You see what I mean by the 'Frey Curtain of Sound'?" Frey rhetorically asked a visitor in the control room as he came back in. "It's not at all ping-pong. I like broad panorama of sound so that each one of the elements is placed—and heard—according to where he'd actually be standing in a performance."

The next *Avalon* was superb with a thrilling high-note ending by Louis. The musicians relaxed, and listened to the playback.

"Louis sure is making the Dukes sound good," said a visitor. "Almost like jazzmen."

"There's more to them than you think," said manager Delaney defensively.

"Well," said the visitor, "you know what jazzmen and the critics think of them. Circus-playing, mechanical routines, a thumping rhythm section, and very predictable solos."

"I don't think you've heard them enough," Delaney countered. "For one thing, the boys spend a lot of time digging modern jazz. And they've never gone in for hokum like funny hats. They walked off a Firestone TV show on ABC because they wouldn't wear straw hats and they absolutely refused to put on corny uniforms on another show."

Delaney had become manager of the Dukes a few years ago when he was at Tulane getting his law degree. Previously he had been an executive at Decca, Coral, and London. The Dukes had started some eleven years ago as a neighborhood band in New Orleans, formed by Frank and Fred Assunto. First called the Basin Street Four (or Five or Six, depending on their manpower), they later toured with a Horace Heidt troupe as the Junior Dixieland Band and finally named themselves the Dukes of Dixieland. The band first realized its drawing power during a forty-four-month run at the Famous Door in New Orleans.

When Delaney became head of the now defunct Victor subsidiary, Label "X," he recorded the Dukes for that label. During one of their Las Vegas engagements, however, Sid Frey heard them, thought they could become big record sellers, and finally convinced Delaney of his point. Since October, 1956, the Dukes had made eleven albums for Frey with a total sale of over 1,300,000.

Louis Armstrong walked into the control room. "You really like playing with them?" asked a newcomer who was an old friend of Louis'.

"Sure," said Louis. "They're home boys. Whenever we're playing in the same town, I go and sit in. We have a ball."

"Well, Louis likes Lombardo too," said another hanger-on.

"What you forget," Delaney bristled, "is that the Dukes draw a wide range of ages. They appeal to more than the usual jazz audience. Their fans include many adults and many people well above the average in income. Before the Blue Note in Chicago folded, for example, we would draw less people than Count Basie but they'd spend more."

"This is good-time music," Frey moved into the discussion. "It's not complicated and it's happy. If an appliance dealer is hip, and many of them are, he'll drop a record by the Dukes on a turntable when he's selling equipment. The adults who buy tables and amplifiers generally like their kind of music and will take a record home for the kids too."

The break was over. Frey asked for *Avalon* once more. Armstrong, sitting down and warming up, asked Frankie Assunto, "What key, baby, is that again?"

"F," said Assunto.

"What's here Thursday?" Frey was asking Ray
Hall. "We may need more sessions than I'd counted on."

"A beefsteak party at four o'clock," said Hall, dead-
pan.

"Hmph," Frey commented.

By the time he reached the vocal in the new version,
Louis had changed the words again:

> "Yes, I found my love in Avalon,
> Beside the sea.
> Oh, she was awful nice in Avalon,
> She was cute as can be.
> But now we in Harlem, Lord,
> And boy, you know,
> She knocks me out in Avalon,
> And she's here with me today."

Louis followed the vocal with a climbing, explosive
solo. Frankie Assunto, sitting on a stool with trumpet in
his lap, gazed trance-like at Louis, and smiled seraphi-
cally. Louis tore the trumpet from his lips at the end of
the solo, laughed in satisfaction, and walked away from
the mike.

The tune ended, but Frey held up his arm dramati-
cally for silence. At the end of ten seconds, he put it
down.

"We must get those ten seconds of cymbal ring," he
explained. "It's a natural sound."

During the playback, Louis was talking with grey-
haired "Papa" Jac Assunto. Assunto had brought up the
subject of famous New Orleans restaurants. Louis was
guarded. He is bitter about discrimination in his home
town, and no longer enjoys playing there.

"They still have Antoine's and all them places?" Louis
finally warmed a little to the discussion.

"Yes," Assunto assured him.

The musicians had been confident that the previous take was the final one, but Frey strode out into the hall. "I heard an engineer," he announced, "who said he could do better on another shot."

"Were you the engineer?" a suspicious onlooker whispered to Frey.

"No, no," said Frey, "Ray really wants to do another. He says he knows what he wants to do now."

The Dukes were clustered around Louis.

"That's a very religious family," Frey pointed to the Assunto brothers, "but with them, Louis ranks second to nobody, not even Jesus Christ."

After another take of *Avalon*, Frey resumed lecturing. "The point is that if you can get the cleanest possible sound with the least possible distortion, you can put more volume on the tape, and you get a better signal-to-noise ratio."

Ray Hall raised his eyebrows, but said nothing.

Dixie was proposed as the next tune. Louis began to read the lyrics, but stopped, chuckling. "No, I can't sing that. The colored cats would put me down."

"You know," said Ray Hall, a Negro, "I always thought he was an Uncle Tom. But he's not. And such a cooperative guy."

Several friends of Louis had come into the hall—greying Gene Krupa and trumpeter Max Kaminsky among them. Armstrong and Krupa embraced, and then Louis caught sight of a Long Island neighbor, Dizzy Gillespie. Dizzy, though a key representative of the modern jazz that Louis once contemptuously called "Chinese music," is an admirer of Armstrong; and the two have become friends.

"I was in his house just yesterday," Dizzy was saying to a jazz writer. Dizzy listened for a few minutes to the playback of *Avalon*. "He sure can play, can't he?"

Dixie was shelved, and *Wolverine Blues* took its place. Wordlessly, Louis sang the way he wanted the

ending to go. "You see what I mean," he said to Frankie
Assunto, "you got to watch it close."

"I think we're ready for a take," Frey boomed from
the control room; but photographers from the *Daily News*,
oblivious of Frey, were shooting Louis, Krupa and Gillespie for promotion pictures in connection with a jazz concert the paper was sponsoring.

"I'll be glad when those photographers get out of
here," Frey said to Delaney.

Max Kaminsky, whose jazz renown has faded in
recent years, stood against the wall, watching the picture-
taking.

"Hey," a sensitive friend of Louis shouted to the
photographers. "There's Maxie. Get him in there too."
Kaminsky was duly included in the next set of pictures.

"Gentlemen," said Frey icily, "May we proceed—
please?"

The picture-taking stopped.

"I want all the spectators," Frey's voice cannonaded
from the control room, "to be as quiet as possible. The
mikes are wide open."

"It's getting to look like a Sinatra recording session,"
Joe Delaney pointed to the crowd outside the booth.

"Yes," said Frey, "and I don't like it."

After the first take, Frey expressed dissatisfaction
with the opening. "The beginning is always the most important part of a record. Let's do it again."

By 4:15 a take on *Wolverine Blues* had been tentatively approved. Armstrong had played excellently, but
he wasn't satisfied. He and the Dukes began discussing
changes.

"This is the way we play it," Frankie was saying.

"Yeah," answered Louis, "I'll listen and find a little
part for myself."

The Dukes, standing around the seated Louis, started
to play. Louis fingered his horn, and finally joined in.

"Now," Louis said to Frankie, "when you finish that

chorus, I'll take over and play the obbligation to your
solo."

The Dukes laughed at Louis' play on the word.

"I," Frey announced to Delaney in the control room,
"would rather have excitement and mistakes than no excitement and no mistakes. That's why I try to get complete
takes whenever I can, and I try not to have them do too
many. By the fifth or sixth time around, the arrangement
may get more polished, but the playing begins to lose
excitement."

"Can the drummer tighten the snares," Ray Hall
asked Frey, "so they won't echo so much?"

Frey instructed the drummer.

After the next take, Frey asked if the musicians
wanted to try another right away.

"Pops," Frey added, "you've got to stay on mike
more."

"I'm trying," said Louis.

"Sid," Delaney spoke softly, "have Ray lower the
volume when you're talking from the control room. You
come on like Ethel Merman."

"Yes," said Hall, "and step back a little."

"O.K.," said Frey, looking somewhat surprised and
chastened, "I'll talk softly."

"Now," Frey announced with self-conscious gentle-
ness, "at the end of this next take, everyone please be
quiet. We're trying to catch the cymbal to the very last
ring."

During the take Louis stood, arms wide apart,
stomach out, enjoying the music. He then unleashed a
brilliant, stop-time solo (a solo in which the rhythm section does not play continuously).

The take was approved, and Louis and the Dukes
began to work out an instrumental version of *Dixie*.
Louis started to walk around the hall, playing without accompaniment, until he found the tempo he wanted. The
Dukes soon fell into the same groove.

During a break in the recording, Sid Frey and Louis began to swap jokes. Frankie Assunto was shaking his head. "The old man is too much," he said. "I always thought I'd be afraid to play with him, but he's the easiest person in the world to work with. That first time we recorded in Chicago, however, was an experience. I had such an emotional let-down after that first recording session last year that while I was driving down to the Loop, it took me several minutes to realize I was only going fifteen miles an hour. It was like I was in a trance. I was so depressed and tired but later that night, Louis walked into the night club where we were playing. As soon as he said, 'Hello,' I was all right again."

The playback was ending.

"It sounds like an old marching band," Frankie called over to Louis.

Louis broke into an exaggerated strut. "Yes, indeed," he laughed. "And they've all got their caps on!"

II—*"What's to Understand? Play Them!"*

On a grey November Sunday afternoon, Miles Davis, arranger-conductor Gil Evans and nineteen other musicians were scheduled at Columbia's huge 30th Street studios on New York's East Side. They were to record a unique album concept—Spanish themes rescored by Evans and improvised on by Davis.

The instrumentation was Davis, four trumpets, tuba, three French horns, two trombones, bass, drums, percussion, harp, five woodwinds. Davis and Evans had already collaborated for Columbia on two brilliantly integrated orchestral albums, *Miles Ahead* (CL-1041) and *Porgy and Bess* (CL-1274, CS-8085). Both had sold well, especially the broodingly dramatic intensification of the Gershwin score.

By 2:15 nearly all the musicians had arrived at the studios, which had once been a church, then a brewery, and was now in constant use by Columbia. The majority

of the musicians were dressed in sports clothes. The one
woman was slender, auburn-haired harpist Janet Putnam.
Miles, short and wiry, is somewhat of a stylesetter sar-
torially as well as musically among the younger jazz
musicians and on that afternoon he wore a green Italian
sweater, grey polo shirt, green and red silk scarf and
tapered chino pants. He looked, however, as if he'd
rather be at home swearing at television, a continuing
avocation of his.

Miles moved wearily into the control room. The effects of a recent attack of flu lingered. "I'm breaking up,"
he said in his croaking hoarse voice. "I'm breaking into
pieces."

The a&r man, Teo Macero, a composer and erstwhile
experimental jazz musician, was briskly giving instructions to engineer Fred Plaut and Plaut's assistant, Lou
Belok.

The first session had taken place unsuccessfully the
previous Tuesday. Miles, even more racked by flu then,
hadn't arrived until more than half the date was over,
and the three hours had been spent mostly on the orchestra's finding the right tempos for the main piece in
the album, Evans' re-arrangement of the middle section
of the *Concierto de Aranjuez* for Guitar and Orchestra
by the contemporary Spanish composer, Jacquin Rodrigo
(Columbia ML-5345). As planned, it would take up one
album side.

Miles had first heard the work several months ago
on the West Coast when a friend gave him the record.
"After listening to it for a couple of weeks," Miles said,
"I couldn't get it out of my mind. Then when Gil and I
decided to do this album, I played him the record and
he liked it. As we usually do, we planned the program
first by ourselves for about two months. I work out
something; he takes it home and works on it some more;
and then we figure out how we're going to do it. He can
read my mind and I can read his."

E

Fred Plaut meanwhile was beginning to express firm ideas of his own on the best way to balance the session. Plaut, a Parisian who came to Columbia over twenty years ago is witty, conscientious and multi-lingual. He engineers many classical dates, most of the Broadway shows, and a large percentage of the jazz albums. Plaut is a superb photographer and many candid shots he's taken during Columbia dates have been on exhibition and in magazines.

The balance set by Macero had the trumpets, trombones and regular jazz drums (played by Miles' regular drummer, Jimmy Cobb) on the right. On the left were woodwinds, harp, and Elvin Jones on various percussion instruments, including tympani, tambourine and castanets. The French horns, bass and Miles were in the middle.

Teo started checking out each section of the orchestra to hear if all the microphones were working. Nine microphones had been set up—one each for brass, harp, woodwinds, horns, Miles, castanets and percussion, drums, bass, and an opening trio of flute, trombone and trumpet.

"We're going to cross-feed some of the instruments," Teo explained, "to get a true stereo picture."

In the studio, Gil Evans was checking the parts with his characteristically preoccupied look. A lean, greying man in his late forties, Gil looks like a gently aging diplomat who collects rare species of ferns on weekends. Though always polite, he is in firm control of his record dates and insists on hearing exactly what he has written. Now, while Evans moved to one of the spare pianos at the far end of the studio to play part of the score, Fred Plaut and Teo Macero were debating the placement of the jazz drums.

"I never put rhythm drums with brass," said Fred. "It's a big mistake having the drums on the right side."

"No," countered Teo, "they'll wash out the wood-winds if they're on the left."

"The drums are very bright," Fred persisted. "And the brasses are bright too."

"I'd rather not move them," said Teo.

"All right! I give up," and Fred continued checking out the microphones.

Miles had joined Gil at the spare piano and they started discussing Miles' part which spread out, accordion-fashion, over many sheets of manuscript paper. Teo walked out into the studio from the control room, and Plaut turned to his assistant. "I'm still sorry the jazz drums aren't on the other side."

As each section of the orchestra was being checked out, Gil kept looking at Plaut from the studio to see if any new problems were arising.

"Remember, we want lots of bass," Teo said over his shoulder to Plaut. "And Fred, there's a lot of leakage in the center."

Miles went back in the control booth. "I always manage to put my foot in it," he said of the Spanish experiment. "I always manage to try something I can't do." The statement was mockingly self-deprecating and no one bothered with the logical rebuttal that Miles is usually able to accomplish exactly what he sets out to do, and even rarer among jazzmen, he's always clear as to what it is he does want.

"I'm going to call myself on the phone one day," Miles continued, "and tell myself to shut up."

At ten minutes of three, the remaining music parts were passed out. The copyist had been late. What with further checking of equipment, elimination of a crackling noise that suddenly developed on one control room speaker, dry runs with the orchestra, and other complications, it wasn't until half past three that Teo said, "Stand by, please." And then stopped. "All right, who has a radio on in the studio?" he snapped into the microphone.

"Please!" he ordered, and the offending French horn player put a transistor radio back in his pocket.

The take began with Miles sitting on a stool; a trio of trumpet, trombone and flute behind him; and Gil directing in the center of the orchestra. Evans conducts with an almost ballet-like flow of motion. He uses both arms, and keeps the beat going like a firm Poseidon calming the waves. Evans is extremely careful that all the dense textural details and markings for dynamics are performed precisely and are recorded so that all the interweaving parts emerge clearly.

At one point an hour later, Evans cut off one take and said into the microphone, "Are you getting a blending of the three flutes? I only hear one flute out here." Macero assured him that all three were distinctly audible in the control room. Gil went into the booth, heard for himself, and was satisfied.

Miles came in for a sip of vodka. "I can't eat. That's what's wrong with me." After the vodka, he chuckled as he went out, saying, "Me and Buddy Bolden," referring to the first quasi-legendary jazz trumpeter, a New Orleans barber with a reputation for high and hard living.

By four, the shape of the piece was becoming established. The characteristic, fiercely mournful Spanish melody was a strong one. Evans' sketch for Miles looked complex, but Miles seemed to have no difficulty improvising around it. The orchestra's function, as in other Evans scores, was to provide partly a support for and partly a commentary on Davis' solo statements. The range of colors was extensive and they changed often, sometimes subtly dissolving into slightly different shades and at other times breaking sharply from ominous cool to brighter blends. By means of more complete instrumentation and varied voicings, Evans gets an unusually full-bodied orchestral sound for jazz from the deep bottoms of the tuba and French horns to high-register woodwinds and brass. "These look like flute parts we're playing," lead trumpeter Ernie Royal said during one break, shaking his head in respect and exasperation.

The rhythms were complex and several of the musicians found it hard to keep their time straight. Gil stopped one take as the rhythms became tangled. "The tempo is going to go," he waved his arm in an arc, first to the left and then to the right, "this way and that way. Just keep your own time and let the rhythm *go*." He again made a slow, even wave to further illustrate his point.

As more and more takes, most of them fragmentary, were tried, Miles' confidence in his own role grew markedly. He had already demonstrated in his *Flamenco Sketches* (*Kind of Blue*, Columbia CL-1355, CS-8163) and *Blues for Pablo* with Gil Evans (*Miles Ahead*, Columbia CL-1041), a basic affinity with the Spanish musical temperament and sinuous rhythms. He played as if all by himself, his tone becoming burningly dark in the somber passages and then cutting through with sharper loneliness as the music grew more animated.

In the control room, the visiting Hall Overton, a classical composer who has also been involved in jazz as a pianist and arranger, said, "This is the toughest notation I've ever seen in a jazz arrangement. It could have been written more easily for the players and the result would have been the same, but Gil has to have it exactly the way it happens in the piece. Another thing that makes it tough is that he's using so many different levels. Like the little trio part at the beginning that has to be balanced with Miles on his microphone. Then the three players go back to their places and that makes for another balance problem. And that's just at the beginning. Fortunately, these guys are among the best readers in town. Two of those horn players, Jim Buffington and John Barrows, were in New Jersey last night playing a Beethoven sextet for string quartet and two horns."

In the studio, the French horn player had his radio

at his ear again. Gil, listening intently to a playback a few feet away, had his ears cupped in his hands, and shook his head sadly. "We lost the beat." Miles meanwhile shouted from the studio into the control room, "Hey, Teo, it doesn't matter how loud those castanets are. It's *supposed* to be that way." Then Miles bent over, cupping his ears in his hands, and listened.

"This," said trombonist Frank Rehak between taking pictures of Miles and Gil during the playback, "is a tough one. To count at all, you have to count four on every beat."

For the rest of the afternoon, the takes continued to improve. On one, Miles began to play in the lower register with deep feeling and a fuller tone than is usual in his work. "Beautiful," Teo said. "The writing there is almost Gregorian," he turned to Overton. "It's all diatonic."

"Fred," Teo said quickly, "there'll be big brass after the next little solo if Gil doesn't stop it there." Gil did stop it.

"Ach," said Plaut, "why did he cut it *there?*"

Gil was back at the piano checking chords with Miles.

"This," said Plaut to no one in particular, "will be *some* splicing job."

"Gil will come up for that," said Teo, "and probably Miles too."

Gil and Miles came in to listen to a playback. "I *love* that chord," said Miles, "and the end of that section with the flutes way up there. That's all I could hear last night in my sleep. Hey," he turned to Macero, "don't forget take three. That was a good one."

Teo asked Evans if the tympani came in too softly. "I wanted it to be just a whisper," said Evans, "a little cushion of air, something to keep the thing floating. I think it's all right. The tuba is too loud, though."

"You know," Miles returned to the conversation, "the melody is so strong there's nothing you have to do with it. If you tried to play bebop on it, you'd wind up being a hip cornball. The thing I have to do now is make things connect, make them mean something in what I play around it."

"Why don't we do it from the beginning again?" said Plaut after Evans and Davis had left the control room.

"No," said Teo, "not unless Gil and Miles want to."

"If you don't do it again," said Plaut, "you'll swear at me afterwards."

"The trumpet was a little weak on bar thirty-three," Teo changed the subject.

A little later, Plaut shook his head. "I'm still sorry the jazz drums aren't on the left side. Well, anyway, there's no ping-pong."

"This will be good stereo," Teo agreed.

"Yes," said Fred with more than a touch of irony. "We're playing football now in there."

By four-thirty, the musicians were a little more than a third of the way through. "There's more confusion in there," said Plaut, "than on a Broadway show recording."

As if in counterpoint to the engineer's comment, Gil announced to the orchestra immediately afterwards, "It's in *three* flats," and sat at the piano to demonstrate.

"Can you *please* put that radio away," Teo's voice came into the studio from the control booth. "We're picking it up." The French horn player grimly put the radio away.

The orchestra had now reached the sixty-fifth bar, and from then on it was all new territory for them. At a break, Miles was back in the control room.

"How many copies will this sell?" he asked Teo semi-seriously.

"A hundred thousand. I guarantee it."

"Two!" Miles laughed. "Actually we're making it just to have a record at home we can play for ourselves."

"I think," said Teo, "that's what some of the artists really do."

A few minutes later, a take broke down, and one of the musicians said, "I can't understand those triplets."

"What's to understand?" said Gil. "Play them!"

At a few minutes past five, Fred Plaut began taking pictures during a playback. So did the regular Columbia photographer and a couple of the musicians.

Several more takes were tried, and a few minutes before five-thirty, Teo rushed into the control room. "We're going from the top of the whole thing." Plaut smiled. "Put on another load of tape," Teo said to Belok, Plaut's assistant.

It was the best take of the afternoon, lasting some twelve minutes, and there was no question now that the piece was going to work. During one passage, Miles played a series of notes that made Evans spin around and smile at him.

"This," said Plaut when the take was over, "is a lifetime project."

"What I like about Columbia," Miles reached for a little more vodka, "is they spare no expense." As often with Miles, it was hard to separate the satire from the seriousness of his comment. "We can have seventeen flutes playing one note—in unison. Right, Teo?"

Miles dropped the playfulness entirely when a visitor asked him about a recent album. "My records sound so funny to me," Miles grimaced, "once I've made them. I can't hear them anymore. I'm still on the *Kind of Blue* and *Jazz Track* albums though."

Howard Scott of Columbia's classical a&r department entered the control booth. He had a session scheduled with the Russian cellist, Mstislav Rostropovich for that evening, and had to call him to confirm the time. Scott, however, speaks no Russian. He reached the cellist at his hotel, tried French, was relieved to find it worked, and hung up, happy at having confirmed the arrangements for dinner and the recording time.

In the control room, Evans was listening to the last

playback. "Damn! Miles can play beautifully down low." In the studio, the musicians were packing up. It was a few minutes before six. "This," said Gil, back in the control room, "is where the heroine is crying for the dead bullfighter."

"Really?" said a visitor.

"No," Gil smiled, "it's an old Spanish vamp."

"I would have preferred the drums on the other side," Fred Plaut said to Belok.

"That melody," Miles was still marveling at the piece, "is so strong that the softer you play it, the stronger it gets, and the stronger you play it, the weaker it gets."

"Yes," said Gil, "it's distilled melody. If you lay on it too hard, you don't have it."

"It should take two, maybe three more sessions to finish the album," Teo was speculating.

"When Gil and I start on an album," Miles was relaxing, "we don't know how it's going to wind up. It just goes on and on out there. Gil," he turned to Evans, "our next record date will be silence."

"You," said Gil, "and your big ideas."

8

A Brief Note on the Romance of
'The White Negro"

In his essay, *The White Negro,* Norman Mailer describes the *echt* hipsters "in the sub-worlds of American life" as those who divorce themselves from society, exist without roots, and "set out on that uncharted journey into the rebellious imperatives of the self." Aside from the validity of Mailer's diagnosis of the "essence of Hip" and "its psychopathic brilliance"—a subject not germane to this book because few jazzmen are any longer hipsters in his sense—Mailer's essay illustrates a romanticization of jazz that is increasingly common and increasingly inaccurate. He declares that "the presence of Hip as a working philosophy in the sub-worlds of American life is probably due to jazz, and its knife-like entrance into the culture, its subtle but so penetrating influence on the avant-garde generation. . . ."

Yet nowhere does Mailer detail convincingly what this specifically jazz influence has been. It is true, as he points out, that much of the language of the hipster is taken from jazz and from the larger street dictionary of the Negro from which most jazz terms originally come. But the hipster's reactions to the music itself are usually as superficial and unknowledgeable as those of the

138

hungrily impressionable adolescents who watch Stan Kenton imitate the American eagle.

Mailer does say that the influence of jazz on the hipster came through the fact that jazz was a music of the Negro and it carried his knowledge that "life was war, nothing but war" since "any Negro who wishes to live must live with danger from his first day, and no experience can ever be casual to him. . . . The Negro has the simplest of alternatives: live a life of constant humility or ever-threatening danger." In his music, jazz, "he gave voice to the character and quality of his existence, to his rage and the infinite variations of joy, lust, languor, growl, cramp, pinch, scream and despair of his orgasm. For jazz is orgasm, it is the music of orgasm, good orgasm and bad, and so it spoke across a nation, it had the communication of art even where it was watered, perverted, corrupted, and almost killed, it spoke in no matter what laundered popular way of instantaneous existential states to which some whites could respond, it was indeed a communication by art because it said, 'I feel this, and now you do too.'"

There is nothing untrue in what Mailer says, but he fails to acknowledge the other elements that became part of a much more complex jazz message than he describes from such uncomprehended icons of the hipsters as Charlie Parker, Miles Davis, Thelonious Monk, and for that matter, the hammer of emotions that is the Count Basie band. It is true, as James Baldwin writes, "There is no Negro living in America who has not felt, briefly or for long periods, with anguish sharp or dull, in varying degrees and to varying effect, simple, naked, and unanswerable hatred; who has not wanted to smash any white face he may encounter in a day. . . ." The other side of that rage—the vein of irony that runs through the blues— was described in *Sports Illustrated* by a Negro baseball player:

"I have the most interesting life in the world," he said. "Why? Just being a Negro. I know that when I wake up in the morning and look in the mirror I have a challenge. Where can I find the humor in it?—that's what I try to do. It's so ridiculous you have to find the humor in it. If you didn't you'd go crazy."

Both grinding humor and angry bitterness are at the base of much jazz. "The blues," one wandering singer said, "is revenge." And among the modern "hard boppers," there are several musicians who have played with un-alloyed hatred. "This guy doesn't fit on the date," one critic observed while listening to a "hard bop" session. "He doesn't hate enough."

It is also true that in the beginning years of jazz, many of the blues roamers and players in the barrelhouses were hip in Mailer's sense—amoral, with no roots in or allegiance to a society that tried to make them crawl. They made out any way they could and they lived in a sub-world with its own rules of convenience and its own dangerous, the-only-life-is-right-*now*, asocial existentialism. But also from the beginning, much jazz was made by cigar makers, dock workers, artisans, sons of small businessmen—and there have also been the children of the middle class. Their lives, including those of the Negroes among them, varied widely, as did their temperaments.

It is too simple to hear their music as only hatred—or joy or lust—as only orgasm. Every Negro in America has been made to feel hatred but there have been infinite variations in the way Negroes have lived with that hatred. Those who have become musicians communicate many of those variations. Some have retreated and their music shivers with inhibited fear and rage. Others have become Norman Mailers—insatiably searching and experiencing the present while looking for a center of gravity. Others have brought the middle-class values of their childhood into their music and their jazz is a constant battle be-

tween raw feeling and what it takes to buy a Cadillac.
A few, notably Thelonious Monk, have come very close
to building their own private worlds in which they
can hide, forming their music until it's ready to speak for
them. There is also Charles Mingus, angrily trying to give
and accept love without conditions and without the
barriers that come not only of being a Negro but of
being part of any society in which most of its members,
white and Negro, juggle their values in suspicion and
greed.

The experience—and the music—of the Negro jazzman has been heightened and sharpened because he is a
Negro, but so long as he works, makes time, and gets paid
in the American society, his music also tells of his life—
and not only as a Negro—in that society.

The amoral hipster, in short, is now a rare figure in
jazz. As the music has become an object in itself, a discipline and responsibility is required of the jazzman which
the "authentic" hipster cannot regard as worth that much
time and trouble if the only values are right now. The act
of Sonny Rollins—withdrawing from the jazz life entirely
for more than a year to re-examine the content and
technique of his playing—is not the act of a hipster. The
months of listening and sketching through which Miles
Davis prepared a flamenco album signifies an involvement with the future that is not "hip" in Mailer's sense.

There are some hipsters left. Philly Joe Jones, for
one, lives his own way. If you're in his band and he's not
there one night, that's tough. But not even Philly Joe is
purely hip. He's become hung on his pride in his skill as a
drummer and in the many ways he can talk through his
music. That music takes time to work on and the supple-
ness of his fingers requires practice time to sustain. Philly
Joe keeps coming back to the future, because there are
satisfactions there as well as in the amoral present.

As I hope several of the biographical chapters will
indicate, the conception of the jazz musician, particularly

the Negro player, as the apotheosis of the purely existential "hipster," the Prometheus of orgasm, is not too far from the legend that "all God's chillun got rhythm," particularly the darker ones. The music of jazz—and the jazz life that produces the music—is much too pragmatic, too variegated, and too unpredictable to support such oversimplified romanticizations of the "holy" role of jazz.

"There is not," as Marc Blitzstein has observed, "a single emotion that jazz cannot encompass. Not only joy and depression, but indignation, anger, and scores of specific emotions." Jazz *is* specific. It is what each musician feels as he plays; and that concatenation of emotions comes from specific experiences in each player's life. There is no one "philosophy" of jazz. Each player is his own prophet, and the messages range from picaresque defiance to comfortable acceptance of whatever values are negotiable at the moment.

9

Count Basie

In describing the scope of jazz, Marc Blitzstein has also noted that in addition to the jazz of joy, depression, indignation and anger, there is "the incredibly powerful jazz of fear." Some of that kind of jazz can be heard in several performances by Charlie Parker, the older blues singers, and Billie Holiday toward the end of her life. There is also the much more elusive but quite provocative jazz of courage battling caution, of playing it hard but safe—the jazz of Count Basie.

Personally, Basie is on the surface the most enigmatic of the major jazz figures. Even Duke Ellington, behind his multiple masks, is often openly mocking and elegantly sardonic. There is in Ellington hatred of Jim Crow and the merciless economic facts of keeping a band together. There is also love of pleasure, fear of age, and the intense, endless satisfaction of making form and content fuse into an entity that only he could have created. These parts of his character are in his music and are evident in him. But who is behind the perenially bland face of Basie?

No member of the jazz pantheon smiles so much and says so little as Count Basie. "Except for Freddie Green, the guitarist, nobody really knows Bill," says a veteran member of the band. "He keeps in most of what he feels, and the face he presents to the public is usually the one we see too. Once in a great while he'll explode or do something else that isn't in keeping with the usual picture of him, but he quickly picks up his customary role. And from time to time, we'll see Freddie Green lecturing him off to one side—never the other way around. But I don't know what those conversations are about."

1960 was Basie's 25th anniversary as a leader. Of the big band organizers, Basie, along with Ellington, has had the most influential impact on jazz. His rhythm sections made possible the later liberation of the jazz beat by such early modernists as Kenny Clarke and Max Roach. His soloists—particularly Lester Young—anticipated the long-lined, asymmetrical, bar-crossing adventures of Charlie Parker. And no jazz band has yet come close to achieving the floating unity of the best Basie performances between 1936 and 1942. Within the past decade, moreover, the renaissance of the Basie band shocked many young modernists into a reappraisal of their origins. I remember Stan Getz shaking his head in 1953 after hearing a Basie set: "I haven't been swinging enough; I got too lost in sound."

Although by 1960 the Basie band had become rather mechanical and heavy-footed, musicians still congregate where it plays for the physical pleasure of being shaken by its mass of driving sound. In his career, Basie has solved the jazz paradox uniquely. He has come to connote subtlety and power, wit and ferocity, understatement and a tidal wave.

Nobody as bland as the public Basie could have been responsible for so vigorous a music. His sidemen have no difficulty appraising Basie in terms of his effect on their music. "The band," explains former sideman and arranger Johnny Mandel, "doesn't feel good until he's up there. He makes everybody play differently. There's no going against him; it's almost like having a big father on the bandstand. And not just with his own band. I was working with a poor band Buddy Rich was leading in 1945. One night Basie sat in, and suddenly, everyone was playing differently."

Yet the irresistible strength Basie projects as pianist and leader clashes with another quality—caution—that has also been pervasive in his life on and off the stand. Although, for one example, he plays a great deal more piano technically than he now indicates in public, he has not revealed his capacity since his 1932 recordings with Bennie Moten's orchestra—except at private sessions. He prefers to sustain the image of himself as a functional band pianist, not a soloist; and as a band pianist, he has known no equal.

Basie's caution is also the despair of several arrangers who have seen him accept new scores and not play them or reject pieces they've written specifically for the band because the men can't run them down smoothly on the first or second try. "I just gave up," says one writer who is very fond of Basie personally. "I've got a lot of stuff just lying there. It's no wonder I no longer felt like knocking myself out for him." "He seems to be afraid of new tunes," says one of his trumpet players. "There have been times when he's walked off the stand if one of us calls a new piece early in the evening."

Basie, however, is not complacent in his caution. He worries about freshening the book, and he worries about the band. When one of his oldest friends told him bluntly three years ago that the band was becoming sloppy, Basie admitted the justice of the criticism and soon afterward changes were made. "He *loves* the band," says guitarist Freddie Green. "He loves to hear it. It's not because of the public that he's on the job before we are most nights. It's to hear the band for his own kicks. He'll never stop playing. We still work overtime quite a lot because he gets so much enjoyment out of the job."

For all his love of the band, the Basie caution and disinclination to displease have led him at times to be somewhat less than a dauntless leader. "I've never seen a bandleader like him," says George Wein, producer of a gaggle of jazz festivals. "He's generous beyond belief with the time he gets on the bill. Several times, he allowed the vocal group, Lambert, Hendricks and Ross to work with the band until the band itself had hardly any chance to play. Another year at Newport he let Jo Jones and some other alumni take over for so long that again, his own men had no solo time. Can you imagine Duke Ellington permitting anything like that?"

When TV producer Robert Herridge was assembling the musicians for the CBS-TV *Sound of Jazz* in 1957, his advisers, Whitney Balliet and this writer, felt strongly that the current Basie unit would be less effective than a band composed of alumni and such ringers as Roy Eldridge and Ben Webster. Basie agreed without any complaint although his booking office was querulously perturbed.

Basie's malleability in these areas isn't due simply to good nature. He finds it difficult to defend his own interests directly. Often, rather than risk friction, he'll retreat. "After we'd hit big around 1954," says a featured soloist who has been in the band since 1953, "he was surprisingly timid in asking for things for us during our appearances—billing, money, etc. And although we played all the big package shows, he wouldn't try for one of his own even though there would have been a lot more money involved."

The caution, though, is not impregnable. Like all Negro musicians, Basie is bitter about conditions on the road—filling station operators in New England as well as the Midwest who lock the men's room as the bus approaches; unpredictable restaurants; towns, such as Las Vegas, where for years only Negro headliners could stay in the hotels where they worked.

"The first time I was in Vegas with the band," notes tenor saxophonist Billy Mitchell, "the swimming pool in the motel where we stayed was 'broken' all the time we were there. But hell, it happens in New York too. I've had it happen at 53rd and Seventh. And you *know* that El Morocco and the Stork Club are Crow." "Geography isn't dependable," adds arranger Johnny Mandel. "Indianapolis is one of the worst cities in the country on that."

Basie and his men rarely remonstrate when they run into prejudice. They go somewhere else. But one afternoon about three years ago, the band rolled into Gettysburg, Pennsylvania. They were due at a college dance that night. Some of the musicians went into a restaurant and others found a small tavern. In the tavern, they were refused service. Basie walked up to the manager, looked at him coldly, and said, "You want us to go out in the street and drink it? You want us to get arrested for breaking the law?" The manager was shaken but stubborn, and the musicians decided to at least leave a memory behind. The biggest men in the band—"The Killers"—Eddie Jones, Billy Mitchell, Henry Coker—began to roam around the tavern in the manner of lions deciding just which part of their prey they'd savor first. Basie watched the scene, made no move to stop it, and in fact quite evidently enjoyed the morality play. The band wasn't served, but at least it hadn't slunk away.

Basie has gradually become more vocal about civil rights. In the spring of 1960, for instance, he publicly endorsed the sit-in movement of southern Negro students. Referring to the pressures on the students, he added: "They're trying to knock us down but we get right up again." Basie is also an admirer of Martin Luther King: "Like the cats would put it, he's *saying* something."

There is also a slight relaxation of caution in Basie's handling of the band's rebellion against playing the same arrangements night after night. He yielded to the sidemen's pressure and began to program more of the pungently individual work of his trumpeter Thad Jones as well as scores by band members Frank Foster and Frank

Wess. Basie also occasionally allows sidemen to call a
tune. Almost invariably, they'll call a new number. "But
if we don't play it well," says a reedman, "it'll be a long
time before the guy who calls it will be asked again."

The way Basie fulfills his role as disciplinarian reflects the mixture of strength and reserve that character-
izes nearly everything he does. The "straw boss," the man
who handles rehearsals and is in charge of minor disciplinary problems, is reed section leader Marshall Royal.
Royal is an indifferent soloist and is nowhere near the lead
player Earl Warren was in the old Basie band; but Royal
is self-confident and efficient. Final decisions, however,
are always made by Basie, and if Royal exceeds his authority, Basie immediately steps in.

It's the feeling of Jo Jones, Basie's drummer from
1936-1948, that a major influence on Basie's conception of
leadership was Bennie Moten. After an apprenticeship in
Harlem where he was befriended by Fats Waller and influenced by the reigning ragtime pianists—Luckey Roberts, James P. Johnson, Willie "The Lion" Smith, Abba
Labba—Basie toured for a time with vaudeville shows.
Stranded in the Midwest in 1927, when he was twenty-
three, Basie played for silent movies in Kansas City,
joined Walter Page's Blue Devils (the best of the territory
bands there), and moved over to the Moten band when
the Page unit was absorbed by Moten.

"Bennie," recalls Jo Jones, "was cool. He didn't brow-
beat his men. Whenever Bennie wanted something done,
he'd call the band together and he'd always speak softly
enough so that you had to hear him. After it was all over,
he'd produce a gallon of whiskey."

Basie is also cool until provoked beyond patience.
Most of the time, however, even his rages are somewhat
staged. "The cursing," notes a sideman, "seems controlled.
Sometimes, if we've been goofing at a rehearsal, he'll ask
any women present to leave the room, and then he'll blow

up. But always, after the steam is out, he'll make some kind of funny crack so we'll know he's not still mad."

The Basie wrath can also be set off by men being continually late on stand. When Basie begins to play the piano, that's the signal for the men to return to work. Occasionally, a few sidemen are rather lackadaisical about leaving their avocational pursuits. If their carelessness continues, Basie is likely to hold a meeting of the band in back of the club after a set and lecture the band on the ultimate wages of the sin of tardiness.

"There are other times," says another band member, "when Basie gets angry like a little boy. He'll go into a corner and mumble to himself." "Once," recalls Mandel, "two guys in the band were scuffling, and Basie got as mad as he can get. He shook his head, and said aloud, 'It sure isn't easy to run a band.' The way he said it, I really felt sorry for him."

Whenever possible, Basie tries to mask his anger in play. During the last set early one morning at Birdland, only a few people were in the room. Eddie "Lockjaw" Davis, the featured tenor soloist at the time, was "catting" with a young lady at ringside, sending eyebrow signals for a later tryst. Basie became increasingly irritated and finally, with a smile, wadded up an arrangement and hit Davis hard on the head.

A man who represses as much emotion as Basie has to let some of it out or else suffer with ulcers or hypertension. One of Basie's indirect methods of expelling aggression is to try to catch his men off guard. "If a man comes in juiced," says an aggrieved trumpet player who has been the target of a Basie curve, "Basie is likely to call a number on which that guy is featured." "If he's been having trouble with somebody," adds another employee, "he'll catch him by calling a number with a tough solo before the guy has a chance to warm up."

Of all his contemporaries, Basie is most in awe of

Duke Ellington. He has held Duke's suave dignity as a model for himself, a model he knows he doesn't have the temperament to emulate convincingly. But the two leaders are alike in their extreme reluctance to fire a musician. The discipline in Ellington's band has always been remarkably lax. Basie actually runs a tighter crew, but he too has to be driven to acute irritation before applying the guillotine.

In recent years, the three most notable firings were of drummer Gus Johnson, reed player Bill Graham, and trumpeter Reunald Jones, Senior. No one—in or out of the band—is clear as to exactly why Basie fired Johnson, the best drummer he's had since Jo Jones. The consensus is that Basie felt the band needed some "flash" and accordingly he fired Johnson to replace him with Sonny Payne, who is inclined to send up rockets when the music calls for indirect lighting. The sidemen have long been disturbed at Payne's playing—though he is personally liked—and Basie realizes that he made a mistake. But Basie is not likely to dismiss Payne unless Sonny becomes a disciplinary problem. Basie did look on approvingly during a period when Freddie Green, aggravated by Payne's tendency to rush the beat, kept a long stick on stand with which he poked the drummer when the beat began to run away.

Billy Graham, an extrovert and prankster, "played himself out of the band," as one of his fellow roisterers puts it. "Billy was not only too playful, but he used to get a little too familiar with 'Chief' himself. He'd even heckle Basie on the bandstand. As usually happens when a guy goes, Graham got the news during a layoff. When we came back, he just wasn't there."

The patrician Reunald Jones was quite a different case. For several years, Jones, who has the bearing of a British officer in pre-Gandhi India, was the most conspicuous member of the band. Seated at the extreme left end of the trumpet section, Jones was always one level higher than his colleagues. He played with one hand, as if in derision of the simplicity of the music. When the rest of the section would rise in unison, Jones invariably remained seated. His expression—no matter how much joking was going on among the men—was constantly sour. Jones' childish campaign of passive contempt was in protest at the fact that Basie never assigned him any solos.

Jones was fired finally because, as a section mate says with satisfaction, "he drank too much water." Jones was a clubhouse lawyer, and occasionally complained to the musicians' union about overtime matters. He went to the union one time too often.

Jones has not been alone in summoning Basie to the union. Basie is quite conservative concerning money. He has to be pressured into giving a raise, and he deals with each man in the band individually in a divide-and-conquer technique that lessens the possibility of mass mutiny with regard to basic pay. This absence of collective bargaining exists in many other bands. Basie was not always so close, but he has been mulcted outrageously in his years as a leader.

John Hammond has written about Basie's first Decca contract in 1936, which called for twenty-four sides for a total payment of $750 without a cent of royalty. Hammond later complained to the union and Basie at least was raised to scale, but he's never received any royalties from his big early hits—*One O'Clock Jump, Swinging The Blues,* etc.

It took Basie many years to learn to examine his own books. Relatively unconcerned with financial details, Basie was a "professional baller" during the 1930's and 1940's, hanging out with his men after hours and generally exploring the pleasures and challenges of hedonism. "When he woke up," says a friend, "he had no band, no wardrobe, no money. The managers had swimming pools."

Basie disbanded and toured with a small group in 1950
and 1951, mainly to pay off his debts. He was so careful
of fiscal details in the first years of the new big band that
for a time, he himself was the paymaster.

Basie has held on to his recent profits, investing
some in his informal Harlem night club, Count Basie's, at
132nd Street and Seventh Avenue. Some members of the
band feel occasionally that while Basie is entitled to save
for retirement, so are they. In the spring of 1959, the band
was flown down and back to an all-night barbecue dance
and breakfast given by Roulette Records for visiting
students of communications at the Miami Disc Jockey's
Convention. The sidemen complained to the union that
they were paid less than had been agreed. They won.
"We always win," says the band's unofficial shop steward.
"We take him to the union once or twice a year, but
there's no strain afterwards. It's as if it never happened."

But there are sidemen who are embarrassed by the
trips to the union, and blame not Basie but his booking
office. "That Miami business," says Thad Jones, "wasn't
Basie's fault. The office should have taken care of it
before we left."

As a whole, despite the split about the handling of
labor problems, the Basie unit has fewer cliques than
most big bands. Many of the men spend their spare time
together, and until fairly recently, Basie traveled in the
bus with his sidemen all the time, as he had in the 1930's
and 1940's. The present band, composed of tough professionals, has a team pride, but as one says, "it takes
quite a lot to really excite us. We've been in the business
a long time, mostly for a lot of glory and no money. We
still want a certain amount of recognition, but we won't
stand on our heads for it. We're at our best under strain—
on an opening night or any night when important people
are in the crowd."

Basie has picked his men carefully. He is concerned
with a man's temperament as well as his musical ability,

and will not knowingly hire a congenital complainer or anyone who is addicted to drugs. The Basie band is the cleanest of all the big bands.

Just as he has greater capacity as a pianist than he indicates, so Basie's organizing capacity is more impressive than is generally realized. "Think of what he was able to do in 1953," says Jo Jones. "He'd lost all of the band, and yet he was able to remember guys he'd heard that he'd liked, take some other suggestions, fuse them into a unit, and take over the whole band business."

Basie as an organizer is also in evidence at rehearsals. Sitting on the sidelines, he'll stop the band, make changes, usually cuts, and otherwise shape a score into the Basie vein. He does not read music easily and prefers to absorb a new arrangement by ear, but once he has it down, it becomes inescapably his and the band's.

Age is beginning to tell on Basie, not so much in any diminution of his pleasure in playing, but in his after-hours pursuits. "We used to go to sessions," remembers vocalist Jimmy Rushing of the first Basie band, "or to people's homes and drink and sing. Basie was a pretty nice singer, a more or less baritone. We were all like brothers, and he was with us most of the time."

Basie still socializes with his men after hours on occasion, but his avocations are increasingly solitary. While there are some good golfers in the band—Freddie Greene would be a match for most professionals—Basie's own golf clubs are seldom used. His major outdoor activity is attending and playing the races, and he's also much involved with the fortunes of the New York Yankees.

Basie came from an inner-directed family that emphasized respectability and accomplishment. His father, Harvey Lee Basie, who died in April, 1960, at 88, had been a gardener, and his mother was a domestic. Basie grew up in the Negro ghetto of Red Bank, New Jersey, and learned from watching his parents how much dissembling was necessary to "get on" with the whites. He was a shy child besides and the consciousness of being a Negro intensified the shyness. His wife, Catherine, has known him since his mid-twenties and remembers him as always having been reserved.

As Basie grew older, he found an outlet for some of his emotions in a certain amount of self-gratification— women, food, liquor—though characteristically, he has rarely lost control in any of these areas. In the days before television, he used to read more than he does now. On the way to a job or at home, he'll go through the papers, scan the trade press with the usual musician's skepticism, and look through such magazines as *Jet*. He has a particular affection for certain kinds of comic books, not because he lacks intelligence or interest in other material, but because the horror tales to which he gravitates serve as a partial outlet for all the aggression he keeps down. "Basie was disappointed," says a band member, "when they started to clean up the comics, because they hit most at those shockers he liked so much."

Much of Basie's current means of release are what he terms the "fast draws" on television. The TV set can't talk back or cause any trouble short of refusing to function, so Basie has become a TV addict. "It's the most relaxing thing in the world," he observes. "When I'm home, I usually get up at about 10:30, go downstairs, put on the set, and fall asleep by it because it *is* so relaxing." He's usually up again by noon for the re-runs of westerns. "I especially like playing California because the shows start earlier there and that gives me an extra hour." Characteristically, Basie is drawn to those westerns with the most gun play.

Another solitary avocation of Basie is a large model train development in the basement of his home. Upstairs is a further aid to relaxation, a Hammond organ. The St. Albans, Long Island, house is ample but unostentatious although it does have a swimming pool. Basie, his wife, and their fifteen-year-old daughter Diane have lived there for some fourteen years. Catherine Basie first met the pianist in Philadelphia during an eastern tour by the Moten band. She was one of the dancing Whitman Sisters. (Her maiden name, however, was Morgan, and at one time she was professionally known as Princess Aloha.)

In contrast to her husband, Catherine Basie is a brisk, energetic clubwoman who hurls herself into an astonishingly full round of activities. She is on the boards of nearly a dozen organizations, works for the Urban League and the National Conference of Christians and Jews, and is actively involved in local politics. Although Basie broke through his reserve long enough to support the sit-ins, he leaves other family stands to Catherine. He declined to reveal his 1960 choice for President, suggesting instead that Catherine be asked.

Basie keeps talking rather vaguely about plans to curtail his traveling drastically and center most of his activities in and around New York, but his wife and friends doubt if he'll ever leave the road. "They'll carry him to his grave from a road trip," says trumpeter Joe Newman. "Just like Louis Armstrong. In the band and on the road, he can forget himself and throw away his worries." The road *is* another way of life. You keep moving most of the time and you can avoid becoming too deeply committed to anyone or any one thing. "Bill," says a man who's known Basie for many years, "likes to have that little cushion of privacy between him and everyone else. It's easier to keep air in that cushion on the road."

It is true that while Basie is apt to become rather fretful when based in New York for too long, he is a model of stoicism when traveling. "It's strange to watch him in a crisis," says trombonist Benny Powell. "He lets everybody else panic. We'll be doing a one-nighter, and everything will be going wrong. The bus breaks down; there's no time for dinner; we get to work late; the promoter is angry. Basie couldn't be calmer, and funnier."

Once in a great while, however, Basie's public mask slips momentarily. "One night at Newport," recalls pianist Billy Taylor, "I saw Bill off to one side, listening intently to a modern small combo. He was listening wistfully, it seemed to me. The group was pretty adventurous. Somebody interrupted Bill, and suddenly he was Count Basie again—the smile, the detachment. I just don't think he's as happy musically as he mostly convinces himself he is. There was more he wanted to do, but a while back, he decided to play it safe."

10

Charles Mingus

The jazz players of the 1930's from Louis Armstrong to Roy Eldridge were much more complex in temperament than most of their listeners and the critics realized—except for such obviously complicated loners as Lester Young. The Negroes among them, for one example, were as embittered by pervasive prejudice as all Negroes; but like many other Negroes in the 1930's, the Negro jazzman's public face was deceptively "accepting." ("Bend, you hungry fathead! Bend!")

The Negro modern jazzman, however, like the increasingly aggressive "new Negro" in many areas of American life, began to release and display his hostility more openly. One result, the acting-out of reverse prejudice in jazz, has already been noted. The writers about jazz, most of them white, were simply not prepared at first for this genre of jazzman. The "put ons" became more frequent and more elaborate. In time, many writers became so conditioned to the anger in these musicians that they identified all hostility in their behavior and music as a striking out against whites, or against all of society.

For one instance, Miles Davis has often been criticized because he walks off the stand when a sideman solos and because he does not acknowledge applause. Yet, when Davis was finally asked for an explanation of his behavior, (*Playboy*, August, 1960), his answer was simple and logical:

> "I get off the stand during a set because when I'm not playing, there's nothing for me to do. It's ridiculous for me to just stand there and make the other guys nervous looking at them while they solo. And if I don't look at them, what's the point of my standing up there and looking at the audience? They're not interested in me when somebody else is taking a solo. I don't announce the numbers because I figure the people who come to hear us know everything we play. We have a new record about every three months, and they sell, so the audiences must know what's on them. A lot of musicians think the public is stupid, but the audiences know what's happening. It's like the public is blamed because TV shows are so bad, but hell, what choice do they have in what to watch? . . . Look, if I go to a club and hear a good friend take a solo that I like, I don't applaud him. It's silly. I had a girlfriend once who always used to look at me as if I should applaud her. Hell, if she didn't know I liked her, that was *her* problem. I don't mind if the guys in the band bow and all that, but I figure I'm doing the best I can with my horn, and anybody out front who has ears knows that. What am I there for if not to try to make people like what I'm doing? I have to bow, too? I pay attention to what counts—the music. People should give me credit for that. I try to make sure they'll have something *to* applaud. After all, I don't have the reputation of bringing a sad band into clubs, do I?"

Or, as André Hodeir wrote in reviewing a Paris concert by Davis, "He will not make concessions. When Miles cuts short the applause and moves efficiently from number to number, it's not from contempt of the public. On the contrary, he restores to the public its dignity by refusing it any concession in terms of choice of program or 'showmanship' on the part of himself and his musicians."

Yet, the jazz public and the jazz writers were not at first accustomed to this kind of approach to an audience by a jazz musician. It took many people a long time to understand—if not always to approve—the ubiquitous seriousness with which many of the modernists, white and Negro, took their music. It was a seriousness that in some cases approached pompous solemnity; but there were many jazzmen who did begin to work on the development of their own playing or writing styles with quite as much discipline as their counterparts in classical music, painting or writing. There had, of course, always been players in jazz who had also been intensely involved in developing their music; but as I've tried to indicate earlier in *The Changes,* the audience context in which the earlier jazzmen operated made it much more difficult for many of them realistically to sustain their concentration on the music itself for as long as the modernists are often able to.

The demands that some modern jazzmen make of their society and of themselves (in terms of what they feel their music *can* become) inevitably place them under a greater strain than most of their predecessors exposed themselves to. Those of the modernists who are essentially adolescents have adolescent goals and sometimes take self-destructive routes to reach them. More of them are engaged in a continually shifting battle between the relatively mature and the more childish elements in their characters. A few have matured. But nearly all the modernists, whether temperamentally or musically qualified, do now regard themselves as "artists" first, and "entertainers" only by necessity.

Charles Mingus, for example—big, explosive, ruthlessly honest, is the most astonishing virtuoso on the double bass that jazz has ever known. He is also a disturbing, uneven, unyieldingly original composer who tries for wider range and depth of mood than any other

modern jazz writer so far. In his frequently turbulent relationships with critics, bookers and other jazz musicians,
Mingus is quick to feel a draft because of his color, often
much too quick. His sensitivity to prejudice, however,
goes back a long way.

John Lewis, musical director of the modern jazz
quartet, and Miles Davis, to cite two of many examples,
do not see mirages of Jim Crow as Mingus frequently
does. Nor, when they do scrape against its real manifesta-
tions, do they hit out as wildly and with as uncontrollable
a hurt as Mingus. But John Lewis, growing up in
Albuquerque, New Mexico, knew little personally of Jim
Crow until he left home. Miles Davis, from East St. Louis,
Illinois, came from an upper-middle-class family and was
relatively well protected in his early years. Thelonious
Monk, on the other hand, grew up in New York, where
the consciousness of being a Negro is inescapable; but
quite early in his life, Monk began to construct an inner
refuge into which no one and nothing that might bother
him could enter.

Mingus was born in Nogales, Arizona, April 22, 1922.
His mother died soon after, and when he was three
months old the family moved to Los Angeles. Mingus
grew up in Watts, about three miles from Los Angeles.
An older sister, now in the Los Angeles post office, studied
singing for several years. During one period of his own
withdrawal from the pressures of music, Mingus too was
a post office worker. Another sister has been a pianist. A
step-brother, now dead, was a guitarist who specialized
in Spanish music.

Mingus was made stingingly aware he was a Negro
from his first days in school. One teacher's most frequent
way of summoning him was, "Come here, you yellow
nigger." He was often slapped by "Miss Virginia" with the
accompanying threat that any report home of the violence
would inexorably make the blows come harder and
oftener. The teacher, convinced that by definition a

Negro could not keep up with white pupils, reported Mingus as an exceedingly slow learner. She herself had already effectively curbed his motivation to learn, and another factor in his confusion was the fact that he had been sent to school when he was very young, probably too young.

"I found out later," Mingus recalls, "that they were thinking of sending me to a dumb school. My father and mother were told to come to the principal's office. My father was lighter than anybody else in the room, but he was a proud Negro and contemptuous of most whites. I remember the principal, a fairly conscientious man, didn't want to make a hasty decision. While we were all there, he checked by telephone to find out what my I.Q. tests had shown. It turned out, as my father later explained to me, that 'even by a white man's standards, you're supposed to be a genius.'"

Mingus stayed in the school. And that afternoon, his father made it clear that if he heard of *anyone* slapping the boy again, he would reciprocate tenfold on the principal.

In the meantime, Mingus' development as a musician was beginning. "A lot of my music," he explains, "came from church. All the music I heard when I was a very young child was church music. I was eight or nine years old before I heard an Ellington record on the radio. My father went to the Methodist church; my stepmother would take me to a Holiness church. My father didn't dig my mother going there. People went into trances and the congregation's response was wilder and more uninhibited than in the Methodist church. The blues was in the Holiness churches—moaning and riffs and that sort of thing between the audience and the preacher. My sisters and I had a trio, and we used to play in the Methodist church occasionally."

One Christmas, when he was five or six, Mingus was given a trombone. "His teacher," Ira Gitler reported in a

F

Down Beat interview with Mingus, "didn't bother to distinguish between bass and treble. Mingus asked his sister, who played piano, to help him. She taught him the treble clef. When he recited it verbatim to the teacher, instead of the bass clef, the man told Charlie's parents that their son was too stupid to learn." For a time, Mingus believed the teacher, but tried to play anyway—without much success.

About four years after Mingus picked up trombone, he relates, "I heard there was a kid named Britt Woodman who was very good and I went to where I knew he was playing because I wanted to cut him." Woodman, who has since worked with Duke Ellington, recognized the music in Mingus. Woodman was only two years older, but because his father was a musician, he'd had more training. He advised Mingus that the trombone didn't seem meant for him, but also suggested that the younger boy, who obviously had an excellent ear, should continue in music.

Woodman also convinced Mingus, who shied from physical battle although he was big for his age, to work out in a gym and learn self-defense. In recent years, Mingus has achieved a reputation he does not welcome as a fighter. Usually, however, he does not hit unless he's been extremely or suddenly provoked, and then he strikes in fear that if he doesn't get in the first punch, the other man surely will.

In writing a liner note for one of his Atlantic albums a few years ago, I tried to distill my own impressions of the man:

"Mingus is one of the very few largely ingenuous people I have known, and I remain surprised at how he remains ingenuous after all he has experienced and seen in the cities of his country and in the *Tonight at Noon* (as he has named one of his pieces) that is part of the world of jazz. He doesn't give up. He continues to trust,

to give, to flagellate himself emotionally to be 'better' and
more understanding of others; to have the courage and
the strength to look for help when he feels he needs it.

"He can be very wrong. He sometimes reacts to an
actual or invisible hurt with instantaneous, unreasoning
out-of-proportion emotional directness. And yet sometimes he does all he can to avoid a situation he knows
will detonate his rages. I've seen him leave the room
when a drunken Southerner began to make all too explicit
racial allusions. Mingus didn't want to embarrass his
hosts, and he was in the midst of another of his frequent
resolutions not to explode, whatever the provocation. The
drunk followed him, backed him into a corner, and
finally, with shattering quickness, Mingus knocked him
out. He was shiveringly upset, angry at himself more than
at the man. 'I wouldn't have hit him at all,' he said,
'but I was afraid he was going to hit me.'"

To return to Mingus' musical odyssey, Woodman
convinced the Mingus family to buy their son a cello.
Again Mingus found the wrong teacher. Realizing the boy
had an excellent ear, the teacher didn't bother to show
Mingus the correct fingerboard positions. Mingus' mother
was pleased because her son was playing tunes, but in
high school, when he had to read relatively difficult
music, the inadequate training forced him to leave the
orchestra, another official dismissal of his musical capacity.

Previously, Mingus had played 'cello in the school
band and in the Los Angeles Junior Philharmonic. There
was also a jazz band at Jordan High School, a unit that
also included some students from Jefferson High School.
Among the undergraduate players were such later well-
known jazzmen as Woodman, Buddy Collette, Chico
Hamilton, Dexter Gordon and Ernie Royal. Mingus tried
to play 'cello with this band, but the instrument didn't
really fit and he himself still needed more training. Collette finally suggested he switch to bass and took him to

Red Callender, a long-term professional jazzman in Los Angeles. Callender helped him considerably, and Mingus then studied for five years with H. Rheinschagen, who had been at one time with the New York Philharmonic.

With Rheinschagen, Mingus began to master the instrument and to drive himself through hours of daily practice, a discipline that resulted in his becoming a virtuoso soloist. "I'd practice the hardest things incessantly. The third finger is seldom used, so I used it all the time. What happened, however, is that for a while I concentrated on speed and technique almost as ends in themselves. I aimed at scaring all the other bass players. I stood right, and I was conscious of every note I ran. There seemed to be no problems I couldn't solve. Then one night (when I was eighteen or nineteen) all this changed. Vernon Alley had set up a session to see if I could cut Oscar Pettiford, but Pettiford wasn't feeling well and didn't show. I began playing and didn't stop for a long time. It was suddenly *me*; it wasn't the bass any more. Now I'm not conscious of the instrument as an instrument when I play. And I don't dig any longer thinking in terms of whether one man is a 'better' bassist than another. You're up there—everyone is—trying to express yourself. It's like a preacher, in a sense. And the instrument, any instrument, shouldn't get in the way. Now, too, a wrong note doesn't completely throw me. I make something out of it that's right. In a way, there are no wrong notes."

Mingus was also absorbing jazz influences. During a symposium at Music Inn in Lenox a few years ago, he recalled: "I tried to hear all the bands that came to town. When I first heard Duke Ellington in person, I almost jumped out of the balcony. One piece excited me so much that I screamed. I also listened to Art Tatum a lot, and later, I tried to sit in with him, but he'd laugh at me." Still later, the determined Mingus attained such proficiency as a bassist that he worked for a time with Tatum.

Mingus has always been what he calls a "protest cat.

In high school I was on the basketball team but the coach did something I didn't dig and the next day, he looked up and saw me practicing with the football team." When the urge to protest is involved with Jim Crow, Mingus often has lacked the patience to see beyond his instant reaction. He did not, for example, like Fats Waller or Louis Armstrong, because he thought they were "Tomming." To some extent they were; but in much of their music, they were also expressing open and irrepressibly spontaneous emotions similar in urgency to his own.

Expansively romantic by temperament, Mingus was also attracted while quite young to such composers as Debussy, Ravel, and Richard Strauss. From the time he began writing—then, as now, his compositions usually start on the piano and their form is determined by their content—Mingus rebelled at too narrow a definition of jazz. He's often refused to even call his work jazz for that reason, hopefully regarding "all music as one."

In the summer of 1957, Mingus was commissioned by Brandeis University to write a jazz work for a concert to be part of that University's Fourth Festival of the Creative Arts. Another jazzman, pianist Dick Katz, reviewed the concert for *Jazz Today,* and his description of *Revelations,* the Mingus composition, pertains in part to Mingus' overall body of work as well: "It is a powerful piece which begins with an almost Wagnerian brooding-like intensity, expressed by way of an insinuating pedal point. It also revealed some beautiful dissonances. . . . I was quite taken by the striking patterns of sound and the way it reached its climax with a kind of centrifugal force. It was a very determined piece of music; and as one of the participating musicians said to me later, 'When it was over, you really knew something had happened!' "

None of Mingus' compositions can be easily compartmentalized as belonging to any one "school" of jazz. Mingus is his own faculty and student body. "If I feel a piece a certain way, it'll work that way," he explains. And he describes in the notes to one of his albums, *Mingus Ah Um*, one of the methods by which he composes and tries to give his sidemen freedom of expression while retaining control of the shape, direction and basic emotional content of the composition: "I 'write' compositions on mental score paper. Then I lay out the composition part by part to the musicians. I play them the 'framework' on the piano so that they are all familiar with my interpretation and feeling and with the scale and chord progressions to be used. Each man's particular style is taken into consideration. They are given different rows of notes to use against each chord but they choose their own notes and play them in their own style . . . except where a particular mood is indicated."

As Whitney Balliett has observed in *The New Yorker*, "Mingus, as a jazz composer, daringly asks of his musicians even more than the classical composer asks of his—that they carry both the letter and the spirit of his basic composition over into their own improvisations instead of conventionally using them as a trigger for their own ruminations."

One of his works snaps derisively at Governor Faubus; others pay critical tribute to Duke Ellington and Lester Young; several plunge into a re-examination of the gospel roots of some modern jazz with a ferociously individualistic remembrance of time past that makes most of the other neo-gospel tunes sound as if they'd been cut out of a pattern book. Many Mingus originals are broodingly lovely, long-lined ballads of unashamed tenderness and nostalgia.

Until setting up his own principality, the Charles Mingus Jazz Workshop, in New York in the mid-1950's, Mingus worked with a surprising variety of musicians— Lee Young, Louis Armstrong, Kid Ory, Alvino Rey, Lionel Hampton, Billy Taylor, Charlie Parker, Stan Getz, Duke Ellington, Bud Powell, and Tatum. He has brought to all of them his voracious appetite for new insights and he's taken away a passionately jumbled and constantly re-explored series of impressions. He was, for example, happy with the New Orleans-styled band of Kid Ory, but was kidded out of the band by young musicians who told him it was "square" to be playing "old-timey" jazz. Now Mingus determines the shapes of music, including degrees of squareness, for himself. "I remember," Mingus says, "Fats Navarro telling me, 'That's not it, Mingus; that's what they *used* to do.' Well, I'm not going to worry about that sort of thing any more. I'm going to be *me*. If Bird were to come back to life, I wouldn't do something just because *he* did it. I'd have to feel it too."

Mingus is a thorough-going autodidact. He felt his teachers didn't care what happened to him because he was a Negro. Accordingly, he paid little attention to assigned reading. When he was still a youngster, however, he struggled on his own with Freud's *Introduction to Psychoanalysis*.

It has taken Mingus a couple of marriages to learn that he has first to be able to live with himself. Several areas of knowledge remain even more remote from his consciousness than the grammar of women, but his mind stays remarkably receptive to new ideas and new disciplines.

Mingus remains as sweepingly passionate in his verbal denunciations as he is in his music. He uses terms such as "fascist," "white-citizens-council-thinking" and less printable denunciations with spontaneous, irresponsible abandon. He still reacts with sudden rage to the smallest hint of malice toward him, Negroes, friends, jazz, music, or the new African Nations. But he does react as honestly and completely as he can at any moment. Given the chance, he reacts more often in love and acceptance than he does in fear and anger. But the reactions are seldom clear-cut.

Mingus tells a story that reveals something of himself

and of the peculiar harshness that can result from personality dissonances in the jazz life.

"I was driving to work with a blind pianist—white—
and two other Negroes. The pianist asked why we objected to being called 'niggers.' 'Hell,' he said, 'you use it
among yourselves all the time.' The way he asked showed
he was just bugging us. He knew. He kept it up and
everybody was getting pretty tense. Now this was a guy
I really loved, and especially at that time, I listened to
everything he said about music. But this was too much.
I finally told him: 'You keep this up and when we get to
the gig, I'm going to turn off all the lights and kick your
ass.'

"He laughed, kind of. Then he was silent for a while,
and finally told us about something that had happened to
him at Birdland a few nights before. A very well-known
band leader, a guy who's supposed to be a very nice guy
and a funny one, came over to him. He asked the pianist
if he were *really* blind. 'Yes,' the pianist said, 'I can't see
anything.' The band leader wouldn't let up. He kept
passing his hand over the pianist's eyes. 'Can't you see
something?' 'No, I can't. I told you I can't.' 'Good,' said
the band leader. 'Good, you m—— f——, I'm glad you
can't see!'"

"The car got very still. The other guys were shocked
at such wanton cruelty. But I knew this pianist; I knew
how destructive he could be. And I asked him, 'But what
did you do to get that guy so hurt and angry?' It tore the
pianist up. It was the first time I'd ever seen him tremble."

Mingus may never "grow up" in the usual sense in
which most of us who leash our feelings use that term.
Just as he's likely to remain unpredictable personally, his
music is difficult to chart ahead, although it's sure to remain stormily individual and restless. Mingus has been
blessed and cursed with insatiable curiosity and an un-
ceasing compulsion to cut beneath the words he and
everyone uses to describe feeling. He's constantly probing

through his explosions, musical and others, to find out who he is becoming. As a result, he's sometimes inchoate in his conversation and compositions, but he never plays it safe and never hides. At the end of one set not long ago, he looked hard into the audience which he had earlier lectured for not paying attention. "If you think this is weird, just take a look at yourselves."

II

Three Ways of Making It:
John Lewis, Miles Davis, Thelonius Monk

The lives of Count Basie and Charles Mingus are only two of the many ways of making it in jazz. There is also the quiet but single-minded determination of John Lewis, who has molded the Modern Jazz Quartet into an internationally admired and financially successful unit without altering any of his musical concepts to attract a wider audience. Thoroughly trained in classical music as well as jazz, Lewis has sung in the Schola Cantorum and collects rare books on baroque music, but at base, he is very much a jazzman.

The first time I met him, Lewis had a copy of the *New Statesman* in his pocket, a journal that is not regular reading for most jazz musicians. Lewis does have a considerably wider range of interests than most jazzmen, including those in his own quartet. A carefully softspoken man, he is nonetheless an implacable disciplinarian and the Modern Jazz Quartet's consistent level of musical cohesiveness is due to Lewis' unremitting coaching. Several years ago, a jazz promoter walked into an empty room backstage at a concert and found Percy Heath, bassist with the Modern Jazz Quartet, in tears because of the scalding criticism of his music director.

170

Lewis is carefully tailored and a gourmet. A bache-
lor, his freedom is constricted only by his group's schedule
of engagements and his own schedule of compositions. He
has been known to fly to London from New York for a
few days rest walking around the city. He has a similar
affection for the surface quiet of Boston. When he does
accept an assignment, however, Lewis can be overwhelm-
ingly conscientious. His position as musical adviser to the
Monterey Jazz Festival is not at all nominal. Lewis' stern,
lonely grandeur at Monterey is in contrast to the embar-
rassingly large list of prominent music names listed on the
Newport Jazz Festival letterhead as advisors. The Newport board of advisors hasn't met for years. At that last
meeting, there was some opposition to a plan of the
festival's director. The plan was adopted, in any case,
but the murmur of dissension was enough to insure that
the Newport advisory board's functions would for-
evermore be decorative. Lewis, however, is consulted
on every detail of Monterey and he is one of the primary
causes for that annual series of concerts being the only
festival thoroughly respected by jazz musicians themselves.

Lewis has also been the leading reason major jazz
players have agreed each summer to relinquish three to
four weeks of bookings to teach at the School of Jazz in
Lenox, Massachusetts. The school is an experiment in en-
listing men who have contributed to the development of
the jazz language to teach young players exactly what it
was they had in mind. The School began in 1957, and there
has been disagreement among jazz players ever since as to
how effective it can be under even optimum conditions.
Yet, a number of graduates have become professionals or
teachers, and most feel that their intensive work at the
school with men who could answer their most difficult
questions on their horns, if in no other way at times, was
the most useful jazz instruction they've had.

Almost as important has been the fact that the

youngsters have been required to take history-of-jazz
courses at the School—non-technical history with Dr.
Marshall Stearns and an analytical history of the music
itself with composer Gunther Schuller. For most, such
new experiences as the ingenuity of pre-Parker composer
Jelly Roll Morton and the passion of pre-Sarah Vaughan
singer Bessie Smith have been a revelation. Disappoint-
ingly few Negro applications have been made to the
School. One reason may be the comparatively high tuition
fee for three weeks, although scholarships are available
each year, but the more likely answer is that young Negro
players still feel jazz is a route to proving one's manhood
and that the most impressive proof of virility is to make it
yourself, to "pay the dues" and not run the danger of
someone saying, "Hell, you're just repeating what they
told you up at that school."

In any case, Lewis is the one who keeps the School's
standards up; and along with Phil and Stephanie Barber,
who underwrite it, he worries much of the winter about
funds for the next year.

Lewis is also one of the few jazz leaders to have
given serious thought as to where his own group can best
be heard. (The Modern Jazz Quartet is a co-operative
economically, but Lewis is boss.) He is convinced that
certain types of jazz (Lionel Hampton's for one) are best
in a theatre; others are most in context in a night club;
and some, such as that of the Modern Jazz Quartet, is
most effective in concerts. Accordingly, Lewis has opened
up several concert opportunities for jazz, especially in
Europe where the quartet now spends at least half its
year. It has been the first jazz unit to play at festivals of
contemporary music in Germany (Donaueschingen) and
Italy (Maggio Musicale Fiorentino). Increasingly, the
MJQ has also been touring European university towns.
In America, it plays only a few night clubs, preferring
concerts where the subtle shadings of its dynamics and

the four-part strands of its collective improvisations can best be heard.

Except to very close friends, Lewis externally is formal, polite and rather distant. The MJQ presents a similar surface impression. Benny Green, jazz critic for *The Observer* in London, has quoted with a relish a British musician's reaction to a concert by the Modern Jazz Quartet: "It suddenly occurred to me that there were three thousand of us sitting there watching a man with a small beard hit a small bell with a small stick." Referring to the Modern Jazz Quartet's formal dress for concert appearances, Miles Davis observed: "I don't go with this bringing 'dignity' to jazz. The way they bring 'dignity' to jazz in their formal clothes and the way they bow is like Ray Robinson bringing dignity to boxing by fighting in a tuxedo."

Lewis is rather touchy about the criticism of the MJQ's appearance. "It has taken a long time," he lectured a London interviewer, "to perfect the material that this suit is made from." He fingered the cloth. "We don't want to come over here looking like a bunch of tramps."

At times, there are farcical elements to the MJQ's wardrobe problems. At the end of a rehearsal one afternoon, the group debated for fifteen minutes concerning which suits they'd be taking to Philadelphia the next night and which were the proper shoes and other accessories for those suits. "Are they going to be in *Vogue* again?" muttered a hanger-on.

An interesting partial insight into the MJQ's way of "having it made" is that of Francis Newton in a 1957 *New Statesman:*

"These gifted Coloured musicians belong to a generation which passionately rejects the old, full-blooded, spontaneous jazz, for the same reasons as Shaw's Larry Doyle rejected conventional Irish ebullience: because it

reminds them of oppression, illiteracy, of Negroes clowning to wheedle crumbs from the whites. They know as
well as the Zionists, who rejected Yiddish, that there is
more in the old styles than this; but like the Zionists they
must first prove to themselves and to the world that they
are not dependent for their achievements on these things.
It is natural for men who feel like this to abandon the
warm, shouting, vocalising instruments which are one of
the glories of jazz—the 'horns'—for impersonal ones ('because we want to prove that jazz needn't be noisy'), or
for Mr. Kaye to ration his use of drum-sticks. It is natural
for them to take pride in the intellectualism and struc-
tural complexity of their music, and, in their public and
private behaviour, to maintain an impassive reserve
which would do credit to the late Phineas Fogg ('because
jazz needn't be vulgar and exhibitionist'). And it is not
only natural, but also necessary, for more white jazz-
lovers than care to admit it accept the William Faulkner
view that Negroes are not people like anybody else, but
a sort of divine innocent, whose contribution to the world
lies in their simplicity.

"It is not for us, therefore, to argue with the MJQ.
This is their way, and even if it turns out not to be the
main highway of jazz, its achievements are still considerable, and its attempt to build a classical architecture on
the foundation of blues rhythm and feeling is of extreme
interest."

I expect there is more validity to Francis Newton's
appraisal than John Lewis will ever consciously admit.
Yet, Newton's diagnosis is faulty in several respects. It is
not true that most other Negro jazzmen of Lewis' generation are rejecting "full-blooded, spontaneous jazz." The
prevalence of "hard bop" (which was no less spontaneous
for all its hostility) and the subsequent apotheosis of the
"funky" and "soulful" indicate that Newton was oversim-
plifying. It is true, however, that some Negroes do consciously react to what they consider to be the white
stereotype of the Negro by adopting a studied reserve and

priding themselves on their urbane deportment. The cryptic, nearly motionless hipster is, in part, a further much more hostile variation of this detachment.

An illustration of this conspicuous non-vulgarity was a conversation I had with Benny Carter, one of the more expert arrangers and band leaders of the 1930's and 1940's and a superior, uniquely graceful alto saxophonist. I had been involved as one of the musical advisors to the CBS-TV hour, *The Sound of Jazz,* a few months before. The producer, Robert Herridge, wanted to avoid all the artificial trappings of most jazz television programs. The bare studio and the cameras were the set. There were no dancers and the commentary was compressed to a minimum. The musicians were told to dress as comfortably as they liked, and to smoke if they wanted to. Billie Holiday discarded a $500 gown she had bought for the show and appeared on camera in slacks. Several of the older players, long habituated to keeping their hats on when playing at jam sessions, did so on the program.

Carter, who had watched the program, was furious. "What was all that caricaturing going on?" he asked me. "Jazz has achieved stature and dignity. It's an insult to see people smoking and wearing their hats on a jazz program." It was impossible to convince Carter that the musicians that day dressed as they wanted to, enjoyed smoking during the show, and that the dignity of jazz was made entirely clear by their music and their faces. As Eric Larrabee noted in *Harper's:*

"What made the jazz musicians extraordinary, when the camera put their features through its harsh examination, was how much it found there. Children and animals make the best movie actors, as Douglas Fairbanks said, because they are unselfconscious and unable to fake. No more could these musicians be anything but themselves, for they are committed to independence and to a headlong attack on the cosmos. It showed; here—and no kid-

ding—were individuals of stature and profundity, of
flesh and substance, of warmth and bite. The music was
good, yes, but what lifted "The Sound of Jazz" to a level
hitherto unattained was the sight of it being made. As a
lady in White Plains sat down and wrote CBS as soon
as the show was over, one so seldom has the chance "to
see *real* people doing something that *really* matters to
them."

There are other musicians who deplore what they
call Dizzy Gillespie's public behavior. He doesn't wear a
hat on stand, but he "clowns." Yet his critics fail to catch
in his japeries the frequently sardonic judgments on the
mores of jazz musicians and audiences and occasionally
stinging references to Jim Crow. Gillespie's relationship
with his audience is, in fact, often refreshingly candid.
"Thank you," he noted during one hopeless outdoor jazz
festival concert, "for your wonderful indifference."

As for John Lewis, it is not true, however, that for all
his attention to clothes, he is in any way ashamed of the
basically unreserved roots of jazz itself. The blues make
up the main ingredient of much of what the MJQ plays—
as Francis Newton admits—and Lewis himself is a much
more intense blues pianist than most jazz listeners realize.
Lewis was listening one afternoon to the director of his
record label planning the accompaniment for a forth-
coming album by the distinctly unselfconscious blues
singer, Joe Turner, whose tailoring, I expect, appalls Mr.
Lewis. "You know," Lewis said wistfully, "I'd very much
like to make that date. I'm not a bad blues pianist myself."

My point is that the interactions of sociological, psychological and musical stresses on the development of a
contemporary jazzman are not easily traced and categor-
ized. Lewis, for example, born in 1920, had in retrospect
a relatively conventional background in modern jazz, such
as writing and playing for the Dizzy Gillespie big band
of the late 1940's; helping to formulate the music for the

influential "chamber jazz" Miles Davis recordings on
Capitol in 1949-50; working and recording with Illinois
Jacquet, Lester Young and Charlie Parker; and serving as
accompanist to Ella Fitzgerald. His family background,
however, was upper-middle-class, cultured, and not especially conscious of prejudice. He was early exposed to intellectual as well as purely musical interests and majored
in anthropology for three years at the University of New
Mexico before switching to music.

His music, although it often incorporates classical
forms, is seldom self-conscious in its blending of these
forms with the jazz improvisations of the players within
the piece. Lewis, for example, has never been as naïve as
Charlie Parker, Billie Holiday and Lester Young in be-
lieving that certain appurtenances of classical music—
particularly strings—helped in themselves to enhance their
music and gave it added respectability. Norman Granz,
for instance, has often been criticized for recording Parker
with strings, but Parker wanted them. Billie Holiday believed that her best records were those with strings, although almost invariably they were her worst as the
mockingly unsaccharine impact of her sound and phrasing
had to struggle against the glucosely commercial writing
for the violins. Lewis too has performed with violins, and
while I don't think those combinations he recorded in Europe have been successful, partly because the European
players involved could not phrase idiomatically, Lewis'
attempt was more of an experiment in coloration and dynamics than an ingenuous grasp for the lace-curtain,
lower-middle-class "prettiness" that was desired by the
otherwise nonassimilationist Parker, Young and Holiday.

In short, while Lewis occasionally has fallen into
some of sentimentality-as-aesthetics of Holiday, Parker
and Young in their more insecure moments, his preten-
tions were different because he came from a different
class.

As for the main body of Lewis' work, British critic

Max Harrison has rightly observed that Lewis, in his use of actual classical structures, has "consistently been able to regard a performance as a unit of musical architecture. He has been able to see part in relation to whole and to develop an intimate relationship between improvised solos, predetermined ensembles, and general structure. . . . It is his achievement that he has succeeded where all others have failed in grafting a number of classical devices into the technique of jazz without doing violence to the spirit of the music. . . . In all the MJQ's fugues, the episodes are improvised and are based on predetermined harmonic sequences. A considerable amount of the counterpoint in the group's other pieces would seem to be improvised too. . . . The MJQ presented more improvisation per concert than any other group that has visited us."

Gunther Schuller has summarized the other half of Lewis' achievement at his best: "In a very simple, unspectacular way, he combines the romantic and the classical in a judicious blending. His great melodic gift is very much in evidence. John has that rare ability to create a melody which is thoroughly conventional, immediately hummable, sounds as if one had heard it somewhere before, and yet is in fact absolutely original. Above all, his music has that unassailable quality of rightness for which there is no substitute."

Distinctly opposite to the cosmopolitan Lewis is Thelonious Monk, a pianist-composer who waited more than fifteen years for steady work and acceptance among the majority of jazz musicians. Monk's compositions, even more than Lewis', have "that unassailable quality of rightness" but are not influenced in the least by classical forms. As British writer Stanley Dance, a late and grudging convert to some elements of modern jazz, wrote: "His music is full of personality, and it's of a piece. It's Monk all through. . . . There are no pyrotechnics . . . no ambigu-

ous folksy ties, no sycophantic debt to European culture.
His work is rooted in jazz and has a good, clear sense of
the jazz beat."

In the late 1950's, a number of jazzmen, led by Miles
Davis, became increasingly interested in using space as
part of their improvisations, in getting free of the contin-
uous, chord-choked substructure of modern jazz. They
had begun to realize, moreover, that much of the "advanced" harmonic language of modern jazz, though used
quite differently, had long been familiar to classical composers. Monk, however, had preceded Davis. "Monk," as
Davis has said, "had been a big influence in giving musicians more freedom. They feel that if Monk can do what
he does, they can. Monk has been using space for a long
time."

In 1948, Paul Bacon had written in *The Record
Changer:*

"What Monk has done, in part, is quite simple. He
hasn't invented a new scheme of things, but he has for
years looked with an unjaundiced eye at music and seen
a little something else. He plays riffs that are older than
Bunk Johnson—but they don't sound the same; his beat
is familiar but he does something strange there, too—he
can make a rhythm seem almost separate, so that what
he does is inside it, or outside it. He may play for a space
in nothing but smooth phrases and then suddenly jump
on a part and repeat it with an intensity beyond description. His left hand is not constant—it wanders shrewdly
around, sometimes powerfully on the beat, usually increasing it in variety and occasionally silent. . . . And
Monk has a beat like the ocean waves—no matter how
sudden, spasmodic, or obscure his little inventions, he
rocks irresistibly on. . . . Monk is really making use of all
the unused space around jazz, and he makes you feel
that there are plenty of unopened doors."

Also in *The Record Changer,* nearly a decade later,

Martin Williams, in the course of a Thelonious Monk
record review, provided an admirably succinct history of
jazz improvisation up to that time as it related to Monk's
work:

> "The rest of these performances have a disciplined
> *form* that is rare in modern jazz. Monk has begun playing
> variations on melody. That kind of variation, growing
> and building out of the melodic line of a tune, was the
> virtue of the finest achievement of New Orleans jazz.
> Swing style is based on variations played on chord pat-
> terns, on riffs blown within chords, bits of riffs strung
> together (sometimes brilliantly) on the chord progress-
> ions of, mostly, the blues and *I Got Rhythm.* Its very best
> men usually knew enough about the blues to inform their
> solos with the suggested melodic content of the blues—
> that is, of course, Lester Young's source of beauty. The
> boppers were tired of the same old chords and explored
> new ones. But, essentially, most of them were still playing
> a riff style; it is just that their kind of riffs were built on a
> new approach to harmony—but not really so new as
> some thought. Again the best of them leaned on the me-
> lodic background of the blues for a melodic form and
> unity of mood—as Charlie Parker, and as now Horace
> Silver. Monk has gone back to melody, taking his har-
> monies (which some moderns have still to catch up
> with), his personal rhythms (he plays, by the way, a bit
> less behind the beat than most modernists), gone back
> to basing his improvisations and variations on the growth
> out of the melodic line."

A further, exceptionally useful guideline to Monk in
the context of previous jazz has been provided by pianist
Dick Katz, who amplifies Williams' points:

> "The traditional players—particularly pianists like
> James P. Johnson and Willie 'The Lion' Smith—con-
> sciously or otherwise used a style of improvisation based
> on variations on a theme. The theme, the melody, was

always present, and the idea was to see how many different ways it was possible to embellish, restate or 'extend' the theme. The melody, no matter how disguised, always kept reappearing. Willie 'The Lion' would even resort to a change of tempo to set off a new set of variations, but always on the theme. Art Tatum grew out of this style, but he had superior technique, rhythmic imagination and a much larger harmonic vocabulary.

"Starting probably with men like Roy Eldridge and then fully in the period of Charlie Parker and Dizzy Gillespie, the emphasis was placed on replacing the melody or theme with an entirely new theme (and even that was disposed of after the first chorus) and the harmonic structure of the piece dictated almost exclusively what followed. There were many-noted phrases that didn't have any necessary relation to the theme other than harmonically. Coleman Hawkins' 1939 recording of *Body and Soul* is one of the first examples of this practice. So, when the bop virtuoso players let loose their cascades of altered-chord, many-noted runs and multi-rhythms, the idea of the theme was swept along with the flood. Charlie Parker was one of the few who would still suggest the melody occasionally when it suited his artistic purpose, but he too would not stay close to the melody.

"Monk's approach, in one way, is closer to the traditional. He does have an allegiance to the melody or theme in the course of his improvisations. What makes it appear that Monk is 'far out' is his harmonic system which is very personal. What he may do on occasion is to throw out the original harmonic scheme and substitute his own harmonic structure while continuing to refer back to the melody.

"His harmonic approach mostly has to do with an ingenious sense of voicing chords in a dissonant way. Monk has a remarkably natural dramatic gift for using dissonance in an instinctive rather than a calculated way. He'll pick a dramatic time to use a dissonance so that the dissonance is outlined in relief because of the rhythm.

"A good part of the success of what Monk does depends on the particular sounds, the tone qualities he gets out of the piano. He taught me one of his compositions note for note. I learned and played it but couldn't make it *sound* the way it was supposed to. The sound of the entire piece is important in his work, not just the melodies alone. Of how many jazz composers besides Duke Ellington can this be said?

"In his playing, Monk furthermore has a fine sense of equilibrium. He has an expert command of tension. When he bears down and pushes, he pushes in places where it'll work. But he leaves space and time for the scale to come back up. He doesn't tip it so far that it doesn't have time to right itself. Rhythmically, he has such a strong implicit pulse that he can sit in with bad rhythm sections and *make* them swing. He is his own rhythm section.

"There is also his humor. Monk is one of the truly sophisticated jazz musicians because he's not trying to be sophisticated. He has a beautifully developed sense of sarcasm together with a kind of left-handed veneration for things of the past (he can express respect for stride piano on several of his recordings while making some fun of it too). His is a high expression of the negation of maudlin sentimentality, but unlike many modernists who approach the sentimental hatefully, he can spoof it gently while expressing positive feelings, as Fats Waller did."

Another illustration of the insistently personal pragmatism at the base of the jazz tradition, so consistently represented by Monk, is an observation by classical composer and jazz pianist Hall Overton:

"He has a very selective approach to sound. In a sense, he abstracts from the fuller type of jazz harmony. It isn't that he doesn't know the full harmony—he's played it for me—but he does know those particular sounds he wants and so his harmony is lean. He's no primitive; he's highly sophisticated. Incidentally, there's one thing he does that may or may not be conscious, but that does go along with the spaces he leaves in his chords. He plays with flat fingers; his fingers are splayed out, not curved into the keyboard and as a result, he can resist the temptation to play full chords.

"As a whole, Monk is an excellent example of a non-conformist in a field that's very cliquish and conformist despite the legend that every jazzman is an individualist. Monk always stuck to his own way, and it's finally paying off."

Musician Gigi Gryce indicates how Monk's relentless criteria operate when other musicians are involved:

"I had a part he wrote for me that was impossible. I had to play melody while simultaneously playing harmony with him. In addition, the intervals were very wide besides; and I just told him I couldn't do it. 'You have an instrument, don't you?' he said. 'Either play it or throw it away.' And he walked away. Finally, I *was* able to play it. Another time I was orchestrating a number for him, and I didn't write everything down for the horns exactly as he'd outlined it because I felt the musicians would look at the score and figure it was impossible to play. He was very angry, and he finally got exactly what he wanted. I remember the trumpet player on the date had some runs going up on his horn and Monk said they were only impractical if they didn't give him a chance to breathe. The range was not a factor 'because a man should be flexible on all ranges of his horn.'"

Sahib Shihab, who has worked on several of Monk's record dates, recalls: "I had a part that was unbelievably difficult. I complained to Monk. His only answer was: 'You a musician? You got a union card? Play it!' To my surprise, I eventually did."

Gunther Schuller has summarized Monk's approach as a whole by pointing out: "Where many pianists less original than Monk are exclusively concerned with playing the 'right' (or acceptable) notes, Monk, at his most

inspired, thinks of *over-all* shapes and designs or ideas
. . . and, because he is a man of great talent, or perhaps
even genius, he does play the *right* notes, almost as a
matter of course."

In essence, then, Monk is uncompromisingly himself
in his music and is unaffected by what may be currently
hip among musicians, let alone listeners. "I say," Monk
was quoted in a perceptive article by Grover Sales in
Jazz: A Quarterly of American Music, "play your own
way. Don't play what the public wants—you play what
you want and let the public pick up what *you* are doing—
even if it *does* take them fifteen, twenty years."

The music reflects the man, and it's instructive to
trace the career in jazz of so indomitably singular a force.
For many years, Monk not only worked infrequently but
became a stock cartoon figure for writers of Sunday supplement pieces about the exotica of jazz. Pictures of Monk
in dark glasses and goatee would usually be captioned
"Mad Monk" or "The High Priest of Bop." Exaggerated
stories of his personal life were the "substance" of the
articles. There was no attempt to discuss the nature or
seriousness of his musical intentions. Monk became part
of the Sabbath sideshow of resurrected murderers, celebrated divorce cases, and Elsa Maxwell. Even now, although he receives more respect in print in view of his
growing commercial success, the man himself has remained as opaque as in his barren years.

Monk's final recognition seemed to occur without his
active participation. The music, of course, was there to be
argued about, mocked and praised, but there were no interviews (until recently), no friendships (slight or otherwise) with the critics, no letters to trade-press editors or
ghosted articles. There was no personal advocacy at all—
except the playing and the writing. The music formed a
recognizable entity, although a controversial one; behind
it was mostly vapor in dark glasses and a goatee.

Although there were always a few musicians who at

least partially understood and approved of what Monk was playing and writing, he did not—until the late 1950's —derive much moral support from most modern jazzmen. Some felt his fiercely percussive, unpredictable piano difficult to play with. His predilection for leaving large spaces in his playing left unseasoned sidemen with the sensation, in the middle of a chorus, of having stepped into an abandoned elevator shaft.

Others simply did not understand his music, and since many jazzmen are as herd-like as they tell themselves the day people are, they did not try to investigate Monk's conception too thoroughly for fear of being considered too unorthodox by their colleagues. There were those who agreed with most of the critics that while Monk had written a few intriguing tunes ('Round Midnight was the only one at first that had any real currency), he was a limited pianist who was more eccentric than creative, more an historical relic of the Minton's dawn of bop than a lasting influence. And since he was unable to get steady work, he couldn't keep together and thus develop in a unit those few of the younger musicians who were not intimidated by him.

Around 1957, the inside line began to change. Monk was hired at the Five Spot Cafe on New York's lower East Side, and for the first time in years he could be heard six nights a week. The musicians began to come, began to understand, and started to spread the word. In a few months, the first question a New York musician in Los Angeles or London was likely to be asked by the resident faithful was, "Have you heard Monk lately? What's he doing?" At the same time he was being recorded by a company, Riverside, that had come to realize he was developing into its most important property. Riverside promoted his records accordingly, and made new ones available at regular intervals.

The recognition gathered intensity and momentum until Monk's records began to receive nearly unanimous and almost automatic imprimaturs by the critics, and he won more and more polls here and abroad. More and more of his compositions are being played by other groups, and he has become a major formative influence on jazzmen— not only pianists and writers, but players on all the instruments.

Now, on the few occasions when he can be persuaded to leave New York, Monk commands between $1700 to $2000 a week for his combo and somewhat more than $1000 for a single night's work. As late as four years ago, he was being hired—usually as a single— for $350, and might have been able to get $800 a week for a group.

Two of the most qualified critics in jazz pay him tribute usually held for the dead. To Martin Williams, he is "a major composer—the first . . . since Ellington—and one whose work drastically extends the concept of composition in the idiom." The flinty, sternly unsentimental André Hodeir talks of Monk's "urgent beauty" and says it's quite possible that future generations will regard Monk as *the* jazzman of our epoch.

Although he is, of course, aware of the change in the way he is regarded by others, Monk himself has not altered appreciably either in the angular force of his playing nor in the implacably intuitive way he conducts his personal life. He has, however, begun to worry, an affliction he seldom experienced in his bleaker days. "I wonder," he occasionally says to his wife, Nellie, or to Harry Colomby, his gentle manager who teaches English and History at Far Rockaway High School, "I wonder if it'll last."

There are also signs that, like many rebels who gain power, Monk is beginning to regard himself as a guardian of jazz traditions. During an evening in the spring of 1960 at the home of Baroness Nica de Koenigswarter, a friend of the Monks, I heard a discussion between the Baroness, Monk, and his wife about Ornette Coleman, a controversial alto player who was then at the Five Spot and who a few critics had insisted was moving toward new possibilities of jazz improvisation.

The Baroness was uneasy at not having been able to understand Coleman's work. She and Nellie were animatedly discussing the problem when Monk announced firmly: "There's nothing beautiful in what he's playing." The Baroness vigorously nodded agreement. "He's just playing loud all the time and slurring his notes," Monk continued. "Anybody can do that." The Baroness nodded again. "And that sound of his. That's nothing new. I did it on this number," he started to move toward the pile of records, stacked without envelopes, by the bed. "But I didn't do it all the way through. I did it just to get what I wanted in that one place." He played the record, Nellie and the Baroness listening with complete attention. After playing it again to underline his point, Monk flopped down on the bed again. "I think he has a gang of potentiality though," Monk conceded from the pillow. "But he's not all they say he is right now. After all," Monk stood up again, and said with the imperiousness of a jazz critic, "what has he *contributed?*"

As to whether Monk has himself finally achieved a secure position, the answer lies more with him than with external circumstances such as changing public taste. Although recognition dawdled cruelly in arriving, Monk's achievements have by now been so solidly accepted that he is assured of sizable listener support as long as he wants to appear in public, and fulfills his commitments.

Monk acts according to how he feels, and no one is ever quite sure how he'll feel at any given time, nor even what he feels. He may often stay up two or three days, and he does not eat by the clock since his periods of hunger do not always fall into regular rhythms. On a visit, if he feels like napping, he does. There are times, in his home or outside, when he doesn't feel like talking, and he may not for several hours. The latter condition usually

occurs when he's worried; and if he's sufficiently disturbed, he'll answer no one, not even his wife, to whom
he's very close, except to say that nothing at all is bother-
ing him.

In conversation, Monk is of a literal turn of mind.
"Would you," a lecturer in jazz at Columbia University
directed rather than asked him, "play some of your weird
chords for the class?" Monk was affronted. "What do you
mean weird? They're perfectly logical chords." Another
time, a musician began portentously, "Well, everybody
says . . ." "What do *you* say?" Monk stopped him. He is
impatient with interviewers, especially when they ask
him speculative questions about the future of jazz. "I don't
know where it's going," he told Negro novelist and reporter Frank London Brown in *Down Beat*. "Maybe it's
going to hell. You can't make anything go anywhere. It
just happens."

Monk is easily bored, and he will not long bear a
situation he finds dull. He may suggest a walk to whoever
is with him, or just leave. Walking is a favorite avocation,
as is riding around New York in his car. Monk has a great
love for the city in which he was raised. When he does
get into trouble, it's almost always on the road.

Twice in the past few years, he has become involved
in difficulties on the road, and both times were due in
part to his losing his ability to communicate. Even close
associates know times when Monk simply disconnects
and will not be reached.

"Part of that disconnecting," Hall Overton thinks,
"has to do with what seems to be a deep distrust at times
of his own capacity to communicate what he feels and of
others' ability to understand. He may figure at those
times that he won't be understood, so why try?" "Or,"
says another musician, "he may just be escaping from
reality."

In any case, in the fall of 1958, he, tenor saxophonist
Charlie Rouse and the Baroness de Koenigswarter were

driving to what was to be a week's engagement for Monk at the Comedy Club in Baltimore. They stopped at a motel in Delaware and Monk went in to ask for a glass of water. Monk is an imposing figure. Slightly more than six feet tall and weighing around two hundred pounds, he is physically impressive more because of the forceful solidity with which he stands and moves and the intensity of his look than by his mass itself. The motel owner was shocked at this sudden presence, reacted in a way Monk felt to be rude, and Monk, silent all the time, was slow in leaving. The owner, growing more frightened, called the police. Cops tried to pull Monk out of the car to which he had returned, but he held onto the steering wheel, claiming he hadn't done anything to warrant their attention. About half a mile up the road, more police cars appeared, Monk was dragged from the car, thrown to the floor of a police vehicle, pummeled and hit on the hands as the Baroness tried to tell the officers that Monk was a pianist.

Later, marijuana was found in a can in the trunk of the car. Charges of possession filed against Monk were dismissed, since no connection could be proved between him and the marijuana. He was fined for disturbing the peace. He also lost his New York police identity card without which no musician can work in any New York place where liquor is served. His manager, charging race prejudice was involved in the Delaware arrest, asked for a hearing before the New York State Liquor Authority, which must also pass on applicants for a card. Monk, though nervous, was thoroughly articulate and cooperative at the hearing. An incident underlined his concern for absolute candor. "Didn't one of those people at the motel call you 'nigger'?" asked his manager. "No," said Monk. "I didn't hear that. But they were acting weird." He had felt prejudice, he later said, but he would not say what had not actually happened.

From what Monk has told Frank London Brown, he does not consciously believe his experiences as a

Negro, though sometimes bitter, are reflected in his work. "My music," he told Brown, "is not a social comment on discrimination or poverty or the like. I would have written the same way even if I had not been a Negro." Monk's manager, also interviewed by Brown for *Down Beat,* added: "Monk once told me, 'When I was a kid, some of of the guys would try to get me to hate white people for what they've been doing to Negroes, and for a while I tried real hard. But every time I got to hating them, some white guy would come along and mess the whole thing up.'"

As for Monk's other ordeal on the road, in the spring of 1959, he was booked for a week at Boston's Storyville. He had been up for some three days and nights without sleep. When he arrived, he came to the desk of the Copley Square Hotel, where Storyville was then located, with a glass of liquor in his hand after having flitted around the lobby rather disconcertedly, examining the walls. He was refused a room, and at first also declined to accompany his sidemen to the Hotel Bostonian where they were staying. At about ten o'clock, he finally went on stand. The room was nearly full of expectant but patient admirers. He played two numbers, and came off. At 11:30, he played the same two numbers, and then sat motionless at the piano for what seemed like half an hour. His bewildered sidemen had left the stand after about eight minutes.

Monk began wandering around the club, obviously disturbed at not having a hotel room. He finally registered at the Bostonian, didn't like the room, and left. He tried the Statler, was refused there, and took a cab to the airport with the idea of going home, collecting his wife, Nellie, and taking a room with her for the rest of the week. By that time of night planes were no longer running, and he was picked up by a state trooper to whom he would not or could not communicate. Monk later did reveal who he was, but it was too late, and he was transported to Grafton State Hospital near Worcester for observation.

Monk was lost there for a week. No one knew what had happened to him. The local Boston police were checked, but no one thought of trying the state police. A letter the hospital claims it sent to Nellie Monk never arrived. By accident, an acquaintance in Boston heard mention of Monk's whereabouts on a local television show. Nellie rushed to Massachusetts and secured his release. There had been no grounds on which he could be held. "It was the combination," a friend later speculated, "of exhaustion after several days without sleep, the fact that he disconnected at first, and the fact that he was away from New York and Nellie." Yet much of the time Monk is dependable and concerned with fulfilling his responsibilities. Lapses do occur, but they happen less and less. He had a recording date scheduled three days before the CBS-TV *Sound of Jazz* program in December, 1957. Monk never showed up, and the late Billie Holiday's accompanist, Mal Waldron, hastily substituted for Monk on record. Yet during the rehearsals for *Sound of Jazz* and the subsequent program, Monk was on time, wholly co-operative, and turned out to be one of the most stimulating parts of the program. He had stayed up for a couple of days, it was later learned, because he had been worrying about the show.

A few months before, after a rocky plane ride, Monk spent most of an opening night in Detroit playing with his elbows. "I'm sorry," said a musician who has enormous admiration for Monk's work, "but he or anybody else, genius or not, owes it to an audience to give the best he can." Monk increasingly does realize his responsibilities to an audience, and his troubles on the road may be over. After a stay in San Francisco in early 1960, the owner of the Black Hawk avowed: "Mr. Monk can play my club any time. He's a gentleman. I don't know what they're talking about. This guy was straight with me."

Monk, in fact, was often early for the night's work, was on time for every set, and even signed autographs. He was, reported *Down Beat*, "the very model of a model major jazz artist." And club owner George Wein wants him back at Storyville.

Monk, in short, remains self-absorbed, but is growing up in the way he relates to an audience. In 1949, Paul Bacon, one of the very few writers on jazz who understood Monk in the 1940's, wrote in the French monthly, *Jazz-Hot*, that Monk was very egocentric but the fact that he considered the world revolved around him gave him a remarkably direct vision of things, very much like that of a child. "To become an adult," wrote Bacon, "it's necessary to make a lot of concessions."

Monk has stubbornly avoided concessions, musically and otherwise, as much as he has been able to since boyhood. Drummer Denzil Best first began to play jobs with Monk when the latter was fifteen and is firm on the point that although Monk has certainly developed since then, his approach at the beginning was essentially what it is now. "People," says Denzil, who was then a trumpeter, "would call his changes [chord progressions] wrong to his face. If he hadn't been so strong in his mind, he might easily have become discouraged, but he always went his own way and wouldn't change for anything."

Thelonious (a family name which his father bore and his son now carries), was born October 10, 1920, in North Carolina, but was brought up in New York's San Juan Hill section in the West Sixties close to the Hudson River, where he still lives with his wife and two children in the small apartment he's occupied for nearly thirty years. The dominating piece of furniture in his crowded home is a Steinway baby grand. The piano consumes, as Mrs. Monk puts it, "most of the living-room part of the kitchen."

The neighborhood, as it was when Monk was a child, is largely underprivileged. There were scholarships available for children of musical capacity; but from the beginning, Monk's playing was too unorthodox to qualify him despite the fact that his mother had three children to support on a minute income and the boy obviously was deeply involved with music. His mother, a former Civil Service worker, is said to have been a strict disciplinarian and there were rigid demands on Thelonious to be neat, obedient, and polite. She also, however, was thoroughly protective of him.

When he was about six, Monk began tentatively to trace melodies on the piano by ear. He had some formal lessons when he was eleven, but he's essentially self-taught as pianist and composer. While quite young, he listened to all the jazz pianists he could find, partly as an antidote to the two years he played organ in a church. He had soon wearied of the plush, conservative chords of the religious music and he found the Dixieland and much of the swing music of the time too limiting. "I never picked no special musicians to follow. Of course, you have to go through certain stages to learn how to play the piano, but that doesn't necessarily mean you're copying somebody's style. I've learned from numerous pianists. But I never had what you might call a major influence."

"Didn't have to study hard," Monk told interviewer Grover Sales for *Jazz Magazine*. "Used to amaze all the teachers! No one had to make *me* study. I was *gifted,* you know—music. I learned to read notes before I took lessons. My older sister took—the girls always took in those days— and I learned to read by looking over her shoulder. Got interested in jazz right from the start. Fats Waller, Duke, Louis, Earl Hines—I dug all kinds of music—liked everybody. Art Tatum! Well, he was the greatest piano player I ever heard. . . . My first jobs I got in house parties; used to hear all my favorites at those parties. . . . I started composing around 1942 when I was at Minton's. Parker, Dizzy, they all come in to hear me. Bird never excited me like he did the others. 'Bird is a god,' they said. He wasn't to me! No, and no one else was, either. . . . Music theory? Well, when I was a kid, I only knew I wanted to make it better."

Monk began playing in local bands when he was about thirteen, learning how to read orchestrations at a local community center. Some four years later, he traveled the country as part of a unit accompanying a rocking evangelist. "Rock and roll or rhythm blues," Monk said of this experience, "that's what we were doing. She preached and healed and we played. And then the congregation would sing."

One of the cities the healer visited was Kansas City, and Mary Lou Williams, the perennial modernist, heard Monk there for the first time. "He was playing the same style, to a large extent, that he is now. He told me that he was sick of hearing musicians play the same thing the same way all the time."

Back in New York, Monk began twenty years of scuffling to find steady work. "I worked all over town. Non-union jobs; $20 a week, seven nights a week; and then the boss might fire you any time and you never got your money. I've been on every kind of job you can think of," said Monk, remembering dance halls and bars all over New York. "I really found out how to get around this city. There are a lot of things you can't remember— except the heckling." The work was infrequent, the heckling recurrent, because Monk's style was unexpected, and he would not change.

In the late 1930's, Monk began playing occasionally in Harlem with a few musicians with whom he felt some degree of rapport—the late Charlie Christian, Dizzy Gillespie, trumpeter Idrees Sulieman, Charlie Parker and drummer Kenny Clarke, with whom Monk wrote *Epistrophy*, one of the first modern jazz standards. Just as early jazz history has been romanticized into the "up the river from New Orleans" oversimplification, there also has been a fanciful condensation in the familiar yarn about the birth of bop at Minton's in Harlem with the young insurgents like Monk, Parker and Gillespie depicted as carefully planning raids on the established harmonic and rhythmic order.

Monk recalls of the Minton's era: "I was just playing a gig, trying to play music. While I was at Minton's anybody sat in if he could play. I never bothered anybody. I had no particular feeling that anything new was being built. It's true modern jazz probably began to get popular there, but some of these histories and articles put what happened over the course of ten years into one year. They put people all together in one time in one place. I've seen practically everybody at Minton's, but they were just there playing. They weren't giving any lectures."

But while Monk wasn't lecturing either, he did become a valuable example. "He opened people's ears," says Mary Lou Williams. "If I hadn't met Monk shortly after I first came to New York around 1945," adds Miles Davis, "I wouldn't have advanced as quickly as some say I did. He showed me voicings and progressions, and I remember Charlie Parker would take me down to listen to Monk all the time and make me sit in with him."

Monk was the earliest champion of Bud Powell, whose influence on modern jazz piano became as pervasive—until the Monk renaissance—as Charlie Parker's on all instruments. It was Monk who insisted Bud sit in at Minton's when Kenny Clarke, Dizzy and others were eager to expel him from the stand. Bud, strongly influenced by Monk musically, a few years later helped convince Cootie Williams to record Monk's 'Round About Midnight, a wounding melody that Monk wrote when he was nineteen. As often happens with jazz writers, in return for the first recording of the tune, Monk found Cootie Williams

listed with him as co-author. (Among other Monk jazz
"standards" are *Ruby, My Dear; Well, You Needn't; Off
Minor; In Walked Bud* and *I Mean You.*)

The 1940's were a harsh time for Monk, as the era
was for most of the younger modernists whose music took
a number of years to be accepted by even the basic jazz
audience. Since Monk, however, was even more uncate-
gorizable than the others, his jobs were fewer. There
were quick stands like a week or so at the Savoy with
Lucky Millinder in 1942 and a 1944 date with Coleman
Hawkins on 52nd Street. Hawkins, unlike many jazzmen
of his generation, was intrigued by and encouraged the
modernists. Monk's first record date was with Hawkins on
four 78 r.p.m. sides made in 1944 on the Joe Davis lab
Thirteen years later, Hawkins played as a sideman on a
Monk Riverside album.

Monk made his first records under his own name for
Blue Note, beginning in 1947. The company is consistently
exploratory, and its artistic integrity—it has never, for
example, issued a "jazz" version of a Broadway show—
has sometimes led it to the brink of economic suicide.
The main difficulty with recording Monk, recalls Alfred
Lion, the label's recording director, was finding musicians
who could play with him, since what he was writing and
playing was not in the conventional "bop" vein. "He
didn't then," remembers Lion, "write much of anything
down. The musicians had to learn what he was doing
by ear. And even if he had written it all down, he might
have changed his mind fifteen times between the time
a musician had learned his part and the final take. You
really had to have ears to play with him."

The first Blue Note singles received some attention
in Harlem and in the Negro sections of a few other large
cities, but it took several years before white jazz listeners began to buy Monk. "They thought," Lion reminisces
sadly, "he lacked technique."

Lion managed to get Monk jobs from time to time,

often uptown, but underlines that "in those days, Monk was completely isolated. He rarely worked with the boppers—when they did get a little work—because he was going his own way; and so, in all those years into the '40's and '50's, I doubt if he ever had a job that lasted more than two weeks at a time. Yet the audiences that did come to hear him were usually fascinated and were held by the fact that he always had a beat going."

What scattered night club work Monk had been getting in and around New York was cut off completely in 1951. Monk and a friend were arrested on a narcotics charge. Also along were a girl and a pusher whom Monk didn't know. The consensus among relatively disinterested observers at the time was that Monk, innocent, took a rap rather than risk being regarded—by himself—as a "drag" for putting full blame on his co-defendant. Monk served sixty days, a particularly nightmarish penalty for someone who abhors restraint as he does. "He kept his dignity though," said a friend. "He never grovels, no matter how bad things get."

In the July 2, 1960, New York *Citizen-Call*, Maely Daniele Dufty, who was close to the Monks for a long time, insisted Monk was innocent of the narcotics charge in that 1951 case and that he did indeed keep silent rather than "inform." At the time, Nellie Monk was working in a tailor shop for $45 a week, had recently been released from the hospital after a major intestinal operation, and was desperate at her inability to raise bail or attorney's fee for Monk. Maely Dufty's account of what happened when Nellie Monk came to her for help is a representative illustration of the jazz life for Monk during that period:

"A musician, a girl and a man Monk had never met before came to pay a visit. The apartment was tiny and Monk's mother permanently bedridden. Monk suggested they sit in the car. Shortly after, two men approached the car flashing a badge. Narcotic Squad. Monk, during the ensuing excitement, didn't feel the small flying deck of white powder brush against him. He wasn't worried about anything. He was clean. You need money to be an addict. The cops bent down and picked up the small glassine envelope between Monk's feet from where it had landed and arrested everybody, without a search warrant or proof that the envelope contained narcotics.

"I called a man in the Narcotics Division of the Treasury Department. 'Please help Monk,' I begged, 'all you have to do is make the local police throw him into an isolation cell for 72 hours. The cops didn't find enough heroin to accuse him of selling. They're holding him as a user. He can disprove this within those 72 hours.' No user could stand those three days without a 'fix.'

"'Call me tomorrow, I'll see what I can do.' Next morning he told me he was sorry but he couldn't interfere. I was so angry I hung up without even a goodbye. My next call was to an official in the legal department of the NAACP. 'Sorry, but we don't touch anything involving narcotics.' His voice had become very cool. 'This involves a man being prejudiced against and robbed of his civil liberties,' I argued, 'he is being prevented from being able to prove his innocence in the *only* manner it can be proven—isolation.'

"'Sorry, Madam,' he said, "but it is a matter of policy.' 'O.K.' I conceded, 'but will you at least give me the name of a lawyer who'll take a case like this where there is no money?'

"He gave me Andrew Weinberger's name.

"Nellie and I turned the case over to Weinberger. But there was still a matter of getting money for bail. I went to a disc jockey. He laughed at me. I went to the owner of a hip jazz joint. He laughed harder. Everywhere I went for help, people would burst into gales of laughter as soon as I said: 'Thelonious Monk.'

"My dear friend and fellow European Alfred Lion from Blue Note Records, who had been the first to record Monk, paid the attorney's fee. (And those were Alfred's lean years before jazz became big business.)

"I was never able to raise bail. Con Edison turned Nellie's electricity off. The girl in the case was clear and free. The pusher was out on bail. Monk, alone, in deepest depression, remained in the Tombs till his case went into court.

"The judge accepted the time Monk had already done as full payment for a violation he never committed. The police department deprived Monk of his police work permit."

Worse than the jail sentence was the loss of his police card. He was sustained by a few record dates for Prestige to which label he had switched in 1952; very infrequent engagements out of the city; and mostly by his intensely loyal wife, Nellie, who worked during most of Monk's nearly silent years. When he did finally get steady work at the Five Spot in 1957, Nellie would leave their children with a baby sitter for part of most nights so that she could be with her husband. If she didn't arrive, Monk would usually become restless and would eventually call her at home.

Nellie is tall, thin, nervous, and singularly attractive in the way that many people with oversize strength of spirit often are. "Thelonious had trouble getting work even before he lost the card," she looks back. "Therefore, it wasn't a sudden total calamity. People had told so many stories about his being unreliable and eccentric that it had always been hard. But during the worst years we didn't feel the struggle as much as other people might have because we were very close. We felt each of us was doing the best he could, and we didn't suffer for things we couldn't have. In fact, nobody talked about them. If it was a matter of clothes, for instance, I felt it more important that he have them since he's before the public.

"During those long stretches when he wasn't working," Nellie Monk continues, "it was torture for him not

to be able to play. But you'd never know it from looking
at him, and he didn't get bitter. Anybody else with less
strength would have snapped. And he was continually
omitted from things—records, concerts, and the like.
We'd listen to the all-night Birdland radio show, and
maybe once in two months they'd play a record of his.
There was no money; no place to go. A complete blank.
He wasn't even included in benefits. He even had to pay
to get into Birdland."

In 1957, with the help of a lawyer retained by Baroness de Koenigswarter, Monk regained his police card.
The Baroness, who is becoming somewhat of a misty
legend on the New York scene, has befriended other jazzmen. She has helped Monk financially in the past, and
Monk has occasionally found her home a good place in
which to concentrate on composing. In fact, a few times
the whole Monk family has lived there.

Once, when the Baroness was staying at the Algonquin Hotel in New York, visits from Monk caused a
contretemps between her and the management. Monk
had taken to walking around the lobby wearing a bright
red shirt, dark glasses, and carrying a white cane when
the mood took him. A few elderly ladies who had been
living at the Algonquin for some time took flight at his
bemused appearance and packed their bags. To the
Baroness' annoyance, the hotel asked Mr. Monk not to
come visiting again. "They claim," she says, "they like
to have talented people staying there, but apparently
my friend was too much for them."

Monk's ability to concentrate can be formidable, no
matter what the environment. His manager has recalled:
"I once spent the night at his house, and when I woke up,
I saw Monk at the piano composing while the radio on
top of the piano was blasting away, playing hillbilly
music." Monk does not, however, work on a daily schedule. When he feels "right" he will compose. He won't
force himself. When he does work, as Dick Katz observes,

"he works very hard, very intensely. He has a lot of fragments in his mind that he'll keep coming back to in the process of composition, and he's always especially concerned with getting the right bridge (the 'inside,' he calls it) for his songs. The inside, he insists, has to make you appreciate the outside."

A few years ago, when Nellie was quite sick, Monk began to release some of his worry in music, and worked doggedly at *Crepuscule with Nellie*, one of his most tender compositions. It took him a month before he worked out the "inside" he felt was right.

"Everything fits so well in Monk's work," adds tenor saxophonist John Coltrane, "once you get to see the inside." Another musician discovered that "When you learn one of his pieces, you can't learn just the melody and chord symbols. You have to remember the inner voicings and rhythms exactly. Everything is so carefully interrelated; his works are *compositions* in the sense that relatively few jazz 'originals' are."

When rehearsing musicians in his works, Monk will take a long time to make sure they understand exactly what he wants. A couple of years ago, he was showing an orchestra how his piece, *Little Rootie Tootie*, went. Until they had absorbed his instructions, he had them take the number at a slow tempo, a tempo they assumed was the one he wanted. After he felt satisfied with their grasp of its inner workings he took it at a considerably faster tempo. He hadn't wanted them to be any more flustered at first than they needed to be.

During the same run of rehearsals, a young trumpet player persisted in taking conventional "bop" solos on Monk's *Friday the Thirteenth*. The musician based his fluent improvisations on the chord changes of the tune with little concern for the rest of its parts. "If you know the melody," Monk stopped him, "you can make a better solo." "Do you want me to *play* the melody?" the youngster asked impatiently. "If you know the melody," Monk repeated, "you can make a better solo, and you won't sound as if you're just running changes."

Monk's intentness on securing precisely what he wants occasionally results in his suddenly leaving the piano at a club or recording session, standing in front of the musicians, and lunging into a dance. Onlookers usually regard Monk's flailing steps as just another badge of his "eccentricity." He dances, however, for a specific reason. "It's as if he were conducting," says Gigi Gryce. "It's the way he gets what he wants. At one record date, some of the musicians were laughing as he danced without realizing that meanwhile, by following his rhythmic pulse, they were moving into the rhythm he wanted." "Sometimes, when we're deciding which take to issue for an album," says his recording director, Orrin Keepnews, "he'll do his dance. It's his way of being sure the number is swinging right." "When you're swinging," Monk once told his men, "swing some more!"

Even when seated at the piano, Monk's feet slash into space like the climax of a switch-blade duel. Although physically in repose unto seeming torpor a fair amount of time off the stand, Monk at the piano becomes possessed by immense kinetic energy and plays, in fact, with all of his body.

"Monk is all music," says Dick Katz, "not part piano, part music. A lot of what some fine pianists play is, by virtue of their considerable technique, more piano than music. They'll do things of a mechanical, however fluent, nature that are related to the music only intellectually. Actually, Monk does many technical things other pianists would have difficulty with—long, unorthodoxly fingered whole tones runs, for instance. They may sound slightly crude, but try to do them yourself. Or he'll play a fast succession of chords built on fourths with every note clear as a bell. He gets into areas where the normal pianists wouldn't go. It's like what happened in early jazz history when self-taught musicians would extend the range and capacity of their instruments because they had no instruction books to tell them what they couldn't or shouldn't do."

Thelonious can be challenging in other ways than music. "I used to have a phobia," says Nellie, "about pictures or anything on a wall hanging just a little bit crooked. Thelonious cured me. He nailed a clock to the wall at a very slight angle, just enough to make me furious. We argued about it for two hours, but he wouldn't let me change it. Finally, I got used to it. Now anything can hang at any angle, and it doesn't bother me at all."

Monk's own sense of gravity remains secure. "He needs," as Hall Overton points out, "very few things in life. He's got his one girl, Nellie, and the kids, and the music. And I think that to him the music is the most important of all. And the dearest."

John Lewis has reached one kind of success in the jazz life. He has respect among his professional peers (even those musicians contemptuous of the MJQ's calculated "dignity" in music and appearance admit that Lewis and the other members of the quartet have "paid their dues" and are authenticated members of the club). Lewis enjoys considerable personal self-satisfaction because he does believe in the validity of his work; his playing and compositions are an accurate, honest expression of the man. Lewis now also has the income to satisfy many of his avocations, all the more easily because of the mobile nature of the jazz life. He can indulge his penchant for superior restaurants in many cities, here and abroad, as well as his pleasure in collecting music, books, furniture and excellent clothes.

Thelonious Monk has always been clear about his life-goal—time to work on and play his music, an apartment in New York City, and enough money to provide the basic needs for himself and his family. He has always

insisted on securing the first two conditions, and now
he has the recognition to assure the third. Being so self-
contained, however narcissistically, he needs considerably
fewer stimuli, psychic and musical, than Lewis for a
thoroughly satisfactory existence.

Miles Davis is somewhere between the two. He has
a number of epicurean tastes similar to Lewis'. He is even
more concerned with his appearance. Recently, Davis appeared in a list of best-dressed American men compiled
for *Esquire* by George Frazier: ". . . an individualist who
favors skin-tight trousers, Italian-cut jackets. His seer-
sucker coats, which have side vents, are custom made.
His tailor: Emsley (New York), who charges $185 a
suit."

Davis also enjoys the fastest, most expensive sports
cars; and like Lewis, is somewhat obsessive about physical
culture. He is much more persevering than Lewis in the
latter concern, working out at a New York gym regularly
when at home and often visiting gyms in other cities
while on the road. He has a boxing ability to match his
quick temper. Unlike Lewis, he has little trouble in releasing aggression. After several altercations with a jazz
concert promoter who was shepherding a traveling package, including Davis, the trumpet player floored the entrepreneur backstage in a Chicago theatre. Asked the
reason by a newspaperman, Davis only muttered, "I
should have hit him in Detroit yet."

Like Lewis, Davis, though often thorny and reserved,
can function in most social contexts when he wants to.
While not especially well read, he is exceptionally intelligent and can be a vivid and sometimes epigrammatic
conversationalist. Thelonious Monk, except with a few
intimates, is relatively non-verbal and non-gregarious.
Davis remains more conversant than Lewis with the
hedonistic-hipster periphery of the jazz life and is more
sophisticated in his personal life than Monk. Looking into

Davis' music and background illuminates one of the many ways of making it.

Francis Newton in the *New Statesman* terms Davis "a wraith-like artist . . . a player of surprisingly narrow technical and emotional range." He admits Davis communicates an absolutely unmistakable sound and mood ". . . The mood, as one might expect, is one of total introversion and ranges from a reflective melancholy to naked desolation; but these sound as though felt by someone who, though not quite suffering from nightmares, is never quite awake. It is a sleepwalker's art, a lonely sound which plays before, after and besides, but rarely *with* other players." Newton, from hearing only the music, reacts to Davis as "this strange personality whose power lies in Davis' uncompromising hostility to the outer world." He concedes that Davis has "the rare ability to suggest vistas beyond the sound of his horn, stretching into some sad sort of infinity. I do not think that he is a great artist, because as yet he lacks both the tragic and the comic dimension. But there are few more genuine poets in jazz. . . . The present vogue for him is justified; but I should feel happier if the young men and women for whom jazz is the only adequate expression of their view of life, chose for their symbol a player whose art was less close to self-pity and the denial of life."

It's understandable that the brooding intensity of Davis' music should have led Newton to so misunderstand the man. Far from denying life, Davis enjoys existence more than most of his contemporaries, in or out of jazz. He is subject to moods of depression and extreme irritability, but more often in recent years has "made it" in most areas of his life.

Davis is more solvent than most jazzmen. He invests successfully in the stock market and in real estate. Characteristically, Davis makes his own decisions on what stocks to buy, often based on his own empirical testing

of a company's product or his observance of current sup-
ply-and-demand balances in the various areas through
which he travels. Davis owns a brownstone in New York's
West Seventies, is buying additional real estate, and
does not worry about when his career will end and what
will happen to him then. As a property owner he gets
grim satisfaction when, as recently, an electrician rang
the bell, took Davis for the janitor, and asked to see the
owner.

"You're looking at him," says Davis.

Concerning his music, Davis has said in *Playboy*,
"I'm too vain to play anything really bad musically that I
can help not doing. If ever I feel I *am* getting to the
point where I'm playing it safe, I'll stop. That's all I can
tell you about how I plan for the future. I'll keep on
working until nobody likes me. If I was Secretary of De-
fense, I'd give the future a lot of thought, but now I
don't. When I am without an audience, I'll know it before
anyone else, and I'll stop. That's all there is to life. You
work at what you do best, and if the time comes when
people don't like it, you do something else. As for me, if
I have to stop playing, I'll just drive my Ferrari, go to
the gym, and look at Frances."

Frances is Mrs. Davis, a lissome dancer who is devoted to her husband. He also has two boys and a girl by
a previous marriage. He enjoys playing with them and
teaching the boys boxing. His children's reactions to him
are not usually those set off by a man who denies life.
His teen-age daughter said to him shortly after his marriage to Frances, "I know some girls have an infatuation
for their father, but I tell you that if Frances hadn't married you, I would have."

Miles is similar to Thelonious Monk in the close-
ness he feels to his family and the extent to which he can
be absorbed in his music. He is seldom satisfied with anything he has done musically, but his impatience with himself leads not to frustration but to the constantly re-

newed excitement of finding and coping with the next challenge. Like creators in many fields, Davis is more involved in the continuing process of discovery than in what *is* discovered at each stage.

Davis' disinclination to coast on clichés is similar to the credo of Duke Ellington—a musician Davis admires more than anyone else in jazz—as expressed in a conversation I had with Ellington some years ago. As a composer, Ellington was saying that "the fun, the challenge is writing for musicians who have weaknesses. The fun of writing and participating in music is the motivating force that keeps me going on and on. . . . I enjoy solving problems. Take *Boy Meets Horn*. There's one note with a cocked valve on the trumpet that has that sound I wanted—E natural. The big problem was to employ that note logically and musically within the over-all structure of a composition. It was something to have fun with. It has nothing to do with conquering the world. You write it tonight and play it tomorrow, and that's it."

Ellington added his regret, in a sense, that the young jazzman can now "play anything you set down. I remember when cats with trombones used to say, 'Man, this thing ain't got no keys on it, you know.' Now they don't say it; they just play it. The problems of writing for individual musicians with their particular advantages and their particular weaknesses are reduced. So, you try to make new problems for yourself another way. You try to think in terms of combinations. . . . It's gotten so adult and civilized and that sort of thing. The other way, the old way, was like a kid playing with blocks. The first time he sees a Q, he says, 'Now what'll we do with this?' He hasn't perhaps gotten beyond A, B, and C in his alphabet up to that point."

As a player, Davis is fortunate from Ellington's point of view in that he does not have the seemingly effortless facility in all registers that many other modern jazz trumpet players do. Conversely, not having technical

bravura to rely on when ideas falter, Davis never gives
the impression of vacuous glibness. As trumpeter Art
Farmer has said of Davis: "When you're not technically
a virtuoso, you *have* to be saying something. You've got
no place to hide."

Davis has made maximum use of his assets. He plays
with a burnished tone that can be more expressive in the
lower register than that of any of the modernists; and
his general musical conception and temperament are annealed to a spare style that fits well with the fact that his
technique is somewhat limited.

Davis has an exceptionally keen and subtle chord
sense but his avoidance of bobsledding through changes
is due less to his technical limitations than to his increasing concern with melodic improvisation. Davis has
come to prefer a minimum of chords in most compositions. "When you go that way, you can go on forever. You
don't have to worry about changes and you can do more
with the line. It becomes a challenge to see how melodi-
cally inventive you are. When you're based on chords, you
know at the end of thirty-two bars that the chords have
run out and there's nothing to do but repeat what you've
just done—with variations. I think there is a return in
jazz to emphasis on melodic rather than harmonic variation. There will be fewer chords but infinite possibilities
as to what to do with them. Of course, several classical
composers have been writing this way for years. Too much
modern jazz became thick with chords."

Davis' capacity for the tragic dimension, Newton
notwithstanding, is startlingly evident in his Columbia
Sketches of Spain album in which, with Gil Evans' arrangements, he has blended flamenco patterns and jazz
with surprising success, particularly in his personalization
of the flamenco *cante hondo* ("deep song"). Davis' playing in the set is remarkable in its authenticity of phrasing
and timbre. It is as if he had been born of Andalusian
gypsies but had also grown up with American blues. I

doubt if any other American jazz musician could have so
thoroughly absorbed the emotional nuances of an alien
music and still retained his own personal jazz inflections.

Davis and arranger Gil .Evans, who has provided
him with uniquely sympathetic orchestral textures in
several albums, had, as is their custom, planned the Spanish sketches for months. They also took as much time as
they felt they needed to edit the tapes. In contrast to his
earlier attitude toward recordings, Davis is extremely
careful now as to what performances he allows to be
issued.

Newton is as wrong in ascribing self-pity to Davis'
playing in the past several years as he is in finding life-
denial in his work. Davis' personality is complicated, but
he consistently strikes out for what he wants. His direct
aggressiveness is not characteristic of those who soothe
themselves with pity. A small man with deceptively fragile-
looking features, Davis at times resembles a choirboy who
has been playing chess with the Devil and winning. Not
quite in keeping with his freshness of mien is a voice that
was left much hoarser than Louis Armstrong's after an
operation a few years ago to remove nodes from his vocal
chords. When Miles decides to speak in what is now his
characteristic rough whisper, usually punctuated by a
coughed chuckle, the choirboy turns into a mocking de-
flator of pomposity who will usually become serious only
about music.

"Miles is a leader in jazz," says his long-time friend,
arranger Gil Evans, "because he has definite confidence
in what he likes and he is not *afraid* of what he likes. A
lot of other musicians are constantly looking around to
hear what the next person is doing and worry about
whether they themselves are in style. Miles has confidence in his own taste, and he goes his own way."

Davis has become in the past few years the most influential modern jazz trumpet player since Dizzy Gillespie. The bristling introspectiveness of Davis' playing and

his questioning, intensely personal tone have led to a frequent misconception that his music is delicately cool with only glints of the fire that marks more explosive hornmen such as Dizzy Gillespie and Roy Eldridge. In fact, the most quoted and least accurate description of Davis' playing compares him to a man walking on eggshells. If Davis walked on an eggshell, he'd grind it into the ground.

The essence of Miles Davis can be determined by listening to the men he has surrounded himself with on his regular jobs. There is his favorite drummer, for example, Philly Joe Jones (not to be confused with Basie alumnus Jo Jones). Philly Joe is a fearsomely aggressive, polyrhythmically swinging athlete who often uses his sticks as if he had been trained in Sherwood Forest. Philly Joe's excitability propels him at times to play louder than would be necessary for a military band, but Miles was undismayed when Philly was with his combo, because the excitement Joe generates is more important to Miles than any volume problems.

"Look," Davis said before Philly Joe left the band, "I wouldn't care if he came up on the bandstand in his B.V.D.'s and with one arm, just so long as he was there. He's got the fire I want. There's nothing more terrible than playing with a dull rhythm section. Jazz has got to have *that thing*. You have to be born with it. You can't even buy it. If you could buy it, they'd have it at the next Newport festival."

"You must realize," says Gil Evans, "that underneath his lyricism, Miles *swings*. He'll take care of the lyricism, but the rest of the band must complement him with an intense drive. And it's not that they supply a drive he himself lacks. Actually they have to come up to him. There's nothing flabby or matter-of-fact about his rhythm conception. As subtle as he is in his time and his phrasing and his courage to wait, to use space, he's very forceful. There is a feeling of unhurriedness in his work and yet there's intensity underneath and through it all."

"Miles Davis' conception of time," adds pianist Cecil Taylor, "has led to greater rhythmic freedom for other players. His feeling, for another thing, is so intense that he catapults the drummer, bassist and pianist together, forcing them to play at the top of their technical ability and forcing them with his own emotional strength to be as emotional as possible."

When he's not playing, Davis also will not be hurried. Unlike most jazzmen with a reputation as established as his, Davis will not take all the dates he can get, however well they pay. "I never work steady. I work enough to do what I want to do. I play music more for pleasure than for work." And he seldom yields to any of the intersecting, extra-musical pressures in the business. When a powerful entrepreneur once asked him to let a protégé sit in with his combo while Davis was working at his club, Miles refused. The potentate, paternalistically amiable only so long as his demands are being met, threatened Davis: "You want to work here?"

Miles said with obscene gusto that he didn't care and told the man he was going home. The club owner tried to smooth over the hassle, and asked Miles to return to the stand. Later in the night, however, the protégé was sent up to the band. Miles and his men simply walked off.

Miles claims it was one of his frequent arguments with this particular club owner that prevented his throat from healing properly after his operation. "I wasn't supposed to talk for ten days. The second day I was out of the hospital, I ran into him and he tried to convince me to go into a deal that I didn't want." In the course of the debate, to make himself clear, Miles yelled himself into what may be permanent hoarseness.

Miles Davis' albums sell in sizable figures for jazz sets. Most former skeptics concerning his talent—like

John S. Wilson of *The New York Times*—are being converted. For years Wilson had found Davis' playing to have been characterized by "limp whimpering and fumbling uncertainty," but now he feels Miles' recordings of the past few years are examples of "hitherto diffused talent" suddenly taking a turn "that brings it sharply into focus."

Miles is unimpressed by what little he reads about himself, favorable or not, having small respect for any American critics except Ralph J. Gleason of the San Francisco *Chronicle*. Miles does allow that his playing has come somewhat closer to his own exacting criteria in the past few years.

"Do you find," a record company official, George Avakian, once asked Miles, "there are many things you do now that a few years ago you wouldn't have dared to do?"

Miles laughed. "A few years ago I used to do them anyway. Now maybe I use better taste than then."

Some observers feel that Miles' "comeback," after several years during which his career seemed to be on a slowing treadmill, dates from his appearance at the 1955 Newport Festival where all the reviews underlined the ardor and freshness of his brief contribution. Miles, like many jazzmen angered at the way the Newport supermarket is stocked and serviced, and does not agree: "What are they talking about? I just played the way I always play."

Actually, the renaissance of interest in Miles coincided with the fact that by 1955 he had matured emotionally to the point at which he could handle the multiple pressures of keeping a combo together. He has since led a unit which, despite its shifting personnel, is considered by musicians throughout the country to be one of the most stimulating forces in contemporary jazz. Miles' rejuvenation enabled him finally to establish a consistency in his playing and to develop from night to night in the company of musicians who challenged him and whom he in turn fused into a coherent unit.

Miles is now booked—at the highest prices of his career—in the major American jazz rooms, occasionally spends playing time in Europe, and has ad-libbed the score for a French film, *L'Ascenseur pour L'Echafaud*. Among younger American jazzmen, his intransigent musical integrity and strongly personal "conception" (as a man's style is described in the jazz idiom) make him part of the consistory of modern jazz along with Dizzy Gillespie, Thelonious Monk, the pervasive memory of Charlie Parker and a few others, including a protégé of Miles, tenor saxophonist Sonny Rollins.

Miles' playing is still unpredictable and it may be necessary to sit through two or more sets of an engagement before he indicates fully what all the hosannas have been about. "All of us," says one of his sidemen, "are affected in our playing at night by what's happened to us during the day, but of all those in the band, Miles is the most easily influenced by outside events. He reflects everything he feels in his playing immediately."

Despite Miles' contention that he doesn't particularly care what people think of him, he naturally enjoys his position among the jazz nobility. He's been working toward Olympus since grade school in East St. Louis, Illinois, across the river from St. Louis. Miles Dewey Davis was born May 25, 1926, in Alton, Illinois, and the family moved to East St. Louis two years later. Miles' father is a dentist who also performs dental surgery. In recent years, the elder Davis had also bred about $200,000 worth of cows and hogs on 200 acres near East St. Louis. A grandfather had owned about 1000 acres in Arkansas which financied the schooling of his children. Miles' mother, since divorced from Dr. Davis, was conscious of the family's place in local society and tried to uphold it.

She didn't discourage Miles' early interest in music, but wasn't fervently in favor of his making it a career.

"I didn't know until after I'd gone back there for a visit a few years ago," says Miles, "that my mother ever knew one note of the piano. But she sat down one day and played some funky blues. Turned out my grandmother used to teach organ. I was surprised my mother could play because she always used to look as if she'd hit me every time I played my horn. She also plays violin, by the way."

When Miles was very young, he'd peek through the door and watch his sister's piano lessons. As he reached thirteen, his mother wanted to get him a violin for his birthday, "but my father gave me a trumpet, he loved my mother so much." Miles' first instruction was at school. "A guy used to come around and have all the kids hold one note every Wednesday. A doctor friend of my father's taught me to play the chromatic scale right away so I wouldn't have to sit there and hold that one note all the time. The next day in school I was the belle of the ball."

Miles also benefited from a local instructor who had been with Andy Kirk. The instructor's favorite trumpet players were Bobby Hackett and Harold Baker (later a member of the Ellington band) and he was opposed to the pronounced vibrato with which many of the traditional and swing-era jazzmen played. He warned Miles, "You're gonna get old anyway and start shaking." "So," adds Miles, "that's how I tried to play. Fast and light— and no vibrato."

Miles soon began to work weekends with drums, piano and an alto player "who sounded like Guy Lombardo's first alto." He was also part of a high-school band that rehearsed twice a week and sounded, they hoped, like Count Basie. A local professional trumpet player who especially impressed Miles was Clark Terry, who also was later with Duke Ellington for several years. Miles listened to Terry and other local musicians in all-night jam sessions. Miles has always loved to jam and, during infrequent visits home, sits in for a night in a drab neighborhood club with the resident rock-and-roll band. "It's a funky place," he says happily, "with everybody talking and drinking and no time limits on the sets."

"Miles," said a Paris friend, the late Boris Vian, a writer and trumpet player, "could play a hundred hours in a row."

By the time he was sixteen, Miles was playing with a local band, Randolph's Blue Devils. When Tiny Bradshaw's unit came through town, equipped with Sonny Stitt and his stories of the promised land in New York where the Bird reigned, Miles received an offer to go with the band "for sixty whole dollars a week." Miles' mother indignantly refused permission, insisting Miles finish his last year of high school. "I didn't talk to her for two weeks."

Miles had been moved by Charlie Parker's early records with Jay McShann and by what little could be heard of Dizzy Gillespie on the Billy Eckstine band records. Finally, the Eckstine orchestra with Parker and Gillespie arrived in St. Louis. "A friend and I went down to see them. I had my horn with me; we'd just left rehearsal. As soon as I walked in, this guy runs up to me and says, 'Do you have a union card?' It was Dizzy. I didn't even know him. I said, 'Yeah, I have a union card.' 'We need a trumpet player. Come on.' I wanted to hear him; I could always read, so I got on the bandstand and started playing. I couldn't even read the music at first from listening to Dizzy and Bird. The third trumpet man was sick; I knew the book because I loved the music so much, so I played with the Eckstine band around St. Louis for about three weeks. After that I knew I had to go to New York."

After high school, Miles' mother wanted him to go to Fisk University. "You know how women are. She said

they had a good music department and the Fisk Jubilee
Singers. But I was looking in *Esquire's Jazz Book* and
seeing what was happening in jazz in New York, and
that's where I wanted to go. I got hold of my father,
and got permission to go to New York where I enrolled
at Juilliard."

For a week, Miles looked for Charlie Parker, spending his allowance in the search. He found him and moved
in with Bird. "I used to follow him around, down to 52nd
Street. 'Don't be afraid,' he used to tell me. 'Go ahead and
play.' Every night on matchbox covers I'd write down
chords I'd hear. Everybody helped me. Next day I'd
play those chords all day in the practice room at Juilliard,
instead of going to classes. Monk would write out his
chords and tunes for me. Tadd Dameron helped, as did
Dizzy, who advised me to study piano, and I did. I had
some background in understanding progressions from a
book I'd bought in St. Louis, *Georgia Gibbs Chord Analysis*. I finally left Juilliard. I realized I wasn't going to get
in any symphony orchestra. And I had to go down to the
street at night to play with Bird or Coleman Hawkins, so
I decided to go that way all the way."

Miles' close association with Charlie Parker was vital
to him musically. He learned by listening to Bird play,
almost never by hearing him discourse on theory. "He
never did talk about music. I always even had to show
Duke Jordan, the pianist in the band, the chords. The
only time I ever heard Bird talk about music was an
argument I had with him about the naming of chords.
That was the night Bird said you could do anything with
chords. And I disagreed. 'You can't play D natural in the
fifth bar of a B flat blues.' 'Yes, you can,' said Bird. Well,
one night in Birdland, I heard Lester Young do it, and it
sounded good. But he bent it."

"Bird used to play forty different styles," Miles told
a *Down Beat* interviewer. "He was never content to remain the same. I remember how at times he used to turn

the rhythm section around. Like we'd be playing the blues, and Bird would start on the eleventh bar, and as the rhythm sections stayed where they were and Bird played where he was, it sounded as if the rhythm section was on one and three instead of two and four. Every time that would happen, Max Roach used to scream at Duke Jordan not to follow Bird, but to stay where he was. Then, eventually, it came around as Bird had planned and we were together again. Bird used to make me play. He'd lead me up on the bandstand. I used to quit every night. The tempos were so fast, the challenge so great. I'd ask, 'What do you need *me* for?' "

Another musician who impressed Miles in his first years in New York was the late trumpeter, Freddie Webster. "I used to love what he did to a note. He didn't play a lot of notes; he didn't waste any. I used to try to get his sound. He had a great big tone, like Billy Butterfield, but without a vibrato. Freddie was my best friend. I wanted to play like him. I used to teach him chords, everything I learned at Juilliard. He didn't have the money to go. And in return, I'd try to get his tone."

Miles' career progressed through work with Parker, Benny Carter, the Eckstine band, and finally combos of his own. In the early 1950's, caught in the compulsion of heroin addiction, Miles worked infrequently. When he did play he was rawly inconsistent. His personality difficulties had become intensified; and, to avoid the mounting pressures, he tried not to care about anything.

It was after several months of exile in Detroit, an attempt at analysis, and experiencing the nadir of self-contempt that Miles began to re-establish his career. He has since consolidated his style, honing it to its present quality of probing lyricism.

When he had arrived in New York in 1945, Miles' tone and technique had been tentative; and he had been intimidated further by the weighty presence of Parker and the fact that Dizzy Gillespie was the prevailing influence on modern jazz trumpet at that time. Most of the acolytes tried to emulate Dizzy's fiercely careening, multinoted flights that usually reached their climax in the higher register of the horn. Miles, however, had never been able to play very high. When he was thirteen, he'd tried to play *Flight of the Bumble Bee* in the Harry James manner and found he couldn't. "I felt like I was breaking my head. Years later, I asked Dizzy, 'Why can't I play high like you?' 'Because you don't hear up there,' he said. 'You hear in the middle register.' And that's true. There are times when I can't even tell what chords Dizzy is working on when he's up high; and yet he'll tell me what he's playing is just an octave above what I do."

"Miles," notes a French musician, 'doesn't take you by storm like Dizzy. He's more insidious, more like somebody calling you from the other shore." Herbie Mann, a flute player, has explained that Miles, rather than any other flutist, was his primary inspiration when he started trying to make the flute a jazz instrument. "The attraction of Miles to me as a flutist was that he could be masculine, could communicate strong feeling with his horn and still be subtle and rarely sound beyond the volume level of the flute. He proved you don't have to yell and scream on your instrument to project feeling."

According to Gil Evans, "A big part of Miles' creative gift is in the creation of sound. He arrived at a time when, because of the innovations of modern jazz, all new players had to find their own sound in relation to the new modes of expression. Miles, for example, couldn't play like Louis Armstrong because that sound would interfere with his thoughts. Miles had to start with almost no sound and then develop one as he went along, a sound suitable for the ideas he wanted to express. Finally, he had his own basic sound which any player must develop. But many players then keep this sound more or less constant. Any variation in their work comes in the actual selection of notes, their harmonic patterns and their rhythmic usages. Miles, however, is aware of his complete surroundings and takes advantage of the wide range of sound possibilities that exist even in one's basic sound. He can, in other words, create a particular sound for the existing context. The quality of a certain chord, its tension or lack of tension, can cause him to create a sound appropriate to it. He can put his own substance, his own flesh on a note and then put that note exactly where it belongs."

It was with Evans as the dominating influence and young writer-players Gerry Mulligan, John Lewis and others assisting that Miles assembled an influential nine-piece unit for a series of Capitol recordings in 1949-1950 (now available in *Birth of the Cool*, Capitol T 762). These recordings, more than any other single event, shaped the growing active movement in modern jazz toward carefully integrated "chamber" groups. The Davis Capitol sessions helped establish in the consciousness of many modern jazzmen, here and abroad, an unprecedentedly challenging realization of the subtle possibilities of group dynamics and group expression as a whole in which the solos are a flowing part of the entire texture and structure of the work. The records illustrated further how much more colorful the background textures for jazz improvising could become.

Davis has continued to suggest other directions in modern jazz. He has also prospered, but unlike many jazzmen who begin to achieve relatively wide success, he refuses to adhere to the usual rules for celebrities in any field. With very few exceptions, he will not do radio interviews and will not make guest appearances on local television programs for scale to help advertise the club in which he's appearing. First of all, he feels that he's paid for playing and is entitled to spend the rest of his time his own way. Also, he believes that "people either like what you're doing or they don't. If they don't, I'll know it, and no amount of publicity is going to help."

Although often surfacely churlish, Davis often helps younger players with advice and sometimes gets them jobs. As a leader, he is not a strict disciplinarian, taking care to hire only musicians whom he likes personally. He does let a sideman know if he disapproves of a particular way of playing; but in terms of such infractions as being late on the job, Davis is a permissive employer. He rarely rehearses his band, depending on the constant contact between his sidemen and himself on a job to develop the cohesiveness that any jazz unit must have to sustain attention.

Davis has a rare capacity to fuse a unit into an organically integrated whole. Because the performances of his groups often consist of long solos by the sidemen with only rhythm backing and because Davis himself often strolls offstand during a number, some listeners form an impression of a disorganized band. Davis' combos, for all the freedom he gives his sidemen, unmistakably reflect his musical ideas and personality. There is a noticeable difference between a Davis combo with the leader present and the same men if Davis has gone home before the last set.

Davis is less annoyed than many other jazzmen by noisy night club audiences. "I figure if they're missing what Philly Joe Jones is doing, it's their tough luck. I wouldn't like to sit up there and play without anybody liking it, but I just mainly enjoy playing with my own rhythm section and listening to them. The night clubs are all the same to me. All you do is go in and play and go home. I never do know what people mean when they talk about acoustics. All I try to do is get my sound— full and round. It's a challenge to play in different clubs, to learn how to regulate your blowing to the club."

"Miles has changed much in the past few years," says an old European friend. "He has become more master of himself. He knows what he wants to express, and he expresses it well, with control."

"I'll tell you," says Miles with a grin, "if I can play good for eight bars, it's enough for me. It's satisfaction. The only thing is," he puts his finger on his nose, "I don't tell anybody which eight bars are the good ones. That's my secret."

Ornette Coleman

Few forms of twentieth-century music change as rapidly as jazz. "I don't want time to pass me, and go ahead, and wake up someday and I'm old-fashioned," worries Philly Joe Jones, one of the most modern of drummers. "I'm already old hat," Gerry Mulligan says half-seriously. "There's another generation coming along." Only twenty years separated the radical influences of Louis Armstrong and Charlie Parker, but the period in between was filled with constantly shifting and widening perspectives. Similarly, the past fifteen years have also been marked by constant straining at new conventions despite the increasing entrenchment of the newest neo-orthodoxy. Indications now are that the next decade may bring the most organic changes in jazz since the advent of Charlie Parker, Thelonious Monk and other early modernists.

The two major areas for change are, of course, in jazz improvisation and composition. Among the improvisers, it appears clear there will be increasing emphasis, as Sonny Rollins has indicated, on thematic improvisation rather than just "running the changes" (improvising on the chords) of a tune. Eventually, as has already occurred in several contemporary developments in classical music, the melody itself will more and more determine the chord changes. Asymmetrical phrasing, as in the work of Thelonious Monk, will become more daring and unpredictable. The refusal to be limited to symmetrically constructed solos was begun most importantly by the late Lester Young, whose improvised lines flowed through the previously orthodox two- and four-bar divisions.

Charlie Parker, Dizzy Gillespie, and their colleagues went farther, "sending their solo lines," as British critic Mike Butcher noted, "cutting straight through the conventional divisions of a chorus, bridging 'first eight' [bars] and 'second eight' [bars] with an unbroken string of notes, then unexpectedly breaking the string when the average listener would have expected it to continue." Now there are Monk, Sonny Rollins, John Coltrane, Ornette Coleman, Cecil Taylor, and others, who are even freer in their linear designs.

Harmonically, tenor saxophonist John Coltrane (formerly with Miles Davis and now leader of his own group) is influencing many players to improvise on more complex chordal combinations. "I feel," he explains, "like I can't hear but so much in the ordinary chords we usually have going in the accompaniment. I just have to have more of a blueprint." His former employer, Miles Davis, points out: "What Coltrane does, for one example, is to play five notes of a chord and then keep changing it around, trying to see how many different ways it can sound." Coltrane, however, is also concerned with making his development a *total* one. "I know," he says, "where I want to go harmonically, but now I have to work out a melodic and rhythmic conception that ties in with my harmonic conception." In short, the younger musicians increasingly realize that changes in their style have to occur in all three divisions of the music—harmony, melody and rhythm—or else a lopsidedness results.

As for the jazz rhythm section, critic Martin Williams is correct in noting that "since the bop revolution the rhythmic lead in jazz has been carried by the bass. Bop also released the drummer's right foot, left hand, the pianist's left hand, and did away with rhythm guitar. At the same time, both drums and piano began to take on a polyrhythmic-melodic function which swing percussion had largely minimized and simplified over that of previous jazz. . . . The basic beat in future jazz will be carried by the bass; the drummer . . . will be free to provide a separate percussive line, a complex counter-rhythmic pattern. . . . Imagine the release in the music. Those who complain that even the most varied jazz drumming is monotonous are difficult to answer. But when the basic rhythm is passed to an instrument that is both melodic and rhythmic in one, and the drummer completely released, the problem will be solved." Williams cites bassist Charlie Mingus who "can be a virtuoso soloist, but perhaps more important is his striking ability to maintain a beat firmly and clearly while providing a polyphonic line behind the soloist as well."

Jazz writing is obviously going to become more and more important. The writer of original jazz compositions that in turn become standards in the field has so far been relatively rare. The major indigenous jazz composers over the past sixty years have been Jelly Roll Morton, Duke Ellington, and Thelonious Monk. More recently, John Lewis, Charlie Mingus, and George Russell have developed into important writers. Also indicating considerable potential is trombonist J. J. Johnson, while Horace Silver is the young dean of the limited "funky" school of modern jazz writing. These writers, except in part for John Lewis, have developed nearly all their basic forms from within the jazz language rather than trying to graft onto jazz devices and forms borrowed from classical music. Even Lewis, as previously noted, although he uses fugues and other European forms as frameworks for improvisation, has always transmuted them into jazz terms. Moreover, Lewis constantly changes the formal structure of his compositions as he and the other members of the Modern Jazz Quartet feel the need to express changing emotions through the work.

The goal of most jazz writing is to achieve what Duke Ellington has done in his most successful compositions. Francis Newton of the *New Statesman* has described the Ellington accomplishment as music "which is *both* created by the players *and* fully shaped by the composer." In other terms, the aim is to keep the music —the written as well as the improvised sections—*sounding* spontaneous.

In an essay on this subject in *The Jazz Word* (Ballantine, 1960), jazz composer George Russell notes that a composer may "write an idea that will sound so *improvised* it might influence improvisers to play something that they have never played before." Russell added that in his Decca album, *New York, N.Y.*, he tried "to force the soloist into polymodality. I gave him symbols, which, when superimposed upon the music that's happening under it, create a pan-tonal sort of effect. So I speak to the soloist in terms of his familiar symbols, but, as I like to say—you have to fool the soloist into playing *out*." Concerning jazz writing of the future, Russell believes that many different meters will be increasingly used in a single work and that harmonically, "jazz will by-pass atonality because jazz actually has its roots in folk music, and folk music is scale-based music; and atonality negates the scale. I think jazz will be intensely chromatic; but you can be chromatic and not be atonal." Other writers disagree, and in the fall of 1960, an atonal jazz unit began rehearsing in New York.

As important as written jazz is becoming, it's reasonably safe to predict that at the core of future changes in jazz will be, as before, the improvising soloist. The newest example of muttering, grudging reappraisal in

H

the Establishment forced by an unprecedented soloist
is the shotgun impact on the jazz life of alto saxophonist
Ornette Coleman.

Michael Frayne, a *Manchester Guardian* reporter,
wandered innocently into the Coleman wars toward the
end of 1959. Frayne wrote from New York's Five Spot,
where Coleman opened in November of that year and
played for much of the first half of 1960: "Ornette Coleman's quartet was making the most extraordinary noises,
far out on some limb of its own. A famous English dramatic critic sitting about two feet in front of Mr. Coleman's deeply disturbed saxophone shouted to me, 'I think
they have gone too far.' I think perhaps they had."

The drama critic was Kenneth Tynan, who is usually
receptive to avant-garde activists. A few months later, an
equally intelligent British observer, Francis Newton,
came through New York on his way to a summer of teaching at Stamford. He wrote of Coleman in the *New Statesman:* "The far-out boys do him an injustice by insisting
on the revolutionary character of the sounds which, in
defiance of all the rules of all musical games, he produces
out of his plastic alto-sax, and which can only be described in words which carry unwanted overtones of
depreciation: squeaking, neighing, honking and such-
like. Widening the technical range of an instrument is not
enough to make a player more than a freak. The unfor-
gettable thing about this very dark, soft-handed man playing with a vertical fold over his nose, is the passion with
which he blows. I have heard nothing like it in modern
jazz since Parker. He can and does play the chorus of a
standard straight—with an intense . . . lamenting feeling
for the blues which lays this critic flat on his back."

Most jazz musicians were not so ready to be blown
down. For months, grimly skeptical jazzmen lined up at
the Five Spot's bar. They made fun of Coleman but were
naggingly worried that he might, after all, have something to say—and in a new way. The new orthodoxy is

easily scared. Even some of the most venturesome heretics, for that matter, are not immune to worry about fading popularity. The controversial tenor saxophonist Sonny Rollins, at first criticized by writers and the jazz public for his often jarring tone and, to them, difficult thematic improvisations, finally began to win some polls and was booked on fairly lucrative club and festival dates. Then John Coltrane, an even more controversial tenor with an even harsher tone and more complex (this time, harmonically) style, began to upset the firmament. Toward the end of 1959, Sonny disappeared. He may well have had other personal reasons for going into temporary retirement, but he did say, on one of his few nights on the scene in recent months, that he was practicing a yet more challenging advance in his style. "I guess," said another musician, "that John just drove Sonny back into the woodshed." "Sonny," says pianist Billy Taylor, "takes what's written and said about him too seriously. He used to feel that accordingly he had a larger obligation than he could fulfill. He'd come off the stand fuming, after what I'd thought was a very good set, because he felt he hadn't sustained his ideas well enough or communicated deeply enough with the other guys in the band or with the audience."

Coleman arrived soon after Rollins disappeared. He had made a couple of albums on the coast before he came to the Five Spot. Appearing opposite his quartet was a band prototypical of the best of the new orthodoxy. The co-leaders were Art Farmer, a warm, lyrical, inventively melodic trumpet player, and Benny Golson, one of the most consistently skillful writers of indigenous jazz compositions, though less impressive as a tenor soloist. Yet, in contrast to Coleman's marauders, the Golson-Farmer Jazztet resembled a meeting of the Young Republican Club or the ADA in contrast to Ammon Hennacy of the *Catholic Worker* or Woody Guthrie. After the first set, a member of the Jazztet, a capable and clearly

maturing musician, said mournfully, "Well, I guess I'm
out-of-date now."

The worried musicians watching at the Five Spot in
the following weeks saw with mounting envy the space
that Coleman was getting in the general as well as the
music press, including even the small distinction of being
asked to write a column (actually ghosted by the Five
Spot's press agent) for the vacationing Dorothy Kilgallen.
A *Newsweek* summary of modern jazz had begun with
an impressionistically inaccurate description of Coleman's sound: "The deep bass voice of the alto sax rum-
bled darkly, then picked up steam as if driven by the
ferocious intensity of the man at the mouthpiece."

"Some research staff," commented a Five Spot reg
lar. "By them I suppose a piccolo would sound like a
baritone."

The older jazzmen, traditionally suspicious of the
credentials of the modernists, have been further convinced by Coleman that nearly all modern jazz must now
be a shell game. "If that's music," said one, "I've been
doing something else all my life."

Trumpeter Roy Eldridge, who conscientiously tries to
solve any jazz problems that puzzle him, visited the Five
Spot several times to examine the plastic phenomenon.
"I listened to him all kinds of ways," Eldridge told a
friend. "I listened to him high and I listened to him cold
sober. I even played with him. I think he's jiving, baby.
He's putting everybody on. They start with a nice lead-off
figure, but then they go off into outer space. They dis-
regard the chords and they play odd numbers of bars.
I can't follow them. I even listened to him with Paul
Chambers, Miles Davis' bass player. 'You're younger
than me,' I said to him. 'Can you follow Ornette?' Paul
said he couldn't either."

Coleman Hawkins, a jazz patriarch, has always been
sympathetic to experimenters and gave Thelonious Monk
and Dizzy Gillespie work when others of his generation

hooted at them. "Now, you know," Hawkins says of Ornette Coleman, "that I never like to criticize anyone publicly. Just say I think he needs seasoning. A lot of seasoning." Pianist Red Garland is more blunt: "Nothing's happening. I wouldn't mind if he were serious. I like to see a struggling cat get a break. But Coleman is faking. He's being very unfair to the public. What surprises me is that he fooled someone like John Lewis."

Miles Davis, Red Garland's former employer, believes that Garland is jealous. "I like Ornette," says Davis, "because he doesn't play clichés." Pianist-teacher-critic John Mehegan was at first one of the most alarmed of the early Coleman opponents. Mehegan has since calmed down somewhat: "Ornette Coleman simply isn't playing jazz. He's an excellent performer and he knows his instrument, but what he plays is something else. There are kids all over Long Island and New Jersey— and I presume elsewhere in the country—trying to imitate Ornette. Their attitude is, 'I'll play anything I want to; you do the same thing; and we'll see what happens.' That's not the way music is made."

One result of the spreading Coleman debate was that his recordings began to sell. His first two albums were for Contemporary, a Los Angeles-based label, and had small sales. His next and considerably better two for Atlantic, however, had sold over 25,000 by September, 1960, most of them since June of that year. In the jazz field, sales of five to seven thousand still constitute a fairly respectable figure for a single album, particularly by so unorthodoxly challenging a player as Coleman.

Ahmet Ertegun, an Atlantic official, is a unique combination of elegance and expertise in jazz and rhythm and blues. The sophisticated, precisely bearded son of a former Turkish diplomat is better know at El Morocco than the Five Spot, but he has become one of the more voluble Coleman apostles. "I must tell you," says Ertegun earnestly, "that at first I thought Ornette was jiving.

Now, I play his records all the time. I dig his sound *so* much. He has that wild, brash quality the first Charlie Parker recordings contained. In a way, he's much rougher than Parker; but in those days, Parker too sounded rough in comparison to Johnny Hodges and Benny Carter. Now, I must caution you that Coleman doesn't play anything immediately recognizable, and that's why you have to get the feeling of the whole performance when you listen to him. I dig him so much now that I don't care if he *is* jiving."

Mr. Coleman, more perplexed than perturbed by the brouhaha he has caused, insists he is not jiving in the least. Slight, shy but stubborn, Coleman is inordinately patient with his attackers. He has yet to answer his critics with the slightest touch of malice or rancor. I've seen him during a time when he was completely unknown and spent much of his energy trying to invent the month's rent, and I've seen him often during his recent months of turbulent success. There has been no change in his soft-spoken deliberateness of speech or in his implacable self-confidence. Coleman is not at all arrogant, but he does communicate a strength of conviction similar in doggedness to that of an African nationalist or Senator Barry Goldwater.

Long interested in various forms of redemptive religion, Coleman speaks of "love" in much the same diffuse but incandescent way as a successful cult leader. In the winter of 1960, during a stay in Chicago, Coleman's curiosity led him to attend a convention of Elijah Muhammad's Temples of Islam, a racist movement of Negro Muslims. Their leader warns them against trusting any whites and intends, he says, to demand that the government give his followers several of the United States in compensation for 250 years of slavery so that he can form a separate state. Coleman listened to the speeches, observed the Muslims, and noted: "I don't see why I should follow what they say when they're not cooled out themselves. I could hardly play for all the hate around me."

For all his faith in his musical mission and his refusal to strike back at those musicians who mock him—although he's hit his own trumpet player—Coleman does occasionally become depressed at the naked hostility his music has provoked. Until he came to New York and the Five Spot, he had known exceedingly hard times but worse than the worry about money was the acutely disheartening experience of seeing musicians walk off the stand when he appeared at jam sessions.

"When I arrived in New York," Coleman says, "I was surprised that most musicians here too treated me the same way as the ones in California where I'd been for several years. I thought they were more serious in New York. The main support I've gotten here has been from John Lewis; J. J. Johnson; George Russell, the jazz composer; and Gunther Schuller, a classical composer who sometimes writes jazz pieces. But from most of the jazz musicians, all I got was a wall of hostility. They *had* to listen because what we do automatically catches your ear, but I could feel their anger. I guess it's pretty shocking to hear someone like me come on the scene when they're already comfortable in Charlie Parker's language. They figure that now they may have to learn something else."

Buel Neidlinger, a young bassist who played opposite Coleman in another combo at the Five Spot, agrees with Coleman's analysis of the situation. "Those musicians were standing at the bar scared to death Ornette was going to be the thing and that they couldn't make it."

Coleman meanwhile has achieved a vogue among several of the upper-echelon classical composers and musicians. Virgil Thomson, who had said in conversation three years ago that he was not aware that anything significant in jazz had occurred since Louis Armstrong, finds Coleman strikingly impressive. "He's *hot*," said Mr. Thomson, "and he gets an extraordinarily imperious tone on his instrument!" Marc Blitzstein is another Coleman adherent, and the most boisterous Coleman supporter among the "serious" musicians is Leonard Bernstein. Coleman, a shy man, was startled one evening at the Five Spot to see Bernstein lunge at him after a set, roar, "You're a genius!" and lead him to his table. Bernstein later invited Coleman to Carnegie Hall to hear what *he* was doing on the modern jazz scene, a performance of Howard Brubeck's arid *Dialogues for Jazz Combo and Orchestra* with the quartet of Dave Brubeck (a brother of Howard) and the New York Philharmonic. Coleman was bored by the music, and was stunned by the scenes of homage in the Green Room where Bernstein receives visitors after the concert. Ornette, having finally glimpsed the inside world of "serious" music, left as unobtrusively—and quickly— as he could. I would guess, however, that most members of the new orthodoxy would have stayed, hoping also to be invited again.

"Anyway," Coleman notes with satisfaction, "the people seem to like my music. We never did have a night at the Five Spot with a cold audience. A listener need have no trouble with what we do if he reacts only to what he actually hears and what he feels as we're playing. Some people get so involved in trying to figure out what we're doing that they don't pay attention to their emotions." In an interview with Whitney Balliett of *The New Yorker,* Coleman expanded on the point: "Most people fail to hear what is being played at the moment it is played. They pay more attention to behavior and what they see rather than to what is happening musically."

It has been a novel experience for Coleman to have had a chance to reach an audience. His stay at the Five Spot was the first extended engagement as a leader he'd ever had anywhere except Fort Worth. For that chance,

Coleman has had to wait much longer than it normally takes a jazz musician to reach at least the first plateau of acceptance. Despite the widening audience for jazz, the apprentice still does have to "pay dues" for a considerable length of time, but no contemporary I know of has had to pay as much dues as Coleman or travel so circuitous and seemingly hopeless a route to his first job.

Coleman was born on March 9, 1930, in Fort Worth, Texas. His father died when Ornette was about seven, and his mother did domestic work. An elder sister, Truvenza, became a singer and now heads her own band in Fort Worth. A major influence and goad in Ornette's early attempts at music was a cousin, James Jordan, who played alto and baritone saxophones and had been formally trained. In contrast to the careful Jordan who, as Coleman recalls, "had to know exactly what a thing was all about before he did it," Coleman was self-taught and awkward. "I always wanted to earn respect from Jordan because he went to school, and I didn't." Recently Jordan, who is working for a master's degree, took an Ornette Coleman album to class so that it could be analyzed. A Coleman dream of glory had been fulfilled.

Coleman was not only self-taught but he was an inaccurate teacher. He misinterpreted an instruction book he'd bought and believed the low C on his horn was the A in the book. Finally, when he joined a church band, the leader said scornfully, "Look at this boy. Playing the instrument wrong for two years. He'll never be a saxophone player."

Coleman had bought his own alto saxophone in 1944, but switched to tenor two years later because more jobs were open for the heavier, more aggressive-sounding tenor. "At first, I used to be one of those people like Big Jay McNeeley," Coleman admits with embarrassment. "I'd lie on the floor and play and do all those other gimmicks." But Coleman was also listening intently to a local musician—Red Conner, an alto saxophonist, whom

Coleman claims was more inventive than Charlie Parker. "Red died young. He died of several different things. He lived a jazzman's life, and in the late 1930's and early 1940's, that was really a night-time life. It was listening to Red and his group when I was a kid that made me feel ashamed of myself. They were really playing *music*. I was getting all the praise around town, but I wasn't making any contribution."

Conner, according to Coleman, did not influence his style so much as he did his respect for jazz. "No one ever really influenced me fundamentally, although I did listen to many players. I liked Jimmy Dorsey, Pete Brown, Lester Young, Charlie Parker, and many others. I've always been able to play exactly like anyone I've ever liked, but fortunately, I found out pretty early that I could also play myself."

In 1949, Coleman went on the road. Two months after the journey began, Ornette was fired in Natchez, Mississippi. He had tried to teach a jazz number to the other tenor in the combo, and the latter complained to the leader that a subversive in the band was trying to make a "bebopper" out of him. Not wanting his men contaminated, the leader cashiered Coleman. While in Natchez, Coleman made a tape for a local record company, but never heard it or found out what had happened to it. "The police department ran me out of town. I told them I was from Texas, but they thought I was from the North. I was just sitting in a place eating one day, and they said I had to leave."

The Natchez police had seen a Negro with long hair and a long beard, two marks of non-conformity not likely to reassure a southern cop. "I looked that way then," Coleman explains, "because I was so determined not to be commercial that I tried to look as well as play as uncommercially as possible." Coleman went on to New Orleans where he joined a rhythm and blues band that toured the surrounding area.

While in New Orleans, Coleman was invited to Baton Rouge one night by a group of local Negroes who said they wanted to meet him. As soon as Coleman arrived, six men—each larger than the slim Coleman—leaped on him, broke several teeth, kicked him, bent his tenor and threw it away. Coleman limped to the police to file a complaint. "The police said that if the niggers didn't get through killing me, they would. So I left." Coleman believes the beating took place because a number of Baton Rouge men had seen their girls follow previous rhythm and blues musicians out of town. "They had some bad experiences with musicians, and I guess they wanted to make an example of me. It didn't turn me bitter. I figured if they'd really known me, they wouldn't have done it."

Ornette stayed in New Orleans for nearly a year, playing occasionally at night and doing yard work and other laboring jobs during the day. Having left his twisted tenor in Baton Rouge, Coleman returned to the alto. He also went back to Fort Worth toward the end of 1950. Coleman then joined Pee Wee Crayton's touring rhythm and blues band but was stranded in Los Angeles because Crayton was appalled by the bearded altoist's sound and style. "We'd worked around ten one-nighters when Crayton told me, 'You don't have to play tonight. I'll pay you anyway.' The next night I left."

In Los Angeles, Coleman became a house boy. "A wonderful middle-aged lady let me rent out the back part of a converted garage. There was no heat, but at least it was a place to stay. I took care of the kids—she ran a little nursery—cleaned the kitchen, and did other odd jobs.

Coleman started to go to sessions. Having very little money, he would walk the long distance to the Negro section of Los Angeles. After one such walk, he tried to sit in with tenor saxophonist Dexter Gordon, a musician who at that time was influencing many young players. "He made me stop playing, and get off the stand. I had

no money left, so I walked all the way home again in
the rain. That sort of thing happened a lot. Some musicians would promise me I could play but they'd keep me
waiting all night. Then, with the place due to close at
two in the morning, they'd put me on at three minutes to
two. I was getting discouraged. They said I didn't know
the changes and was out of tune, but I knew that wasn't
so. But something, I thought, must be wrong. I didn't
know what."

During much of his first Los Angeles period, Coleman had to play on a rented horn. His own had collapsed.
When the rented alto was taken back, he had no instrument at all. Finally, he decided to go back to Fort Worth
and stayed from 1952 to 1954. There at least he had
an audience. "I got a horn and formed my own band.
We played what the people liked, but I wasn't playing
the way I wanted to." Coleman tried Los Angeles again.
He worked at Bullock's department store for several
years, first as an elevator operator and then as a stock
boy.

Coleman had continued teaching himself music
theory. The only music lesson he'd ever had was given
him in New York during a brief visit he made there
when he was fifteen. He was staying with an aunt who
was then married to jazz trumpeter Doc Cheatham.
Cheatham brought the youngster to Walter "Foots"
Thomas, a big band veteran. "It seemed I made a lot of
faces when I played. Thomas had me look into the mirror
and play for an hour. That was my lesson."

While he was an elevator operator at Bullock's, Coleman continued his more serious musical education, bringing several books on music theory to work. "I used to
go up to the tenth floor, park there, and read the books."
Automation came to Bullock's, and Coleman lost his
study hall. At jam sessions meanwhile Coleman was still
unwelcome. There was little more encouragement at
home. Coleman had married a California girl who was

thoroughly oriented in modern jazz and played 'cello as well. She was not, however, convinced that her husband was leading a new wave of significance. "My wife would start in, 'People say you're crazy,' and she sounded as if she agreed. By then, however, I'd made up my mind I was right. After all, the musicians who were putting me down were playing things I'd known about ten years before. I was only trying to be better, and they didn't like me because I was trying things that were different from what they were used to."

Coleman finally met a few young musicians who were intrigued by his message. Don Cherry, a trumpet player from Oklahoma, had grown up in Los Angeles. He had first met Coleman in a music store in Watts, California. "Ornette was buying the thickest reed you can get. He still had long hair and a beard. Although it was about 90 degrees, he had an overcoat on. I was scared of him." After the fright wore off, Cherry became a disciple, and is still with Coleman's quartet. Bassist Don Payne had been born in Texas but grew up in California. He too became a fervent convert. It was at Payne's apartment in 1958 that Red Mitchell, an established bassist, heard a composition by Coleman. Mitchell advised Coleman, who needed money badly, to take the tune to Lester Koenig, owner of Contemporary Records, on the chance that Koenig might suggest to one of his contract players that he use it on a date. It was inconceivable to Mitchell or Coleman that Koenig would decide to ask Coleman himself to make an album.

Koenig described his initial interview with Coleman to John Tynan, a *Down Beat* reporter, who was the first critic to recognize Coleman's potential: "I took him to the piano and asked him to play the tunes. Ornette then said he couldn't *play* the piano. Then I asked him 'How did you hope to play your tunes for me if you can't play piano?' So he took out his plastic alto and began to play." Koenig was as impressed by the playing as by Coleman's characteristically bold, angular originals. He set up the first of two albums Coleman was to do for Contemporary (*Something Else!!!*, 3551; *Tomorrow is the Question*, 3569, stereo 7569).

At the time he went to see Koenig, Coleman had exhausted nearly all of his emotional, let alone financial resources. "I was going to give up my music and go back to Fort Worth. I wanted to live a normal life again." Not much happened to encourage Coleman after the Contemporary album, but some work did come in, including a stay in San Francisco. More important than the intermittent jobs was the fact that Don Payne brought Percy Heath, bassist with the Modern Jazz Quartet, to hear Coleman. "I jammed with him," Percy remembers. "It sounded strange but it felt very good, and it felt fresh. I don't say I understood it, but it was exciting and that's one quality jazz has to have. But believe me, those guys were starving then, and musicians were still walking off the stand when Ornette came in."

Heath brought John Lewis, musical director of the Modern Jazz Quartet, to hear Coleman. Lewis was the next major factor in accelerating Coleman's career. A man rarely given to unfettered enthusiasm, Lewis told an interviewer in June, 1959: "I've never heard anything like Ornette Coleman and Don Cherry before. Ornette is, in a sense, an extension of Charlie Parker—the first I've heard. This is the real need . . . to extend the basic ideas of Bird until they're not playing an imitation but actually something new."

Lewis made arrangements for Coleman and Don Cherry to become students at the School of Jazz at Lenox, Massachusetts for the 1959 semester. The money was put up by Atlantic records, the company that records the Modern Jazz Quartet. Nesuhi Ertegen, Ahmet's brother and in charge of jazz at the company, signed Coleman, largely on Lewis' recommendation. Les Koenig of Contemporary reluctantly let Coleman go. "We just couldn't support him here in Los Angeles. There was no place for the group to work."

There was some dissension among faculty members at the School of Jazz concerning Coleman's worth. Trombonist-arranger Bob Brookmeyer at first was angered by what he regarded as Coleman's gratuitous formlessness. Brookmeyer is now an admirer. "What can I say? I kept on listening, and now he gives me great pleasure. It was a lesson for me on quick judgements." Other faculty members, led by Lewis, Max Roach and George Russell, were strongly impressed by Coleman from the start.

Coleman and his principal adviser, John Lewis, realized that Coleman now had to base himself in New York if his career were to grow. Coleman took half his advance for his first Atlantic album to transport his men to New York from Los Angeles. He also had to borrow $72 from each of his three sidemen to complete the fare. (His first two Atlantic sets are *The Shape of Jazz to Come*, 1317, S-1317 and *Change of the Century*, 1327, S-1327.)

The guerrilla warfare began as soon as Coleman opened at the Five Spot that November. For every musician, such as John Coltrane, who asked to meet Coleman during the day so that he could understand his musical tenets more thoroughly, there were ten who were scornful. Significantly, most of the more thoughtful and original jazzmen reserved their opinions. *Time*, with its music department's customary inaccuracy in jazz matters, quoted Dizzy Gillespie as asking rhetorically, "Are they kidding?" Gillespie, however, recalls: "I never said no such thing. I don't claim to know what they're doing. I've been traveling so much myself that I've hardly had a chance to hear them. But I do know Ornette is a serious musician, and he's not jiving. We're going to get together at my house as soon as I'm back in town for a while so that I can really get to understand what's happening."

Charles Mingus is not fully convinced that Coleman

knows where he's going, but he told a *Down Beat* ques-
tioner: ". . . The fact remains that his notes and lines are
so fresh. . . . I'm not saying that everybody's going to
have to play like Coleman. But they're going to have to
stop copying Bird. . . . You can't put your finger on
what he's doing . . . [but] it gets to you emotionally."

The most lucid description of what Coleman is, in
fact, doing has come from critic Martin Williams, Coleman's leading critical interpreter. Coleman has been
criticized principally for his tone, which is often pierc-
ingly harsh; the fact that his improvisations seem to have
little connection with the chords underneath his starting
line; and his often unpredictable, extremely asymmetrical phrasing. Arranger Quincy Jones, for example, while
conceding that Coleman was no fraud, was doubtful if
Coleman were a major prophet. He made all the above
criticisms and talked of Coleman's "occasional incoher-
ence." Martin Williams, however, in his notes for *The
Shape of Jazz to Come*, explained:

"What he has done is, like all valid innovations,
basically simple, authentic, and inevitable. . . . The basis
of it is this: if you put a conventional chord under my
note, you limit the number of choices I have for my
next note; if you do not, my melody may move freely in a
far greater choice of directions. . . . This does not mean
that his music is 'a-harmonic' as is the music of a 'country'
blues singer . . . nor that he invited disorder. He can
work through and beyond the furthest intervals of the
chords. . . . As several developments in jazz in the last
few years have shown, no one really needs to state all
those chords that nearly everyone uses, and as some
events have shown, if someone does state them or if a
soloist implies them, he may end up with a harassed
running up and down scales at those 'advanced' intervals
like a rat in a harmonic maze. Someone had to break
through the walls that those harmonies have built, and
restore melody. . . . Like the important innovators in jazz,

Coleman maintains an innate balance among rhythm and harmony and melodic line. In jazz, these are really an identity, and any change in one of them without intrinsic reshuffling of the others inevitably risks failure. Further, he works in terms of developing the specific, implicit resources of jazz, not by wholesale importations from concert music. . . . To say . . . that his solos . . . do not have a relationship to his melodies is quite wrong. As a matter of fact, most jazz solos are not related to their theme-melodies, but to the chords with which the themes are harmonized. Coleman and Cherry may relate to the emotion, the pitch, the rhythm, the melody of a theme, without relating to 'chords' or bar divisions. To a listener such relationships can have even more meaning than the usual harmonic ones."

Coleman himself is quite verbal about his work, and the motif of *pitch,* of wanting his horn to sound as much as possible like the human voice, runs through much of what he says. "There are some intervals," he observes, "that carry that *human* quality if you play them in the right pitch. You can reach into the human sound of a voice on your horn if you're actually hearing and trying to express the warmth of a human voice."

Coleman adds that he always writes the melody line first, because several different chords can fit the same melody line. "In fact, I would prefer it if musicians would play my tunes with different changes as they take a new chorus so that there would be all the more variety in the performance. I would also like the rhythm section to be as free as I'm trying to get, but very few players so far—on horns or rhythm instruments—can do this yet. Thelonious Monk is free in many respects. He sometimes plays one note, and because he plays it in exactly the right pitch, he carries more music in it than if he had filled out the chord. Monk can also play different rhythm patterns; and my drummer, Edward Blackwell, can also play all kinds of time."

"You know," Coleman said in a *Metronome* magazine panel discussion, "my music doesn't have any real
time, no metric time. It has time, but not in the sense
that you can time it. It's more like breathing—a natural,
freer time. People have forgotten how beautiful it is to
be natural. Even in love . . . I like spread rhythm, rhythm
that has a lot of freedom in it, rather than the more
conventional, *netted* rhythm. With spread rhythm, you
might tap your feet awhile, then stop, then later start
tapping again. That's what I like. Otherwise, you tap
your feet so much, you forget what you hear. You just
hear the rhythm."

Coleman is continually stretching the possibilities of
each player's freedom to improvise, even collectively. "If
I don't set a pattern at a given moment, whoever has
the dominant ear at that moment can take and do a
thing that will change the direction. The drums can
help determine direction too. Certain phrases I start
to play with Blackwell suddenly seem backward to me
because he can turn them around on a different beat,
thereby increasing the freedom of my playing. Our group
does not begin with a preconceived notion as to what
kind of effect we will achieve. When we record, sometimes I can hardly believe that what I hear when the
tape is played back is the playing of my group. I want
the members of my group to play what they hear in the
piece for themselves."

Drummer Shelly Manne worked on Coleman's second
Contemporary album, and says of the altoist: "He sounds
like a person crying or a person laughing when he plays.
And he makes *me* want to laugh and cry. The real great
traditional jazz players will do those things to you.
Although he may be flying all over the horn and doing
weird things metrically, the basic feelings are still there.
And when you're working with him, he makes you listen
so hard to what he's doing that he makes you play a
whole other way. When I worked on his session, I didn't

feel I was playing a song as much as that I was really playing *with* a person. And somehow I became more of a person in my own playing. He made me freer."

"Music," Coleman summarizes his credo, "is for our feelings. I think jazz should try to express more kinds of feelings than it has up to now."

Coleman is also lucid in explaining his fondness for the small, white, plastic alto saxophone that has become his hallmark. The plastic alto has served as a target for attacks on Coleman by several writers who lack the ability to criticize the music on its own terms.

"I bought it in Los Angeles in 1954," Coleman recalls. "I needed a new horn badly but I didn't have much money. A man in the music store said he could sell me a new horn—a plastic model—for the price of a used Selmer. I didn't like it at first, but I figured it would be better to have a new horn anyway. Now I won't play any other. They're made in England, and I have to send for them. They're only good for a year the way I play them. The plastic horn is better for me because it responds more completely to the way I blow into it. There's less resistance than from metal. Also, the notes seem to come out detached, almost like you could see them. What I mean is that notes from a metal instrument include the sounds the metal itself makes when it vibrates. The notes from a plastic horn are purer. In addition, the body of the horn is made flat, like a flute keyboard, whereas a regular horn is curved. On a flat keyboard, I can dig in more."

In his customary pragmatic manner, Coleman makes his own repairs, and is one of the relatively few saxophonists who can take his horn apart and put it together again.

Although Coleman—with his plastic alto—has been working steadily for a year and has received unprecedented press attention, the big money hasn't come yet. He had been playing at the Five Spot for six months

before he was granted a raise of $32 a week. By the end
of July, 1960, Coleman was being paid $682 for four men
for a six-day week. In the winter of 1960, he went on the
road briefly for $850 a week; for his tour in the fall of
1960, his price had gone up to between $1100 and $1250
a week.

Coleman has already recorded enough material for
several more Atlantic albums. "In July, 1960," he says with
satisfaction, "we did thirty tunes in three weeks. All
originals. Everything I've ever recorded has been a piece
of my own. Until I heard these last tapes, I hadn't
realized all the different approaches we'd been developing in the past few months. I think the new albums
will give the public and the musicians a more accurate
idea of what we're trying to do. In some of them, we put
what would usually be regarded as the theme in the
middle; and at the end, each man finishes by improvising alone without returning to the theme."

The debate meanwhile continues. Tom Scanlan
writes in the *Army Times:* ". . . let it be known that there
is at least one writer on jazz who not only doesn't understand what Coleman is doing but suggests that it is not
worth trying to understand. Not, that is, if you are interested in music." Whitney Balliett in *The New Yorker*,
however, asserts: "It is hard to think of any jazz musician,
alive or dead, who has ever exhibited as much naked
emotion as Coleman." What intrigues me more than the
chasm between the critics is how Coleman, despite his
reputation for being so experimental, reminds several
listeners of parts of the jazz past that are seldom referred to in discussions of other modernists. Coleman
recalls to syndicated jazz columnist Ralph Gleason "the
Jenkins Orphange Band which used to parade in Saratoga
Springs in the summer thirty years ago." The Jenkins
youngsters, who traveled through the North raising funds,
are still remembered by older jazzmen for their raw,
fiery abandon. Another Coleman interpretation, *Lonely*

Woman, seems to John S. Wilson to resemble "the plain-
tive New Orleans dirges recorded by the Eureka Brass
Band and the Young Tuxedo Band." And Kenneth Rex-
roth observes that "the whole group is from the Southwest, and behind them you can hear the old bygone
banjos and tack pianos, and the first hard moans of
country blues."

Reading these varied appraisals and feeling the
stares of the resolutely unconverted professionals, Coleman has felt at times in New York as if he were being
exhibited on a revolving stand. He has, however, become
fond of the city and has decided to make it his base. He
is separated from his wife who remains in Los Angeles
with their young son, Denardo. Coleman misses the
boy, but is convinced that New York is the city in which
he and his music can most freely grow. His family in Fort
Worth, however, is fearful of his safety so far from home,
and vainly tries to lure him back.

"New York," Coleman explains, "is the best city anywhere for jazz. Even when the snow was thick on the
ground last winter, there were nights when the Five Spot
was so crowded that people couldn't get in. They don't
love music that much anywhere else in America."

Coleman wanders through the city. He stops occasionally at museums—the Guggenheim, Metropolitan,
and the Museum of Modern Art. Having become friendly
with several of the abstract expressionist painters who
have made the Five Spot a clubhouse, Coleman is now
intensely interested in painting. His favorite avocation
though is, as he describes it, "taking long walks and seeing people do things they know how to do. I don't care
what it is—sports or a craft—so long as a man is showing
delight in a skill he's developed. It's relaxing to watch
a man express himself, and what is usually called art is
far from the only medium of self-expression.

"I went to Radio City Music Hall," Coleman becomes excited in reliving the scene, "and saw a Hawaiian

who was balancing four cocktail glasses on a six by four
piece of wood. The board was on the knob of a two-foot
sword. The Hawaiian put a dagger in his mouth and
balanced the dagger—point to point—against the sword,
climbed fifteen feet up a ladder, spread his hands, and
not a drop spilled. It was the most beautiful piece of art
I'd ever seen. I said to myself, 'Where am I at if this guy
can do something so unbelievable?'"

Although his hair is now of respectable length and
his beard is smaller, Coleman also still spends time in-
vestigating routes to godhead. "I've gone through the
Rosicrucians, the Muslims, various 'metaphysical' groups,
and a couple of years ago, I was baptized a Jehovah's Wit-
ness at my wife's insistence. I haven't been active in the
Witnesses though. Spiritually, I'm free-lancing now. The
one thing that did bother me in all the New York musicians' hostility was that some of them said I was playing
God. It seems to me that when someone tries to do the
best he can in his own way, that doesn't mean he's playing
God. He's just showing God exists."

In less ontological terms, Ornette's music has shown
a marked increase in clarity of conception since he's had
a chance to work every night over a long period of
time. Coleman feels, however, that the added clarity
could have come as effectively through steady practice.
"I'm not sure but what I lose more than I gain by working every night. I get so tired I don't have the enthusiasm
to write or rehearse during the day. I'd much prefer
longer sets three or four nights a week, and the rest of
the time off." Coleman reflected the feelings of many
jazzmen when he told Whitney Balliett: "Six hours a
night, six nights a week. Sometimes I go to the club and
I can't understand what I feel. 'Am I here? How will I
make it through tonight?'"

A new dimension to Coleman's musical experience
since his arrival in New York has been his studying with
Gunther Schuller, the young classical composer who is

an active jazz critic and has been exploring in his composing what John Wilson has termed in *The New York Times*
a "third stream" of music that organically incorporates
elements of both the jazz and classical traditions. Coleman has been taking instruction in notation and other
aspects of music with Schuller.

Since observing Coleman at the School of Jazz,
Schuller had been convinced of Coleman's violently expressive power: "His musical inspiration operates in a
world uncluttered by conventional bar lines, conventional
chord changes, and conventional ways of blowing or fingering a saxophone. Such practical 'limitations' do not
seem even to have been overcome in his music; they
somehow never existed for him. Despite this—or more
accurately, *because* of this—his playing has a deep inner
logic. Not an obvious surface logic, it is based on subtleties of reaction, subtleties of timing and color that are, I
think, quite new to jazz—at least they have never appeared in so pure and direct a form. . . . I don't think
Ornette could ever *play at* playing as so many jazzmen
do. The music sits too deeply in him for that, and all
these qualities are the more startling because they are
not only imbued with a profound love and knowledge of
jazz tradition, but are the first new realization of all that
is implicit in the music of Charlie Parker."

Schuller did realize, however, that Coleman could
use added training in certain areas. "He had no concept,
for example, of how rhythms are organized. He feels
rhythms but didn't know what to call them or how to
notate them. I would never have suggested he come to
me for lessons. It would have been presumptuous, and
besides it's like psychoanalysis. You have to want it before training can do you any good. He finally asked
for instruction because he wanted to write longer pieces
and notate them so that other musicians could play them
the way he wanted them to sound."

Schuller is not afraid that Coleman's immersion in

music theory will inhibit his work. "On the contrary, it'll open up new possibilities of expression for him. It's extraordinary, by the way, how much he'd already learned about harmony by himself. His ear is phenomenal. I'm also amazed, the longer I know him, at the degree of inner peace he's attained. He's a remarkably mature, wise person."

Miles Davis, a shrewd, mordant observer of the jazz scene, is skeptical at such talk of Coleman's inner serenity. "Hell," says Davis, "just listen to what he writes and how he plays. If you're talking psychologically, the man is all screwed up inside."

Whether or not Coleman is as Buddha-like as he appears, he shows no sign of making any concessions to other musicians or to listeners now that success seems imminent. "I'm still trying," he says, "to make my playing as free as I can. The creation of music is—or should be— as natural as breathing. Music is a free thing, and any way you can enjoy it, you should. Jazz is growing up. It's not a cutting contest any more—seeing which man can outplay another. More and more, people are listening not for what a man knows about his horn, but for what he expresses through that horn."

"This is just the beginning of something," young bassist Buell Neidlinger prophesies. "Something wonderful is going to happen with that guy. He's going to shake up jazz a lot more than he already has."

In London recently, a young British drummer was listening with a critic to an Ornette Coleman album. He shook his head. "The drummer is unchained. Goodbye ching-chinga-ching. Now the drummer can play with other musicians, not behind them, not waiting for a few breaks, but really playing, giving, saying something all the way through. This is freedom. It's wonderful. But you're an idiot if you think I like it. Who is able to be free?"

Epilogue

My elementary school in jazz, the Savoy Café in Boston, has long since closed. I miss those years with more than nostalgia. I wasn't then professionally involved with jazz. In the French meaning of the term, I was an "amateur." I didn't love the music and the musicians uncritically, but my reaction to jazz was certainly more spontaneous than it later became with the reviewing of records, the assembly of liner notes, and the occasional supervision of recording sessions. My full-time involvement in jazz in New York for several years led to me to more insights into the jazz life than I would otherwise have absorbed, but I have welcomed the chances since 1957 to write more and more on non-jazz subjects. For a non-musician writer to stay entirely within jazz for too long can blunt and narrow his perspective so that he becomes as parochial as some of the musicians. It can also lead to a waspish querulousness about other critics that has poisoned the jazz atmosphere since the beginning of jazz criticism and to which I have contributed far too much.

The area of jazz writing in which I plan to continue is that represented by this book. It is not technical musical criticism but rather an attempt at socio-economic description of the backgrounds of the music and its players.

250   THE JAZZ LIFE

For this approach, Francis Newton of the *New Statesman*
has set standards of research, lucidity of style, and a wide-
ranging knowledge of those many other elements of
the culture that are inevitably reflected within the jazz
life.

As for jazz music criticism as such, the situation appears to me much improved since I first began reading
such impressionistic, Old Testament-like oracles of jazz as
Hugues Panassié when I was a boy. In the past decade particularly, a nucleus of technically trained critics has finally
been developing a durable body of analytical jazz criticism. "I am tired," a Swarthmore professor and jazz collector said recently, "of jazz being treated as metaphor
rather than music." The sentimental, semi-mystical, vehemently contentious approach to jazz criticism is outdated.
Certainly there is still a function for jazz as metaphor in
writing for a non-specialized audience, as Whitney Balliett's exceptionally skillful and conscientious jazz criticism for *The New Yorker* continues to demonstrate.

There is also, however, a growing number of listeners who want particularly to know how the music is
actually made. The criticism of such musician-writers
as Gunther Schuller in America, André Hodeir in France,
and Max Harrison in England, among others, has begun
to fill this need, as is evidenced by Hodeir's book, *Jazz:
Its Evolution and Essence* (Grove Press) and a forth-
coming analytical history of jazz by Schuller for Oxford
University Press.

Although the approach to writing on jazz is changing, I've found little difference since my nights at the
Savoy in the way jazz musicians themselves react to
criticism, and their nearly unanimous hostility also reveals much about the jazz life. If a non-musician is the
writer, the jazzman asks, "How can he possibly know
what we're doing when he can't even hear the chord
changes? And what the hell does 'angular' mean?" If the
critic has been musically trained, the jazzman is no less

intense in his complaint: "How can he tell us what to play when he doesn't swing himself and hasn't made his own contribution? Besides, you can't *write* about something as emotional as what we're doing." Or, as Miles Davis says in his dismissal of critics, "Who can tell you what love is?"

This defensiveness of the jazzman to criticism is likely to last a long time. It's partly due to the fact that from the beginning, jazz has been a stubbornly empirical, self-searching discipline with little regard for "legitimate" standards of tone, fingering, or voicings. The jazzman, particularly the Negro, is proud of what he has developed by himself. Because of the huge emotional investment he has made in his music, the jazz musician generally respects only the opinions of other musicians who have also worked out their problems and styles by themselves and does not always respect even theirs. In addition, the Negro player frequently does not believe that the critics —nearly all of whom are white—have paid the emotional "dues" he has been assessed from the time he was born. Therefore, he reasons, not always with justice, how can the critics possibly understand his message, which is so much more than the notes he plays?

Another reason for the suspicious insularity of many jazzmen is involved with their self-appraisal as a particularly "hip" in-group in this society. They consider their music and lives somewhat of a protest against the square conformity of the day people, not always realizing how conformist and money-directed large sections of jazz have become. As the music became more of an object-in-itself in the past twenty years, this sense of "specialness" increased. Some apprentices are now first drawn to jazz more by its aura of a secret society than by the music itself. Over-concentration on one's own "specialness" is usually an indication, of course, of insecurity. And if the apprentice is not insecure emotionally when he begins to become involved in the jazz life, its economic uncertainties and fierce competition can quickly disturb his equilibrium. Accordingly, he will soon also rail at the critics for injuring his chances to make more money. "If they can't say anything good about us, they ought to write about something else. It's hard enough out here."

The young jazzman also knows, however, that while his career can be advanced through the notice of critics, he almost invariably gets his first important work through accreditation by other musicians. An Ornette Coleman is an exception. Today, as in New Orleans, Dallas and Kansas City thirty years ago, the apprentice, for all the changes in the music and the audience, must first impress the players who have already paid dues. Although there is growing concern with learning music theory, either in regular schools or with such teacher-practitioners as George Russell, jazzmen also still agree with the late Sidney Bechet that "when you come right down to it, a musicianer just has to learn for himself, just by playing and listening. . . . There ain't no one can write down the feeling you have to have. That's from inside yourself. The music has to let you be . . . you got to stay free inside it." Similarly, Milt Jackson, while teaching at the School of Jazz in Lenox, told a student, "We can tell you something about techniques, but we sure can't teach you 'soul.'"

With this almost mystical, sometimes childish, and always aggressively emotional approach to their life work, most jazz musicians resist analysis even when it comes in print from one of their own. As more intellectuals become involved as active jazz musicians, I expect that some of this hostility to analysis will be dissipated, but the process will require a long time; and for the next few years anyway, those "new" critics who hope to affect as well as explain the music are not likely to get through to many of the players and composers. Nor am I sure it would be of value if they could.

In any case, I expect the critic most effectively influences the music in the long run if he is able to raise the standards of enough of the jazz public so that fewer confidence men will be lauded and more of the uncompromisingly original will be recognized.

Apparently, however, little can be done so far by the critics about the wasting of the older musicians in jazz. It is this dismissal of the old that has saddened and angered me more than any other aspect of jazz. The jazz life is relentlessly cruel for most jazzmen past forty. The older players, no matter how much they still have to say—and many are much more personal and powerful than at any previous points in their careers—become almost entirely ignored. To the audiences, the booking agents, and even some of the critics, jazz is still a music for the young and by the young. "What can you say to a man?" the wife of Hilton Jefferson, a prominent alto saxophonist of the 1930's, asks rhetorically, "when he's given his whole life to music, has reached the point where the horn really is part of him and can express everything he wants to say, and then there is no place for him." Her husband works in a bank, and takes what weekend work he can get. Now almost sixty, he plays remarkably well considering the infrequency of his jazz engagements, and with as much individuality as he ever had. Jefferson said recently, "Believe me, I'd leave the bank job, secure as it's become, in a minute if I could go back to music full-time." He will get no invitations.

Yet, for the jazzman of all ages and styles, the jazz life, however uncertain, becomes the most fulfilling way of existence he knows. Few, if any, have ever voluntarily retired. I suppose that as the teaching of jazz becomes a more common vocation, players now in their twenties and thirties may eventually be able to remain in the music as instructors of the young—if the young are by that time willing to listen to their elders. The rushing compulsion to be "hip" to the newest sounds and styles continues to afflict the younger players as pervasively as it does most of the jazz audience. By 1960, a great many apprentices had stopped listening to even Charlie Parker recordings, let alone those of Johnny Hodges, Louis Armstrong, and Bessie Smith.

Which of the young, for example, still buy recordings of Roy Eldridge? For me, perhaps because of my own age, he is the one horn I listen to with the most expectancy of being radically shaken and fulfilled emotionally. At the end of a recording date in November, 1960, Eldridge was telling the bristling modernist, Charles Mingus, who had been on the session: "I'm glad I made this. I wanted to find out what bag you're in. Now I know you're in the right bag. I'm not naming names," Eldridge pointed vaguely to new legions of young trumpeters in the distance, "but a lot of them are so busy being busy on their horns that they forget the basics. They don't get all the way down into the music. You did, baby. It's good to know. There are very few of us left out here."

A couple of weeks later, the 1960 *Down Beat* readers' poll results were published. A minimum of fifteen votes was required for a player to be listed. Fifteen trumpet players made it, but not Eldridge. Although he is quite aware of being past the age of jazz lionization, Eldridge, however, refuses to go gently into limbo. He remains an intense competitor, and plays with no less power than when he was bewildering Dizzy Gillespie twenty-five years ago. The tension that invariably seizes Eldridge as he's about to play sometimes pulls him up too short and makes his playing desperately shrill. But when he's at relative ease, Eldridge, fifty, is a paradigm of jazz power.

At that session with Mingus, several young players had finished their assignments early in the afternoon. A few of them, curious at the name, stayed to hear Eldridge. "He may not be hip," said one, a Dizzy Gillespie disciple from Detroit, after an hour of playing by Eldridge, "but Jesus, he sure fills that horn." At one point, Eldridge ripped out a ferocious solo and then, laughing, pointed at the boy from Detroit. "We're still trying, aren't we?" Eldridge said.

Among the most intense impressions I've had of the jazz life are of those older musicians who still try. Having committed themselves to the music, they keep talking on their horns, even when there's no one to hear. And so will most of those now young in jazz, since jazz is one of the few vocations that allows a man to be himself, to say in his work who he is and what he feels.

From childhood, I've been drawn to those insistent, often raw and often terribly soft autobiographies that are the sounds of jazz. The music may well be a "minor" art, whatever that distinction really means (how does one measure Bessie Smith as against Claudia Muzio?). But many of the makers of jazz have been larger in life than most people in their generation, and they have transmuted their lives into their music. The jazz life, in short, is the total existence of its players. For its makers, jazz is entertainment and religion, pride and temptation, and as unpredictable—or predictable—as they themselves are.

"I can tell you much more about what a man is really thinking," says Jo Jones, the Nestor of jazz, "by listening to him play than by hearing him talk. You can't hide anything in that horn, especially when you think you are hiding." And at base, the continuing attraction and challenge of jazz to many of us is that it does have so few places in which to hide.